MAY 1 9 1987	DATE DUE	
MAR 1 5 1989		
4·4·89		
DEC 5 1989		
JAN 2 9 1991		
JUN 4 1991		

**Looking at Schools:
Good, Bad, and
Indifferent**

Looking at Schools: Good, Bad, and Indifferent

Edward A. Wynne
University of Illinois
at Chicago Circle

LexingtonBooks
D.C. Heath and Company
Lexington, Massachusetts
Toronto

Library of Congress Cataloging in Publication Data

Wynne, Edward.
  Looking at schools.

  Bibliography: p.
  Includes index.
  1. Private schools—United States. 2. Public schools—United States.
3. Educational research—United States. I. Title.
LC49.W94   371'.00973   79-2798
ISBN 0-669-03292-1

Copyright © 1980 by D.C. Heath and Company

Published simultaneously in Canada

Printed in the United States of America

International Standard Book Number: 0-669-03292-1

Library of Congress Catalog Card Number: 79-2798

For
Adam, my son
1959–1978
May this book
help improve the schooling
of other parents' children

Contents

List of Figures
and Table

Foreword

The author of this volume hears a different drummer, and we do well to listen to the beat. There are no captivating rhythms; it is a cadence for a long march, unsuited to the free and often frenetic movement of today. Symbolically, therein lies Wynne's challenge to what he sees as the prevailing climate of American schools, a climate he regards as inimical to the true purpose of education.

That purpose, as Wynne states it, has a paradoxical quality, for it is outmoded and yet perceptively ahead of its time. Wynne harks back to classical tradition in defining character building, not academic achievement, as the principal aim of schooling. For him, the mastery of subject matter, while important, is but one by-product of the educational process. Indeed, academic proficiency, Wynne contends, can only be achieved through character education. Hence, schools must be organized and conducted to foster the development of certain human qualities. These are never set forth in systematic form, but the conventional virtues of a bygone age—industry, responsibility, honesty, self-discipline, service to others—emerge from the pages that follow.

The aura of traditionalism pervades not only the goals of education as Wynne defines them but also the methods to be employed. In the recommendations of this volume, one reads much about rules, maxims, strict discipline, and gold stars for good conduct. It would be a mistake, however, to dismiss this work as irrelevant to contemporary reality—to the schools and children of today and especially of tomorrow. It is the realism and contemporaneousness of Wynne's book that give it importance and power. At a time when much educational research has become lost in the majestic objectivity and airy ambiguity generated by complex statistical models for analyzing classroom interaction or the sociological determinants of academic achievement, Wynne and his students present us with an unashamedly subjective essay, based on a lively ethnography of what has been happening in the classrooms, corridors, and surrounding streets of some forty public, private, and church-related schools in the Chicago area. The recorded events are so powerful in themselves that the author's personal reactions—often illuminating, sometimes moralistic—recede into the background; what stands out are certain hard realities about what is actually happening in American education at the elementary and secondary level.

The first hard reality is that the main impact of today's schools is indeed not so much on academic achievement as on character formation. Moreover, in many schools, that impact is manifestly destructive. By their mode of operation, these schools are unwittingly but efficiently training youngsters in immediate self-gratification, evasion of responsibility, poor work habits, manipulation and exploitation of others, insensitivity and indifference to human needs, and the all-too-familiar vandalism and violence. Wynne documents the emergence of these behavior patterns; he also analyzes their sources in the internal organization of classrooms and schools and (of equal if not greater importance) in the relationship between the school and the community.

The second, equally hard but more heartening reality is that a significant number of schools, whether as an expression of their educational philosophy or in reaction to observed destructive effects, have instituted policies and practices that, in effect, have character education as their aim. What is more, some of the strategies appear to be working.

Herein lies the principal value of this book. It contains a rich store of social inventions designed to bring out the constructive potential of young people. The inventors include all those involved, directly or indirectly, in the educational process. They are mostly teachers, principals, and other staff members, but also include pupils, parents, school-board members, and local citizens. Notably missing are the academicians—educational researchers, teacher educators, and professors of pedagogy.

As for the social inventions themselves, they cover a wide range. Even if one disagrees, as I do, with some of the more traditional, authoritarian policies that Wynne endorses most strongly (including some practices now legally prohibited), the rich repertoire that he and his students have compiled offers many other, more contemporary and expressive options. Varied though they are, all of these strategies have a common, comprehensive aim—the creation and maintenance of a caring community. To be effective and enduring, such a community not only has to exist in the classroom but must pervade the school as a whole and reach beyond its walls to involve local residents and institutions.

It is this revolutionary broadening of the mission of schools in American society, accompanied by concrete strategies for its implementation, that makes this book deserving of the attention of all those concerned with the present and future of American education. The next and equally necessary tasks are to subject these strategies to systematic critical analyses, to probe their implicit theoretical and ideological assumptions, and, above all, to investigate their immediate and long-range effects. Only in this way can we establish a justifiable empirical and ethical basis for the desperately needed educational renaissance envisioned in this volume.

Urie Bronfenbrenner
Jacob Gould Schurman Professor
   of Human Development and Family
   Studies and of Psychology
Cornell University

Introduction

A variety of studies in both Britain and the United States have clearly indicated that the main source of variations between schools in their effects on the children does not lie in factors such as buildings or resources. Rather, the crucial differences seemed to concern aspects of school life to do with its functioning as a social organization. Observers have noted differences between schools in morale, climate and atmosphere but little was known about what staff actions or activities lay behind these intangible but important features.[1]

There are thousands of books on education. There are hundreds of books in which teachers describe their experiences in classrooms or analyze schools from their perspectives as teachers. There are very few that describe real operating schools as total organisms and show how the different parts of a school fit together—or fail to fit. *Looking at Schools* is such a book.

It differs from the many "teacher-centered" books because it tries to see schools from a broader perspective; the vision of individual teachers is largely constrained by what happens in their classroom; but parents, students, and administrators deal with many different teachers over time. And, as *Looking at Schools* shows, the general tone of a particular school is more important than the personality of any individual teacher.

The book is derived from 167 school reports done by my graduate and undergraduate students on schools in and around Chicago between 1972 and 1979. Due to limitations of space, materials from only forty of these reports have been quoted. (A more detailed outline of the underlying statistics is contained in the appendix.) The texts of the reports are based on interviews with students, teachers, administrators, aides, security guards, and parents; actual observations by my students; and collection and analysis of school documents, such as school newspapers, discipline codes, and teachers' manuals. The schools studied were public and private, secular and religious, large and small, elementary and secondary, central city and suburban, and good, bad, and indifferent (see table I-1).

Although the geographic area studied was limited, many of the findings and interpretations have applicability beyond Chicago. For example, the January 1979 *Report* of the chancellor of the New York City school system lists, as typical school problems, "less extra-curricular involvement by teachers, greater reliance on the union contract as the standard of professional responsibility, less willingness to articulate values, the lockout of latecoming high school students, decreasing levels of student achievement, increasing truancy, increasing drop-outs and increasing pressure to maximize the severity of student discipline. . . ."[2] As readers proceed, it will

Table I–1
Tabulation of Schools Described

	Elementary	Secondary [a]	Totals for Each Type of "System"
Chicago city public	7	10	17
Chicago suburban public	1	10	11
Church-related [b]	2	5	7
Private (secular)	1	4	5
Totals for each age level	11	29	40

[a] Includes junior high schools.

[b] All of these schools are related to the Roman Catholic Archdiocese of Chicago.

become evident to them that there are many parallels between New York and Chicago. I must also note that *Looking at Schools* is about "better-run" suburban schools, and here, too, it is my professional opinion that its findings are relatively generalizable.

The reports were researched and written according to an outline and instructions gradually refined over time. The reports have a comparatively high level of coherence and accuracy. The information they reveal is often intrinsically interesting and can engage researchers, educators, college students, and some of the general public. The reports demonstrate the variety of patterns that prevail in schools. This diversity is intellectually stimulating, since it causes readers to realize that there is no one way of doing things—and that many school practices we see and take for granted are not applied in other schools even five or ten blocks away. In every class I teach, I see my students' eyes open as they see how varied—for both better and worse—school practices are. The variety is a great stimulant to their imagination: they begin to see that things don't have to be "the way they are." There are real choices.

The commentary on the information collected is sometimes extensive and accounts for about half of the text in the topical chapters. The fact is that many school policies that seem quite simple—and that can be easily described—often have complex ramifications. Making these ramifications evident sometimes requires careful discussion. For instance, three teachers in a school described their separate penalties for cheating as (1) always flunking the student for the course, (2) always flunking the student for the exam, or (3) usually flunking the student for the exam, but first hearing him out. Actually these are three entirely different policies, with significantly different implications for shaping student conduct. And it is not evident that the teachers involved, or at least the last two teachers, see the differences. Thus some commentary is required to make the differences clear. Naturally, such comments may involve debatable interpretations or analyses. However, readers will first be provided with the facts, and the comments will at least stimulate their own thoughts.

The materials disclosed are significant because they focus on many of the things that students, most parents, and many teachers and competent administrators actually worry about when they deal with schools. Thus the information reports on school spirit and student discipline, as well as on book learning. These priorities are not just matters of personal opinion. For example, student discipline has been listed as the major concern of parents in eleven of the past twelve national Gallup polls on education, and we can assume these parents were not just worried about ghetto schools.

The first two chapters present complete reports on individual schools. The reports show the types of interrelationships that will be considered in *Looking at Schools;* furthermore, since the rest of the text will be comprised of items excerpted from various reports, the two complete reports will help readers appreciate the basic documents from which such excerpts will be drawn. Following the two complete reports are four topical chapters, presenting contrasting interviews, observations, and other data (plus appropriate commentary) gathered from different schools. Chapter 7 presents conclusions.

In the appendix, the schools studied are described, although their identities are concealed. Listed beside each description are the numbers of all items in the text for that school. Some schools have only a few numbered items, but many are portrayed in considerable detail. Interested readers can benefit from using this cross-referencing system to examine some of the schools studied. In effect, *Looking at Schools* describes schools from the two perspectives: first, through grouping items from many different schools under topical headings: and second, through grouping together (via cross-referencing) the items about each school. Readers who examine some schools through a "whole school" perspective may find their ability to interpret school activities in other schools significantly enhanced. The fact is that schools are highly integrated entities. Good practices affecting some operations are usually related to other good practices applied to other operations. Unfortunately, the obverse rule also generally applies. In any case, at this time, many able and concerned people need more experience in identifying the relationships among school policies, and in seeing how visible policy A in a school can lead one to look more carefully for obscure—but equally important—policy B.

It is also evident that there will be some overlap between the materials found in different chapters; for example, the line between character development and discipline can be fuzzy. However, no harm should result if one reader or another occasionally differs with my conceptual boundary. Vital, real-life activities rarely shape themselves to facilitate academic categorization, and *Looking at Schools* describes such activities.

Some readers may question the importance of reports developed as much as seven years ago—except for their historical significance. However, my conclusion is that things have not really changed a great deal in schools over those years. Of course, some individual schools have changed considerably due to changes in principals or other key staff. But many of these changes in individual schools will average themselves out since we are considering a pool of forty schools. Thus, while some of the schools described may now be different from the time of the description, the proportion of "good" or "bad" schools—or practices—in the Chicago area will tend to stay the same; or things will average out unless certain systemic change has been carried out, which has not happened. This is not to say there haven't been any significant broadcast changes; for instance, the proportion of public schools in Chicago with almost all-black enrollment has steadily increased. But such a change does not alter the general nature of each particular all-black, racially mixed, or all-white Chicago public school. The reality is that the systemic elements governing school operations in and around Chicago are (1) the size of school buildings; (2) the procedures controlling the allocation and enrollment of students; (3) the policies covering the hiring, firing, assignment, evaluation, promotion, and granting of raises to teachers and administrators; (4) the general social assumptions about the relationship between students and adults in America; and (5) the degree of administrative centralization or decentralization in different school systems. None of these factors has been static around Chicago during the past seven years, but the changes that have occurred have not been dramatic. And, indeed, the sum of the identifiable changes that have occurred may be for the worse. In any event, the question of what has changed, and what the significance is of any real or proposed changes, will be treated in my concluding chapter.

Sophisticated readers of *Looking at Schools* will become conscious of a contrast between its findings and those of much traditional education research on student learning and conduct. This contrast should be discussed here.

Traditional education research focusing on pupils has generally been highly quantitative in nature: reading and math scores; pupil/teacher ratio in the school; money spent per pupil; or years of higher education or teaching experience the teachers have had. The reports presented here include some counting: how many students put in how much time in extracurricular activities; how often fights occur in the playground; how many schoolwide assemblies are held each year. But events that are not easily quantifiable are also described: Do students really dislike or fear the punishments given for breaches of discipline? Are there symbols which are popularly seen as epitomizing the school's traditions? Obviously, the reports, whether they present counts or descriptions, have been concerned with topics different from the focus of most educational research on school effects on pupils. This difference has two conflicting interpretations: either *Looking at Schools* is studying the "wrong" things, or much educational research has been misdirected.

I favor the latter interpretation. I believe many researchers have been focusing on the wrong issues—or "variables," to use the technical term. This misdirection is easy to explain. The first point is that their research is not necessarily in error: essentially, research tries to find out whether there is a significant relationship between two or more factors. For instance, how much difference does it make on children's reading scores if they are taught in smaller-sized classes? Suppose such research discovers that modest differences in class size—say, one teacher to twenty pupils, compared to one to twenty-four—has no consequential effect. The research is not a "failure." It has shown us something: modest differences in class size do not change scores. That was its basic aim: to discover something. Thus much traditional research has revealed that many of the variables studied bear only small relationships to improving students' reading scores. What is the major lesson of this research? We should look at different variables. And this is what *Looking at Schools* does.

But the "misdirection" of traditional educational research has other causes less laudable than discovering what is not important. Most of the differences studied cost more money to foster—for example, smaller classrooms, or teachers who have taken advanced degrees. For instance, even lowering class size from twenty-four to twenty throughout a school system might increase total operating costs about 15 percent—not a small matter. Also, the differences studied have been cheaper for researchers to describe quantitatively—it is easy to translate numbers of pupils or years of teacher training into data that can be plugged into a computer. In sum, traditional research has continued, in part, because it has aimed at issues that satisfy the interests of some school administrators (the findings might justify larger budgets) and because it is easier to produce "hard" numerical conclusions if easily defined topics are studied.

Furthermore, the focus of traditional research has been congenial to the current graduate and undergraduate programs conducted in many colleges of education (and the faculty of those colleges do much of this research). Thus I know of only one college of education that teaches administrators in its courses how to write discipline codes for students, or how to stimulate school spirit. (I'm not saying there is only one such place, but simply that such "teachings" must be uncommon.) However, almost all colleges of education have courses on how to teach reading. And—not too surprisingly—there is a great deal of research on teaching reading.

Essentially, a complicated relationship has evolved among schools, colleges of education, the bureaucracies that finance research, and education researchers. The effect of this relationship has been to constrain what we look at when we study schools, and what we try to change to foster improvement. Some of the implications of this relationship were suggested in a 1979 press interview of Ellis Page, the 1979–1980 president of the American Education Research Association. He wondered why researchers were so reluctant to study the question of student discipline (or indiscipline), which obviously was of such concern to parents and legislators.[3] He suggested that there was a sort of "liberal bias" against such studies, since they might tend to be critical of current school and college policies and philosophies. In other words, suppose researchers did "discover" ways of improving student discipline. Their solution might not be "conventionally liberal." As a result, it might provide ammunition for generating changes uncongenial to education "intellectuals."

Another inhibiting factor on traditional education research has been its tendency to focus on *public* schools. Of course, over 85 percent of American students attend such schools, but (for a variety of reasons) there are significant patterns of administrative uniformity among these tens of thousands of schools. Thus studies covering public schools generate huge amounts of analyzable statistics, but the differences among these schools in "interesting" variables are often quite modest. It is foolish to make simplistic comparisons between public and private schools (whether the private ones are church-related or secular), since a key element in the operation of private schools is that they are "schools of choice" for the parents, and often for the students. And this matter of choice has many implications for school operations. However, as *Looking at Schools* reveals, many private schools are "different" in ways that might arguably be imitated by public schools. For instance, their buildings are usually smaller, and each school enrolls less students. Again, some school systems and policymakers are becoming more actively interested in the issue of family and student choice, and are talking about such matters as magnet schools and "houses" or subschools or voucher systems. Such efforts at constructively fostering choice can be more usefully managed if we learn from the private-school experience. In sum, I believe that education research, in its failure to make comparisons among public and private schools, has shut itself off from many rewarding insights.

At this point, I should make reference to the recent book, *Fifteen Thousand Hours,* by Michael Ritter and his associates.[4] This British study contrasts with much of the research just characterized. It has made an intensive and imaginative effort to measure a variety of school processes usually ignored by research and to show their relationship to pupil learning and conduct. There are both parallel and divergent themes between *Looking at Schools* and *Fifteen Thousand Hours*. Both studies are concerned with what it "feels" like in schools, the practices that cause these feelings, and the effects of such feelings on pupil conduct and learning. Both conclude that the quality of school life can be clearly described and related to pupil conduct and learning. These common perspectives and conclusions cause both studies—and many of their conclusions—to mutually support each other. They suggest that such research approaches can provide us with important tools for improving school operations.

But the books also have differences. *Fifteen Thousand Hours* describes its schools and their practices with statistical techniques and has related their practices to carefully calculated reading outcomes. *Looking at Schools* lacks such statistical precision and has omitted reading-score data. However, *Looking at Schools* (1) considers more schools than the British study, (2) examines a greater variety of schools and school practices, and (3) has dedicated more attention to the analysis and interpretation of the practices portrayed, partly because their variety provides rich material for analysis. The differences between the two books do not make one right and the other wrong. Schools are extraordinarily complicated, and we have developed many research techniques, which serve different needs. The important thing is that researchers seem to have begun to shift from relatively simplistic nose counting. We have started to look more carefully at the feelings and values of people in schools. And, after all, feelings and values are the roots of human conduct.

One more contrast between the focus of *Looking at Schools* and traditional education research on school effects should be mentioned. Up until now, this research has concentrated on discovering the effect of school operations on pupils' reading and math scores. Such scores are important; they bear a reasonable relationship to a pupil's ability to read, write, or compute. But most vital contacts between human beings are affected by far more significant factors than the parties's literacy. To be specific, parents are concerned about the manners and diligence of their children; students are concerned about the kindness and tact of their fellow students; teachers and administrators want their students to be honest and obedient; and the future employers, coworkers, and spouses of the students want them to grow into adults who display what we call good character. In sum, most of the virtues other human beings display to us, and most of the deficiencies they visit upon us, have little to do with their literacy or computational skills. They have to do with their character, and character is largely a medley of learned traits.

The traits we call character, whether they are good or bad, are formed not through lectures but through the social learning structures maintained around us as children and adolescents. Of course, much of this learning occurs in families. But children are placed in schools for thousands of hours during the formative years of their lives. In these schools, they are surrounded by prestigious adults and diverse peer pressures. Under these circumstances, schools will inescapably have powerful character-formation effects. Schools will stimulate students either to be honest or to be indifferent when they cheat, lie, or steal. They will encourage students to be diligent or they will reward equally the striver and the drone. They will ask students to show loyalty and concern for one another or they will covertly reward selfishness and indifference. In other words, researchers apply a very narrow focus when they look only at the effects of schools on students' book skills, as compared to seeing how schools shape students' character—for better or worse.

Education research has failed to focus strongly on student character, partly because it has relied largely on paper-and-pencil tests, which can be graded by machines and which produce data that can be fed easily into computers. On the other hand, character is largely demonstrated by conduct; by what we do. Sometimes words can constitute "acts," as when we lie or say unnecessarily cruel things. However, hypothetical answers on written tests may not show what we'll do in real life. Character must first be evaluated by observation, by seeing and counting what pupils do (and say) in their daily activities.

The reports in *Looking at Schools* are strongly concerned with good and bad acts by students. Therefore, they help us develop new insights into the role of modern schools in assisting, and hurting, character information.

A book like *Looking at Schools* can stimulate us to move to new perceptions. Essentially, it will show that there are important differences among operating schools. These differences are not the things most researchers have been looking at. The differences are not especially related to the amounts of money spent. The differences are tied to such things as the energy, imagination, and determination of the staff (especially the principal); the level of staff stability in the school; the ability (or determination) of the principal to choose and control the staff; the size of the school (essentially, small is "better"); the congruence among parent, school, and student aspirations; and the ability of the principal and faculty to provide pupils with strong leadership and emotional support. The differences affect not only pupils' reading scores but also the character traits that they display and learn in school.

As the reports show, the differences can be described and identified with considerable precision. In effect, they can be taught to other teachers, principals, and parents. And educators can then change their current policies to imitate those they believe are better. Furthermore, if someone wants to research such differences quantitatively, that task can be accomplished (see, for example, *Fifteen Thousand Hours*). But it must be approached with adequate resources and some vigor—and a willingness to ignore sacred cows.

Finally, the procedures for indexing the material in the book are of interest. After the first two chapters, each item of information in the text (that is, each example or quotation) is preceded by a sequential number, and is concluded by two numbers and a capital letter, all enclosed in parentheses—for example (7, P, K–8). The sequential number will provide a means to identify the item. There are more than 330 items in the text. The first number in the parentheses will identify the school involved. In other words, each school (as well as each item) will have an identifying number, and all items scattered throughout the text that relate to that particular school will be followed by that school's number. The letter will signify if the school is public (P) or private religious (R) or private secular (S). The second numbers in parentheses will designate the school years the school covers—for example, 9–12 for a traditional high school.

Addendum

Professor Bronfenbrenner raised two thoughtful issues. The values that underlic my analytic perspective are considered traditional or conservative by many people. I believe that young people should learn to tell the truth under pressure; should go out of their way to be helpful to others; should receive rewards for good conduct; should be punished for bad conduct; and should be educated (or socialized) to become involved, contributing adults in their communities, families, and jobs. In schools, in particular, students should work hard, should be inspired with pride in their school, and should frequently find themselves participating in an exciting and enjoyable community. All adult institutions that work with youth should be evaluated in terms of their success in pursuing these ends. My values may not be universally accepted, but even readers who disagree with some of these concerns may find this book helpful for the descriptions it contains—and for some of the arguable analyses that evolve from these descriptions.

A large body of educational research is critical of some of the analyses and practices I present in the text. Much of this research, however, uses deficient methodology. The researchers are competent, but much of the research is old and its methodologies are obsolete by current standards. For example, there are studies that show that schools with precise discipline codes have more disorder than schools without such codes. However, discipline codes are often adopted in schools that are already plagued with disorder and not adopted in schools where there is comparatively little disorder. The obsolete methodology I have described might also be used to conclude that, if there are more police in communities with high crime rates, one solution to the crime problem would be to abolish the police; after all, many communities with low crime rates have few or no police. Thus, discipline codes are not necessarily the cause of disorder; the disorder might be even worse without the codes. Whether discipline codes—and many other practices I defend—are good or bad can only be determined by far more elaborate research than is typically now applied.

**Looking at Schools:
Good, Bad, and
Indifferent**

1 A Chicago Public Elementary School

Here then is a real teaching. . . .it recognizes that knowledge is something more than a sort of reception of scraps and details; it is a something and it does a something, which will never issue from the most strenuous efforts of a set of teachers with no mutual sympathies and no intercommunication, of a set of examiners with no opinions which they dare profess, and with no common principles, who are teaching or questioning a set of youths who do not know them, and do not know each other, on a large number of subjects, different in kind, and connected by no wide philosophy. . . .[1]

The School[a] is a Chicago public elementary school (kindergarten [K] through eighth grade) with almost 600 students. It is located near several high-rise housing projects, a few miles from downtown. The population of the neighborhood is almost entirely black, and the student body is all black. Many children come from single-parent families, where the mother receives welfare assistance. The School consists of two buildings, separated by a cement play area. One building, dating from 1915, houses the school administrative offices, library, gym, and upper-grade classrooms; the other, built in 1950, contains the primary and middle grades. In good weather during recess and before school, students play on the campus as well as on two city playlots which are located behind the campus.

The 1915 building has a clean and neat-appearing interior. In both buildings, student artwork and papers decorate bulletin boards in corridors and classrooms. About 15 percent of the total wall space in the corridors is taken up by such bulletin boards. Every month, the bulletin boards are assigned to a different team of two teachers and completely revised. Almost all the wall space in all the classrooms is taken up with examples of students' work, posters, and instructional materials. About 60 percent of the materials on the classroom walls are "current," that is, they are materials placed up during the present school year.

School Spirit

Formal assembly programs take place every other month. They are held in the older building, which was once a private, church-related high school.

---

[a] Throughout the book, the word "School" will be substituted for the names of all schools studied, in order to protect the privacy of informants.

The assemblies usually include onstage presentations to the student audience, by each homeroom class in the School. The assembly hall in the building was formerly the high school's chapel. To prepare for the presentations, usually a copy of the program for the assembly is given to everyone. Since the hall is relatively small, assembly day is handled in three shifts. Students share the assembly period with classes from their approximate age groups, except that kindergarten and eighth graders go together.

The School's four special education classes for handicapped and retarded children participate along with the normal students, both as performers and audience.

Diverse types of interaction occur among students, and students and faculty, at assemblies. The students come dressed in their Sunday best. Each class performs on stage as a group. All performances are greeted with applause. The whole audience often participates in different group songs, including the regular singing of the school anthem, composed by the assistant principal. The principal makes announcements or remarks about varied school policies or programs. The assistant principal tells jokes or performs amusing songs. At the assembly that was observed, the music was supplied by a retired music teacher from the school, who voluntarily returned to play the piano and accompany the performances.

On assembly day, the investigator saw two students who were sitting in the principal's office during their group's assembly. The background of this episode is enlightening. The students had chosen to leave the assembly because they believed they were not properly dressed for the occasion. Their clothing was neat and clean, but not up to the level of that worn by the other students. Their teachers were quite willing to have them remain with the class and join the performance on stage, but the students felt out of place and chose to withdraw.

Obviously the school faculty have succeeded in giving the assemblies some of the attributes of a vital ceremonial occasion.

The principal has been at the school for fourteen years, all as principal. Her assistant principal has served there for twenty-one years. He had been a master teacher at the school, and was appointed assistant principal by the principal two years after her arrival. Their relationship is characterized by informality and trust. Both of them are white.

Faculty members have taught at the School an average of sixteen years. There is a sense of security, friendliness, and shared responsibility among faculty members. New teachers are helped to fit in, and most do very quickly. Those few who may have been unhappy at being assigned to the School "just seem to disappear," as one teacher put it. What generally happens is that the principal will ask for an administrative transfer, or the teacher will ask for a transfer. In some cases, a teacher with initially unsympathetic attitudes and behavior has changed so as to become part of the school community. In other cases, teachers have brought pressure against uncooperative or incompetent colleagues to provoke them to leave.

There are twenty-eight full-time teachers. For a number of years the faculty has been evenly divided between black and white. Race relations among them seem good. Thus teachers are grouped into five separate clusters (or teams); all of the teams are racially integrated, and three of the five team leaders are black. Some of the white teachers live in largely white suburbs, and frequently invite black colleagues to gatherings of teachers at their homes. Again, recently one of the black teachers suffered a prolonged illness that kept her housebound, and shopping for her home was partially handled by a white colleague.

For a variety of reasons, the relationship between teachers and students in the School has some of the character of parenting. The comparatively mature teachers are often parents in their own right. They usually know the older siblings of their students from having taught them in earlier classes. And they have become acquainted with parents as a result of their teaching longevity. As a result, they are unlikely to see students as members of continuing family units, and make remarks and observations that spring from this vision. As evidence of this bonding pattern, 80 percent of the students who graduated last year to the level of high-school freshmen returned to the School at various occasions this year to visit their former classroom teachers.

Faculty members claim they feel "like a family" among themselves, and with administrators and staff as well. Even maintenance personnel and those involved in the preparation of school lunches exhibit a friendly spirit toward all other adults, students, and visitors.

At Christmas time, instead of exchanging gifts with one another, faculty members donate money to a special fund which is used to buy clothes for needy students. One girl who was to receive some clothes and shoes already had a new pair of gym shoes. She gave the second pair of shoes she was receiving from the school to another student who needed them.

Student gift-giving to students, especially at Christmas time, is not a general school practice. Nor does the eighth grade leave a class gift at graduation time. Teachers do not set up expectations of gifts from students. But small personal remembrances from students often take the form of handmade gifts such as those items created in an art class.

On the whole, the School's relationship with parents from the neighborhood is good. Although the level of parent involvement in school policy-setting is only moderate, a teacher aide who is also a parent says she feels "comfortable" knowing her children are at the School. "I wouldn't send them elsewhere," she states. She likes the "family feeling" of the School, and adds, "I have a different perspective now that I'm working here."

The School sends home, through the students, a monthly calendar to inform parents of events. There is a parent advisory council which meets in the early afternoon once a month. When the council was first inaugurated, much effort was given to having good election procedures which would encourage parent representation and participation, and the membership went up to seventeen. In recent years there has been a more informal recreation of the council from year to year, and attendance has dropped off to about six people. Nevertheless, the principal makes oral reports monthly to the council and keeps it informed about school matters. In turn, the council advises the principal about how parents feel on such issues as special programs proposed for the School.

There is little parent fundraising done. A taffy-apple sale provides the money to pay for the trophies and other awards given at the annual honors assembly each June. The profit from school pictures is the only other source of extra funds. The per-pupil appropriation takes care of books and supplies only, so it was with money saved from taffy apples and pictures that the principal was able eventually to buy curtains for the classrooms.

Character Development

On a typical school day, the principal arrives about 8:00 A.M., an hour before starting time. Children coming to school early will greet her with friendliness, and she responds to most of them by name. Once school starts students enter from the playground areas. The assistant principal helps to extinguish any horseplay among the older boys as they come up the back stairs, and his good-humored remarks are met with equal good humor by those students requested to quiet down or remove their hats. Once students are in their classrooms, the school day begins (in all classrooms) with the pledge of allegiance to the flag, and the singing of a patriotic song—either the National Anthem or "America the Beautiful." Primary students sometimes sing "This Land Is Your Land."

The School has a practice of maintaining two students in the office area every day. They come prepared to work independently on class assignments, and to be available as messengers should the need arise. About 75 percent of the fifth- and sixth-year students form the pool from which the office members are selected. They are responsible enough to work on their own and to carry whatever messages are sent from the office to teachers in either of the two school buildings.

There are other opportunities for students to exercise responsibility for helping others during the school day. About 10 percent of the seventh- and eighth-grade pupils tutor, read to, or care for younger students at the primary level. Another 10 percent serve as crossing guards, while 50 percent do duty as hall guards in the old building. In the new building, about 50 percent of the fourth-, fifth-, and sixth-year pupils have the chance to be hall guards. School doors are kept locked, as a safety precaution for those inside. The principal and her staff do not need—and refuse to have—any type of security protection from the police inside the school (though such protection is commonly used in Chicago public schools in difficult neighborhoods).

Wide-scale student fundraising activities are nonexistent. However, students do raise money among themselves when it is needed by a particular class or group for a special reason. Money is contributed to buy flowers for a sick teacher, or to buy a gift for a retiring teacher. The school does participate in the annual collection for the Crusade of Mercy. Contributions by students are mostly in pennies, nickels, and dimes, amounting to a total of perhaps $35.00.

Students feel that among the best things they learn at the School are attitudes like being honest and hardworking, and how to get along in life. Teachers try to instill in students respect for others, and teach children to apologize when they hurt others or misbehave. Students say that their teachers are good teachers because "they want you to learn" and "they don't let you walk all over them." In general, students say they do what the teachers ask. The School's most famous recent graduates are members of a well-known rock group. They are cited to students as an example of recent alumni who have succeeded, and are respected at the School for being good students while there, as well as good entertainers now.

The June honors assembly is the formal recognition of what students have done for the School, for one another, and for themselves. For the purposes of the assembly, the School is broken down into two parts, and two separate assemblies are held (one for K–3, the other for 4–8). A total of about 125 parents attend one of the two assemblies, which are held during the school day. A published program, designed by a teacher, lists the awards that are given in such areas as attendance, citizenship, service, personal academic achievement, and also for scholarship. There are trophies, medals, and certificates for those who have merited them.

At the last June assembly, eighteen students received recognition for perfect attendance, fifty-four for scholarship, fourteen for patrol, and seven for outstanding service as messengers. A total of sixty-eight pupils were honored for their improvement in reading, and another twenty-four for special reading achievement. All of these students were selected by their homeroom teachers. The last two reading award categories make it possible for pupils who cannot achieve in the scholarship area to achieve according to their personal effort.

The ceremony included the posting of Colors, the Pledge of Allegiance, the National Anthem, the school song, and three chorus pieces, two of which were sung by the honorees. The principal presented the awards and gave a speech. Later, many of the honorees attended a district honors assembly with students from other schools (in the Chicago public school system, a "district" is a subunit comprised of about fifteen elementary schools and perhaps two high schools).

There is also a separate graduation assembly for the eighth-grade class. The whole hall is filled with parents and other relatives, and some of the relatives even come from out of state for the occasion.

Maintaining Discipline

Discipline at the School is maintained less by teacher control than by teacher motivation of students to do the right thing at all times. The key factor is that the principal and teachers consistently try to teach students to accept responsibility for their behavior and its consequences. In an assembly at the beginning of each school year, the principal informs students, "This is what we expect of you." Throughout the year, teachers encourage students to continue doing what is expected. Among other things, students are told that maintaining appropriate reading scores is important, as well as showing respect for teachers and other pupils, and that if they feel under severe stress (or must "blow steam") they are free to leave the classroom and visit the principal's office and talk it out with someone else.

Teachers handle minor student infractions in the classroom as they arise. There is no after-school detention available as a punishment, but students are sometimes deprived of an activity like a field trip or gym, or eating lunch with their friends (they will eat alone) as a consequence of bad behavior.

There are seldom any serious misconduct problems. Students know and follow the rules. Things like stealing, cheating, fighting, and vandalism do not usually occur. Students say this is so because they like one another, their teachers, and their principal, and they are proud of their school. However, students are told not to bring valuable objects to school, for example, cameras and radios, and if they do the items are confiscated by faculty and returned later.

Because the faculty has a large number of experienced teachers, most lessons show the results of this experience in terms of good classroom management and a variety of teaching methods that have been acquired over the years. Often, teachers leave the room briefly, while children are working on assignments; at such times an adult teacher aide comes in to keep an eye on things, but there is no change in the class atmosphere. The children simply continue on with their work. Good behavior also carries over outside the classroom, too. The principal frequently receives letters and phone calls from places students have visited on field trips, commending the students.

Teachers are responsible for seeing that their homerooms get to and from the gym and library in good order. Older students eat in the lunch-room of the old building, and their teachers eat with them so they can supervise the lunch period. Bathroom breaks are scheduled for the younger students, and it is each teacher's responsibility to see that students go and return quietly so as not to disturb other classrooms. Teachers take turns supervising the all-school recess period in good weather. Six teachers are on playground duty at all times, but they rotate supervision one week at a time, so that each has three or four turns during a semester. In addition, the gym teacher, the adjustment teacher, and the teacher aides increase the number of supervisors on duty outside.

The School has an average daily attendance of about 92 percent. In winter, attendance slips to perhaps 85 percent, while in September, May, and June possibly 95 percent are in attendance. Parents are instructed to call in on the day their children are absent. If such calls are not received, follow-up calls are made the same day either by a teacher or a community aide.

Tardiness is handled on an individual basis in whatever way seems appropriate to the situation. In general, teachers react to the tardy students by conveying the attitude, "You're late and that's not good, but we're glad you are here. Please try to make it on time in the future."

If necessary, the principal will lay down the law more strongly. How-ever, it should be noted that some students practically raise themselves, and their overall sense of responsibility is praiseworthy despite occasional tardi-ness. The principal cited as an example two brothers whose mother is a drug pusher. The boys, now in sixth and eighth grade, have been on their own to get to school regularly and on time ever since they started.

Serious fighting and stealing are handled by the principal in her office, in conferences with the students involved. The philosophy out of which she operates in such cases is: teach kids what is right. Get them to achieve insights into their own behavior. Once a fight is over you can't undo it, but you can admit your mistake and decide not to repeat it.

The principal reserves suspension as the ultimate punishment. She uses it rarely, and only if a student poses a threat to others. If she suspends one student a year for serious infringement of discipline, that is a lot.

Book Learning

The teaching of cognitive skills is carried out in self-contained classrooms. In other words, all students who are achieving at a certain level are with one teacher in one classroom for all their subjects all day long. Thus their "sub-ject" teacher and their "homeroom" teacher are the same. However, the School is "ungraded," which means that a student will be in a fifth-year classroom rather than a fifth grade. Students who will master the work designated for the fifth level will be promoted at the end of the year to the sixth level. Those who do not complete the requirements are not advanced.

Classrooms have an air of busy informality. If the teacher is working with a small group of students, the rest of the class is quietly doing individual work. Students at listening posts who are plugged into tape recorders continue to work undistracted. So do others who are doing spelling or programmed learning or writing compositions at their desks. Checked-in homework for each student is duly recorded on a bulletin board chart, and teachers are expected to assign homework daily to all students. But cognitive learning skills go on outside the classroom, too. There are field trips scheduled several times a year. And, sometime during the spring, the assistant principal walks the eighth-year students over to the nearby social security office, where they fill out the forms for their social security numbers.

Teacher praise and report-card evaluations are one means for reinforcing student achievement. The Board of Education provides a report-card form and requires reports four times a year. The grades are E (Excellent), G (Good), F (Fair) and D (Failure). However, the principal and teachers found that the official report card lacked some of the more precise information parents wanted to know. The faculty spent one semester of inservice meetings working out their own forms for kindergarten, primary, intermediate, upper, and special education levels. Recently the board revised its report-card form and incorporated some of the School's items.

Parents, too, take an interest in their children's academic progress. Almost 100 percent of them come twice a year for report-card conferences with their child's teacher. On the half-day which is set aside for this purpose each semester, 60 percent of the parents are present. The remainder schedule a convenient time with the teacher. The principal concludes, "Parents will come to school when they figure it's worth their while."

The Board of Education also provides teachers with lesson plan books. These are kept in the teacher's desk, available to the principal. It is her belief that lesson plans are needed by teachers, but the longer a teacher works at the School, the less she looks at their lesson plans. When teachers are succeeding in raising their pupils' score, she infers they are teaching efficiently. When pupils' scores are lagging behind, the lesson plan is the first thing the principal asks to see, because often difficulties arise from poor planning. Informally, the principal sees lesson plans when teachers come to confer about student progress.

Each teacher keeps the cumulative folders on his own students. The principal has a file of cards on each of the 600 students, which she keeps in her office. The card, which she designed, records attendance, reading and math scores, and other significant items. It is a good information summary, always handy for academic or discipline conferences.

There has been a collective scholastic improvement at the School in recent years. Citywide standardized testing indicates the median reading level of the graduating students gained a year and a half during the past two years, from 5.3 to 6.9. At the primary level, scores show 40 percent of students reading above grade level. At the same time, the percentage of low-income families (as classified under the Elementary and Secondary Education Act) has increased from 63.7 percent to 82.1 percent. One reason for the reading improvement is that teachers have worked especially hard at reading. At the principal's insistence, teachers try to help each student achieve grade-level competence regardless of what "the records" show he can do.

A graduation list of eighth-year students is started at the beginning of the year, listing those students who are achieving at grade level (and who thus are sure of graduating). The list is added to as more students reach the standards for graduation. The Iowa Basics test given in the spring increases the list further, so that by June about 88 percent of the eighth-year students have fulfilled the requirements for graduation. The 12 percent who do not achieve begin a ninth year at the School, but do not remain in elementary school beyond that.

Supervising Teachers

In the past, the principal did some recruiting for her staff, and wrote to the personnel department of the Chicago Board of Education to request that certain teachers be assigned to her school. Today racial balance requirements affect teacher assignments, but the principal still makes requests for teachers she knows to be good (and often such requests are honored).

In case of teacher absence, a substitute teacher is obtained from the district list. If a substitute proves to be good, the principal may arrange with that person to return daily for a period of time. Such teachers are put on "full-time basis" substitution for the School. This assures the principal and the faculty of maintaining quality teachers even in a substitute position. It also strengthens the principal as head of her own local institution. Finally, it lets the principal look over potential new permanent staff.

The principal has spent a good deal of time getting to know her teachers as persons and as professionals. She has become familiar with their personal problems and their orientation through conferences and observation. Her office door is always open, and teachers know they can stop in at any time.

Each teacher builds a class learning plan for the year, and confers with the principal about its rationale. Teachers also organize lesson plans, make out quarterly report cards and monthly attendance records, answer Board of Education surveys, and fill out a variety of required forms as part of their job. Most of these documents are scanned by the principal. How teachers handle these kinds of paperwork is one indication of their professional competence. These items also provide a springboard for discussion during conferences with the principal.

Informal encounters, classroom visits, and faculty meetings provide further opportunity for the principal to talk with and observe teachers. She feels that a teacher's value system as a professional is the same as her value system as a person. One indirect way of discovering a teacher's value system is to see how that teacher evaluates students and comments on their progress in the periodic written reports to parents (and the principal scans all of these reports).

Teachers spend twenty-two and one-half hours a week in actual classroom teaching at the School. This does not include gym, library, recess, and lunch. Six and one-half hours during the school week are allowed each teacher for preparation time. About 50 percent of the faculty arrive at 8:00 A.M. instead of at 8:30 (as required), because teachers value the extra time for professional exchange and/or social interaction with one another before school.

At present, faculty inservice days provide the best time for meeting colleagues on a professional level. There are five half-days of inservice scheduled each year, and three full days. Every other week, half an hour is provided during the school day for inservice. The teachers at the School say they prefer their own inservice held at their school to the inservice sponsored at the district level.

Because of the dangerous character of the neighborhood, the principal encourages all teachers to leave the building right after student dismissal. Since this leaves no time for teachers to be available to students after school, most give students' parents their home phone numbers.

The Chicago public school system requires a yearly evaluation of teachers. The evaluation includes a computerized instrument that provides a rating for every teacher. At the School, the principal also evaluates her teachers in an informal way, using a very flexible approach. Sometimes she will have the teacher use a self-evaluation instrument (which she has designed), to provide the basis for teacher self-evaluation and subsequent discussion with the principal at an appropriate time. Sometimes no instrument is used at all, and a conference suffices.

The principal also talks with both teachers and students outside of the classroom or in her office. She observes how students imitate their teachers for better or worse, observes student-teacher contacts in the halls, and notices whether or not students take books home with them. She deals with student discipline problems, hears parent feedback, and is aware of how punctual teachers are when returning reports to the office. As she sees it, all these things provide clues as to how effective a teacher is.

The principal relies on her teachers for input before making administrative decisions. Thus, the School experimented for a while with departmental studies some years ago. Under that plan, a teacher of upper-grade language arts would have four or five groups of students for that one subject area; a teacher of intermediate-level arithmetic would have all intermediate students coming in for that subject, and so on. When teachers evaluated the experiment, the consensus was that students needed the structure and stability which the self-contained classroom could offer. So the decision was made to change back to self-contained classrooms.

Teachers also provide the principal with curriculum input and try out new methods and materials. They have used various materials such as the Board of Education's End of Cycle tests to judge their value in determining whether a student should be promoted. Teachers also help decide which books should be ordered for each level.

Finally, it was a faculty decision which caused the principal to shorten the school day by shortening the lunch period. Such arrangements to create a "closed campus" (no going home for lunch) had been implemented by most other public elementary schools in Chicago, with a 9:00 to 2:30 school day. The School's faculty preferred to keep the longer schedule, in order to keep open some lunchtime meeting opportunities for staff. However, after several years the faculty finally decided it would be in the best interests of the students and parents to shorten the school day.

The principal maintains good relations with the district superintendent's office, which is the next intermediate supervisory unit between the School and the Board of Education. There are monthly meetings for all the district's principals, either at the office or at one of the schools. The meetings are scheduled for a half-day, but frequently continue in an informal way over lunch. The principals cooperate, through committees, to carry on work that has been delegated by the superintendent. Such topics as promotion policy, textbook selection, and inservice program planning are handled this way. In addition, the principal of the School and four or five other principal friends from the district meet weekly for lunch, providing a support network and social interaction for one another.

The principal's eighteen years' experience in administration and twelve years as a teacher have helped her become efficient in handling bureaucratic matters. She is also skillful in running her own school without submitting to the pressures and rigidity that can arise within a large school system. As she sees it, her school exists to educate children, and all other concerns are of secondary importance. Often she asks teachers about the usefulness of materials that come from the Board of Education. If certain forms or procedures will create more problems or work for teachers, the principal will make the final decision about implementing them in her school. This means a communication with the district superintendent, and her willingness to handle the disapproval which may result.

The School has one assistant principal. He has an important role in the school's daily operation. He, too, spends much time getting to know students and teachers, and parents as well. He often acts as an important sounding board—relating people's concerns to the principal. In this way the principal hears and learns a lot, but not in a formal manner. She can thus keep a finger on the pulse of the School, without becoming a threatening presence.

The assistant principal also deals frequently with parents, filtering out problems that do not necessarily need the principal's attention. He offers another administrative personality capable of hearing an individual's concerns. It is he who takes care of scheduling, assigning teacher duties, arranging for substitute teachers, and dealing with student problems.

The assistant principal meets each morning with the principal. Together they discuss the day's agenda and the state of affairs. Since he arrives at 7:30, half an hour before the principal, he already knows what faculty members will be absent and has arranged to cover their classes. He and the principal also discuss scheduling procedures at the beginning of the school year, as well as the philosophy behind any changes in routine. Both administrators operate on the theory that they are there to serve the teachers, so that the teachers can teach the students more efficiently and effectively.

The relationship among the principal, the assistant principal, and the teachers is suggested by the following example of delegated authority and accountability. The School is divided into primary, intermediate, and junior-high clusters. There are about 250 students and eleven teachers in the primary cluster, 200 students and eight teachers in the intermediate cluster, and 150 students and five teachers in the junior-high cluster. Four rooms of special-education students are included in this breakdown, and one teacher represents a special-ed focus when the clusters meet.

Each cluster has a chair—one teacher responsible for helping the group work together, and for being knowledgeable about one another's curriculum and teaching practices. The chair also serves as a liaison between principal and teachers. The additional responsibility placed on and accepted by the chair has encouraged that teacher to become more professional.

Being cluster chair involves extra time and work, but no extra pay. The principal meets with these people every two weeks, and they meet among themselves weekly. They declined the principal's offer of an extra free period each week as a form of small incentive, preferring to meet on their own time rather than to be away from their students. The assistant principal jokingly takes credit "for finally getting the principal to delegate," as he puts it. At the same time, this informal organization of faculty gives the principal a good way of communicating with all her teachers through the cluster chair.

The principal spends about 60 percent of her week in the office. During that time she is usually dealing with teachers, students, and parents rather than with paperwork. When complaints reach her, they are listened to. Whether the source is a parent, teacher, or student, the administration will hear the person out before making a judgment. Some complaints will lead to a change, or suggestions for improvement will be implemented. When a parent felt that the library was not being well used, the criticism was investigated, and as a result library usage was improved.

In general, there is open communication among adults at all levels in the School. Teachers will usually confront one another, rather than take their differences to the principal. Most often, an atmosphere of helpfulness, not competition or bickering, prevails. The rapport between union and management is so good that the union rep complains she hasn't found anything to grieve over in nine years.

2 A Chicago Public High School

Evidence indicates that the large, comprehensive school has not been naturally money-saving, educationally advantageous, or broadly socializing. . . . The data demonstrate that when enrollment rises above 1,000 students, the comprehensive high school's cost per student declines little, while there is abundant evidence that the educational effectiveness of such institutions decreases with size. [1]

The School is a large high school with 3,763 students and 202 teachers. Seventy-five percent of its students are white, and 25 percent of them are classified as coming from "low-income" families.

Character Development and Extracurricular Activities

One way to describe a school is to determine the amount of "prosocial conduct" it generates among students. Such conduct obviously assists character development. We found that the School offers a variety of character-related activities for its students. A list of the major extracurricular activities which we compiled totaled seventeen sports activities and twenty-nine clubs and other student organizations. In the folder which each entering freshman is given (containing two pages of text), most of these activities are enumerated and the "students are encouraged to participate."

What was discouraging for us, then, was the widespread lack of participation. For example, we asked twenty-four students if they participated in a club or activity (with the exclusion of being a teacher aide), and only six responded affirmatively, naming concert choir, band, Girls Athletic Association, and athletic teams as what they took part in. This random sampling suggests that only about one-fourth of the School's student body participates in a structured activity, despite the fact that, for many of these activities, participation is open to all. Later, we will try to discover why this lack of participation exists, but for the moment we would like to consider some of the activities with which we became familiar.

We observed a scheduled pep rally. This was the third pep rally of the year; it honored the School's "girls' teams." The president of the student council (who, by her uniform, must have also been either a cheerleader or pompom girl) did an excellent job of presiding over the rally, being very poised on stage and speaking clearly into the microphone as she announced the team coaches and program highlights. It appeared to be a well-planned rally, with the ROTC presenting the colors, the band providing music, and twirlers performing routines.

Each coach announced her team and usually gave some facts about the season or how one could go about trying out for the team. As the names were read, the girl athletes came up on the stage and formed a line. We could thus determine the number of girls who "had made" each team, which was as follows: volleyball—twelve girls; swimming—sixteen; tennis—six; basketball—eleven; track—1979 team not picked yet, but the coach gave logistics for trying out, number of events, and stated that there could be 30 to 40 girls on the team; and softball—also not yet picked. As an example of the recognition given, the volleyball coach announced that the School's team had taken third place in the citywide Mayor Bilandic Tournament, and two of the team members brought huge trophies on stage.

Most of the students seemed to be enjoying the rally. Previously we had asked nine students if they had ever attended a pep rally and only four said that they had. It was explained to us that one could only attend the rally if his or her class (meeting at that period) was invited, or if he or she received written permission from a P.E. teacher to miss class to attend the rally. Noticing that the auditorium was packed, we inferred that this limit is imposed because of the size of the student body. Nevertheless, all four students who had attended a pep rally said they enjoyed it.

Moreover, nine out of seventeen students we interviewed said they thought there was lots of school spirit for athletic events; eleven out of seventeen had attended at least one game or event; and nine had attended more than one.

We also asked nine girls if they knew what the qualifications were for being a cheerleader and all nine knew (whereas they usually did not know how one could go about participating in other activities, such as the student council or yearbook). We found that being a cheerleader and, to a lesser extent, a pom-pom girl or twirler, was a "status" position at the School. The students knew that "cheerleaders must have a B overall average, a B in gym, and be able to do things like splits and cartwheels." One student estimated that each year about fifty girls try out, but only five are chosen to be cheerleaders.

Another activity we found to be popular, but in this case open to anyone who wanted to participate, is being a teacher aide. When we asked twenty students if they were aides, thirteen responded affirmatively. They listed their duties as running messages, picking up mail, filing, and writing cut slips. We heard from several students that teacher aides or student office aides can often be "bribed" by other students into not reporting cuts and stealing tardy cards (that is, excuse forms) for students. In effect, their work was often not carefully supervised by teachers, and they were not properly socialized for their responsibilities.

Another activity which generates wide participation at the School is drama. The School's dramatic events, especially its spectacular musicals, are very popular with students. Sixteen out of twenty students we talked to had attended at least one play, and they all had words of praise for the professionally done performances. A student who had participated in dramatic productions told us that it was necessary to devote about two hours of work after school every day to prepare for them and that, as the production date drew nearer, rehearsals demanded even more time. We discovered that 100 students are involved in this spring's production of *The King and I*, currently in preparation.

Of course, this number includes students with musical talents who are members of the various instrumental and vocal groups. Music activities, then, are another popular form of participation at the School. Two students out of fifteen interviewed said they participated, and nine said they had attended performances. One student estimated that there were about seventy-five students in the concert choir, thirty-five students in the mixed chorus, and twenty-five in the girls' chorus. We found out that fifty students participate in the band and twenty in the jazz band. We also learned that students receive one-fourth of an academic credit for being in either of the three choruses (concert, mixed, and girls') or the band or orchestra, and that the students rarely put in time before or after school for these activities, with the exception of the orchestra. The orchestra has an annual election for student officers: president, vice-president, secretary, and treasurer. The officers' main functions are to organize fundraisers (for new instruments) and determine who will participate in the annual citywide orchestra competition. Other than the spring and winter concerts, the choruses and band gather as a group for about forty minutes, five days a week, during a class period.

A news article on the School in a major Chicago paper reported that student organizations (last year) had raised $6,000 to help pay for the auditorium's new sound system. We cross-checked this information with students, to test the quality of information flow in the school (and to implicitly assess the accuracy of the report). Fifteen out of seventeen students we asked said there were fundraising programs at the School, and cited such projects as Christmas toy giving, Taffy Apple Day, bake sales, the football team's raffling off a turkey to buy new equipment, and the band's selling candy bars to buy new instruments and uniforms. However, none of the respondents (thirteen were upperclassmen) made mention of what must have been the rather spectacular fundraising project for the new sound equipment. To illustrate the diversity of answers we often got, we asked seventeen students, "About how often do you think a fundraising project occurs?" Some of the answers: "We don't have any"; "Continuously"; "Five a year"; "Three a month"; "Once a month"; "Over the holidays"; "Don't know."

Furthermore, when we asked the seventeen students, "Do you think the student council does a good job?" eight students thought the council was rather ineffective, yet the same article reported that last year the council raised $1,000 toward the new sound system. Of course, it is possible that the students we asked were thinking of this year's student council, which may not be doing a very good job. Still, we thought it strange that no one mentioned the fundraising role of the student council. When we asked the students what the council does do, they cited that it sponsors activities such as Hat Day (everybody wears a hat), Turn-about Day (teachers exchange places with students), Carnation Day (on February 14 secret admirers send carnations), and roller skating parties, as well as doing some of the planning for Homecoming and Prom.

Despite the fact that the folder entering freshmen are given states how council members are elected, most students did not know the election procedures. Many did know that representatives are elected yearly by divisions (that is, there is one division for each year group of students). We asked, "Do the elections create lots of interest? Do students campaign?" The most recurring answer: "Not much. Usually somebody wants to be a member from a division, but it's really no big deal." Then we asked, "Do you know how often the student council meets?" Again, the answers were diverse, ranging from "I don't know" to "I think once a month." So we asked, "Does your representative report back to your division? Is he given a few minutes to stand before the division and report activities the council has planned?" The usual answer: "No, I don't think so." This conflicts with what is stated in the explanation folder. So we asked, "Then how do you find out about what's going on—for example, Hat Day?" The typical answer: "You just find out by talkin' to other kids." Two students did mention that the council often decorates bulletin boards in the halls and places notices of coming events on them. This we observed to be the case.

As observer/interviewers visiting the School, we concluded that many, many students simply don't know what's going on in the School, and don't care. We could cite many examples of factual, not opinion, questions we asked to which we received a myriad of answers. Perhaps if we had talked to the School's "most involved" students, we would walk away with the feeling that the students are highly interested in extracurricular activities. However, as we stated, our random sampling suggests that only about one-fourth of the students participate in a club or activity (exclusive of being teacher aides). And, moreover, communication lines concerning how to get involved seem to be rather poor.

We will close this section on extracurricular activities by taking a close look at what is often a critical means of communication in an educational institution—the school newspaper. While it is only one of many activities in the School, an in-depth treatment of its operations may suggest to us some of the patterns that affect other programs. Part of our information came from the paper's faculty sponsor.

First, we asked twenty-four students, "Have you ever read the school newspaper?" Eighteen responded affirmatively. We then asked, "How often it is issued?" Again, there were a variety of answers, but most students thought it was issued about once a month. Our next question was: "Who prints, edits, and writes it?" Ten students responded that they didn't know; the remaining fourteen generally named the journalism class and the print shop. We then asked, "So how do you go about being on the staff—take the journalism or the printing class?" Most frequent answer: "Yes, I guess so." Finally we asked, "Do you think the newspaper is good?" Twelve thought it was good, five thought is was "just okay" or "so-so," and seven students thought it wasn't very good, giving such answers as "It stinks"; "It comes out late and is very outdated"; and "It's not worth 10 cents."

Mrs. X, the newspaper sponsor, explained that the publication is compiled by students in the journalism class, and students who have seventh, eighth, and ninth periods free and who desire to be on the staff. The printing class uses offset printing to produce the final product. In short, anyone who really wants to work on the newspaper is welcome to do so. When we asked her how many students actually comprise the staff, her response involved counting the list of names on the masthead, which totaled thirty-three.

Away for the summer, Mrs. X, who normally teaches all English classes, found out two weeks before school was to begin that she would be teaching journalism and sponsoring the newspaper for the 1978–1979 school year. However, she wasn't upset or too concerned because she "had had a course in journalism in college." She set as her goal the production of five issues this school year. (Issue three was currently being prepared.) She feels that the size of her staff is very adequate and that her staffers are all hard workers. "I'd rather have ten good workers than twenty lazy ones," Mrs. X said. Mrs. X was also extremely proud of the job her students have done so far.

When asked why there was a charge for the paper, she replied that normally high-school students pay into a "civic fund" but that School students are not required to pay; therefore, a 10-cent charge per issue is levied to help defray paper, ink, and telephone costs. Ads are generally accepted, but not solicited. That is, businesses wishing to place an ad usually contact Mrs X; student business managers do not sell ads.

When we asked her why so few issues were put out a year, she replied that the print shop is very busy because it does "all the printing for the School." She said that in her journalism class coming issues are discussed and story assignments are made. When these assignments are turned in, they are typed and then sent to the print shop class, who, in turn, return galleys to the journalism class for layout. She implied that this procedure is quite time-consuming.

Noticing a Quill & Scroll pennant on the paper's bulletin board and its emblem on the masthead, we asked Mrs. X if there was a chapter at the School. (Quill & Scroll is the national honor society for students interested in journalism.) She said no, and that the teacher who taught journalism last year had his students involved in it.'' We asked her if members of the staff were recognized schoolwide for their journalistic efforts at any type of awards ceremony. She replied that they were not, but that "the newspaper staff itself does hold its own banquet every spring." We asked if students ever attended journalism conferences and she mentioned that she thought some students were planning to attend workshops geared to newspaper and yearbook production which would be held at another Chicago high school this spring.

Now, for a look at the paper itself. The two issues we examined were ridden with errors in punctuation, spelling, and grammar. For instance, thirty errors were counted on the first page of the second issue. The paper has only eight pages, four of which are entirely pictures!

A reading of the paper also showed why some students told us it wasn't very good, or just okay. The front page story for the second issue was on "Christmas around the World." It is a somewhat vapid little piece on different holiday traditions—a typical "World Book Encyclopedia–researched" article. Since the School has students from many ethnic groups, a student reporter might have gone out and interviewed a dozen School students about how their families celebrate Christmas: for example, "Maria Lopez, whose parents were born in Mexico, tells us that every year. . . . '' Not only would Maria and the other interviewees probably eagerly await the paper, but they might even share the article with their families.

The paper has nothing in it that might interest students. There are no student-written editorials, for example, or any guest editorials by faculty members. Instead, a typical issue of the paper is comprised of the aforementioned Christmas piece, an article on the student ROTC, a humorous piece on the hazards of walking in the halls, a couple letters to the editor, a horoscope (the seer who compiled it is unnamed), some artwork, a couple poems, a Christmas spirit story, three ads, and some sports stories. The *School Times* cannot serve to disseminate much information about coming events because of its low issuance rate. The Christmas issue, for example, only informs us of the wrestling schedule. In short, the paper lacks substance, flavor, pizzazz.

It is instructive to see why activities such as cheerleading and drama attract enthusiastic and competent participants at this school, and others, like the school newspaper, do not. Cheerleading and drama are presented to audiences via a literal stage. And when activities are physically "on stage," the participants are under obvious pressure to improve on the quality of their product, and to seek and earn the pleasure of direct plaudits. In the case of the paper, the feedback from readers is somewhat more indirect. It takes ingenuity—essentially by the faculty sponsor—to translate such potential feedback into reinforcements which stimulate students to maintain a high level operation.

The Quill & Scroll matter is another example of insufficient ingenuity. If the journalism teacher were motivated to go about getting a Quill & Scroll chapter, the students might profit: Quill & Scroll has academic standards; it publishes a magazine for its members; it sponsors contests; it gives scholarships. Moreover, the journalism teacher could not only encourage students to attend workshops but she could attend them as well. And if the newspaper staff could be recognized as part of a schoolwide ceremony (rather than having a little awardless banquet all to themselves), students might be more motivated to join the staff and work hard to produce an informative, interesting, and artistic product. As it is, the newspaper staffers are undistinguished from the rest of the student body. When a cheerleader wearing her uniform walks down the hall, everyone recognizes her as such. Chances are when the sports editor walks down the hall nobody knows he's even on the newspaper staff. And nobody probably cares.

Discipline

Certain forms of antisocial conduct are expressly prohibited at the School. The folder given to freshmen makes it clear to students that smoking is not permitted and that failure to obey the rule will result in suspension. Tardiness, absences, lunchroom rules, appropriate dress, and corridor passes are also briefly mentioned in the folder. Since this is the only form of written rules distributed to students, we decided to try to find out if students assumed other forms of antisocial conduct, such as cheating, fighting, and stealing, are implicitly prohibited simply because society at large defines them as undesirable.

We went to the students and asked a variety of questions concerning prohibited conduct and corollary punishment. For example, we asked sixteen students if they ever smoke in school. Thirteen responded negatively, and fourteen knew that the punishment when caught is suspension. The students told us that most teachers enforce the rule, to the extent of telling the student to stop smoking. In other words, rather than report that the student should be suspended for smoking, the teacher merely tells the student to stop smoking. The students told us that failure to stop would then result in action toward suspension by the teacher.

We also asked sixteen students if they'd ever seen a fight in the School. Fifteen replied affirmatively, and five said that they'd personally been involved in fights. All but one student listed the punishment if caught as suspension. Several told us that the male teachers are usually called in to break up fights as soon as possible.

We asked if there were prohibitions against taking drugs and alcohol in school. The students told us there were. We asked, "How do you know? Do you have a handbook with this rule stated in it? How do you know what the punishment is? Is the rule announced to you by teachers or administrators—say, at the beginning of the school year?" Their most frequent reply: 'You just know." We asked these same sixteen students if they'd ever seen anyone intoxicated or "high" in school, and thirteen replied affirmatively.

We asked twenty-two students if they knew of anyone who carried a weapon in school. Sixteen said they had seen knives and razor blades. We asked if carrying a weapon was against school policy, and they said it was, but could not pinpoint how they knew so. Five thought it was written down in a list of rules they'd been given, but none could produce this list or give us its title or other particulars. We also asked the students if they thought schoolmates carried weapons for protection. The answers were varied: six thought they weren't needed for protection, six thought they were needed, and ten thought they were needed partly for protection but also were carried just to "act tough."

We asked these same twenty-two students if they'd ever had anything stolen, and fifteen lamented their vanished possessions, although twelve had had something stolen only once. Again, we asked them if there is a formal school prohibition against stealing, and their answers were similar to those given for using alcohol or drugs and carrying a weapon. Finally, we asked if they could offer any kind of solution to this problem and most said that, because of the size of the School, some amount of stealing was bound to occur and it probably just couldn't be stopped. A few said there could be more and better security, and that the best way to discourage stealing was not to bring expensive possessions to school.

We asked twenty students if they had ever cheated on an exam, and fifteen said they had, but none of them had ever been caught. From the estimates these fifteen students gave us about how often they cheat, we calculated that they cheat about 20 percent of the time. "What do you think would have happened if you'd been caught?" we asked. Most thought the teacher would fail the cheater for that exam; three students thought the teacher might fail the cheater for the entire course that quarter. "You mean it's probably up to the discretion of the individual teacher to determine the severity of the punishment?" we asked. All the students agreed.

We then asked twenty students if there was a rule against swearing. Ten said a student would get into trouble for swearing at a teacher. "What kind of trouble?'' we asked. Four thought the punishment would be suspension; four, detention; two didn't know. "So there's no formal rule stating a punishment for invective speech?" we asked. The students agreed. Some students added that some teachers are "more lenient" about swearing and that the usual practice concerning swearing is similar to that for smoking, that is, when a teacher hears a student using four-letter expletives he says something like, "Hey, watch what you're saying!" Only if the student continues to use inappropriate language does the teacher take further disciplinary action.

Our next questions concerned unexcused cutting classes, or being tardy, or entirely absent from school. We asked sixteen students what the penalty was for cutting classes, and fifteen told us that the student would be "barred" from all classes. "What does this mean?" we asked. "It means you can't go to classes until your parents come to school and reinstate you." "How's it different from 'suspension'?" we asked. All sixteen knew the distinction: suspension involves being sent home; being barred involves being confined to a certain room in the school.

When we asked them how they knew this punishment rule, they replied as they had to our questions about cheating, using drugs and alcohol, and so on. In other words, "you just know." We pointed out that the folder said that "cutting will result in a direct lowering of grades." "Is this so?" we asked. "Yea, I guess so—but you've got to be caught," was the usual reply. We asked sixteen students if they'd ever cut a class and twelve said they had, but that it was fairly easy to avoid getting caught. "What's your trick?" Some of their revelations: forge passes, bribe student aides working in the office, or "feed the teacher a line."

The folder gives the procedure a tardy student must follow upon arriving at school, and states that "continued tardiness will result in severe disciplinary action." This vague warning perhaps accounts for the fact that students gave us a variety of answers when we asked them, "What happens if you are tardy?" Some told us that after a student is tardy five times, a note is sent home to his parents and after ten times the punishment is detention. Still another student gave us an elaborate description: if a student is tardy over 200 minutes or five times (whichever comes first) he gets five detentions; after ten tardies a quarter, ten detentions; after fifteen tardies the student gets barred; and after twenty tardies, suspended.

We asked twenty students if they'd ever been tardy and all but one said that they had. We asked them about how many times they'd been tardy this school year. Their answers resulted in a high of one student having been tardy fifty times, but the majority said they had been tardy about twenty times. Again, they told us that it was possible to avoid the penalties for tardiness by asking friends who worked in the office to let them have tardy excuse cards.

Last, we asked the students about absences, and again the answers varied. Some said the administration called the student's parents whenever a student failed to show up at school, while others thought the school didn't do anything until a student was absent ten days, at which time a truant officer was called in. All twenty told us that, upon returning to school, a student has to present a note from his parents concerning the absence. We asked them how many times they'd been absent this school year. Some of the answers: twenty times, seventeen times, fifteen times, ten times, six times, once, not at all.

The folder gives a few general prescriptions for appropriate dress (for example, "dress and grooming shall reflect good taste"). We asked twenty students if there is a dress code, and fourteen said there is one. The other six replied that there is a code only in warm months, and that at these times students are not allowed to go barefoot and girls are not allowed to wear "skimpy" outfits: for example, halters and tube tops. Other students told us a student would be sent home and asked to change if he or she wore a T-shirt whose slogan was profane or sexually suggestive, and four students thought this rule wasn't fair. The remaining sixteen students thought the dress code was "fair."

We also asked students if there was a prohibition against displaying too much affection (for members of the opposite sex) at school; their answers were similar to those they gave for smoking: that is, if teachers walked by an noticed two students kissing, for example, they would say something like, "Hey, you two better stop messing around and get to class." Others said that teachers rarely made a point of trying to stop this behavior. Four students, all of whom admitted to displaying too much affection in the halls, told us that if a teacher noticed them doing so, they would be asked to show their ID cards. (If one imagines students searching in their purses and wallets for I.D.s, then presumably this works as a temporary means of breaking up the act of sexual affinity!)

We have tried to examine a number of forms of antisocial conduct and their corollary punishments. It is obvious that, while the students imagine they generally know "the rules," this knowledge is inconsistent and vague. This obscurity is understandable, since there actually exist few explicitly written prohibitions aside from the folder, and the language used in the folder is frequently ambiguous, obscure: for example, "Continued tardiness will result in severe disciplinary action." Also, we were not able to determine that parents are mailed any sort of handbook or letter stating rules of conduct. However, parents (or guardians) are required to come to the School to reinstate their barred or suspended children (or wards), so the School does place some responsibility for discouraging antisocial behavior on the parents. We did note that the School attempts to reduce antisocial behavior by restricting students from participation in extracurricular activities as a result of suspension or expulsion. This is clearly stated in the folder.

The students gave us the impression that they thought the faculty generally were pretty strict about requiring students to comply with the rules. For example, we asked ten students, "If you were smoking in the bathroom and a teacher walked in, would that teacher take some action regarding your smoking?" All ten said the teacher would do so. However, such requests for compliance were rarely accompanied with significant punishments. As a result, many students felt there was little to lose in persistently trying to "get away with" modest violations: the worst that would happen was that they would be told to stop it, and such a trivial "punishment" often made it worthwhile to attempt the violation (recall the number of students who cheated on exams, "tricks" students revealed for not getting caught for cutting classes, and so on).

We also presented this hypothetical situation to ten students: "You know you're not supposed to carry weapons to school, right? Well, suppose you knew that this one student had a switchblade—you'd actually seen it. Would you tell a faculty member that your schoolmate had a knife, would you talk to some of your friends and see if all of you together could do something about it, would you personally talk to the knife-carrying student and urge him to leave the weapon at home, or would you do nothing about it because it's really none of your business?" All ten responded by choosing the last alternative.

We also gave ten different students a similar proposal, except that the inappropriate behavior was "smoking in the john" rather than carrying a switchblade. But again, all ten chose the last alternative. Therefore, it appears that only teachers, administrators, and hired adult personnel (that is, hall guards and teacher aides) report violations of student behavior; students do not "tattle" on other students, even if the rules violated are reasonable, and the violations a physical threat to all persons in the School.

Book Learning

We made a merely brief attempt to assess the means of encouragement for cognitive learning at the School. There are two principal honor societies for recognition of academic achievement, the National Honor Society and Laurels. We were unable to determine if any of the community newspapers carry releases about students being cited for these honors, but all three groups have their pictures in the School yearbook. Neither their names nor pictures go into the student paper. Honor rolls are also posted on bulletin boards at the end of every quarter, and at the end of each year teachers in each home room *may* post class ranks. The ten top-ranking scholars from each senior class are announced at graduation ceremonies.

We also asked students a few questions about their schoolwork. For example, we asked eight students if their teachers usually wrote comments on their papers (specifically in the case of writing assignments) in addition to putting a grade on the paper. All eight said their teachers usually made comments. We asked these students about how much homework they were assigned each week. Six of them said they had about four hours of homework a week, one said he had about five hours, and one replied that he had only about two hours of homework per week. We then asked them if they thought their homework assignments were justified and helpful, or if the work seemed to be unplanned or to be of the "mickey mouse" variety. Four thought the homework was well planned and provided useful practice; four thought it didn't serve much purpose and that "it just gives the teacher more grades."

We asked them if any School teachers had ever contacted their parents—either to offer praise for superior work or to talk about learning difficulties. None of them could remember any teacher doing this. We asked fifteen students if they thought their teachers knew their materials, came to class prepared, and taught well. Nine replied affirmatively, but six told us that not all the teachers at the School meet these criteria. Some added that they had had teachers who "didn't care" and who were "lazy."

We asked eight students if their teachers ever gave them syllabi (a written description of their course's objectives and requirements) or reading lists. Only three responded that they had been given syllabi. No one had received a reading list. We asked them if they were given assignments which involved using the library. Four replied that library use had been necessary for some assignments. We then said, "What do you think of the contest the library's sponsoring now?" All eight asked us, "What contest?" We said we'd read in a recent bulletin, routinely distributed to all teachers, that the library was sponsoring a contest right now to see which student could read the most history books. Six of them then recalled that they'd heard about this contest. So we asked, "How'd you hear about it?" All six said they could remember hearing their homeroom teachers announce it. "Is that a good way to find out what's going on?" we asked. They all thought so.

Next we asked them if they thought their teachers used a variety of teaching modes—lecture, discussion, seeing films, role-playing, and so on. Five thought they did; three thought they didn't. We asked them if they could name some of the different teaching activities they'd had in classes. One student recalled that in his English class the students got to act out plays they were reading. Another student told us that in her bookkeeping class each student was presented with a hypothetical customer who had a problem he needed solved. Another student told us her German class had put out a newspaper in German, for which the students wrote all the news and columns. They couldn't come up with many other teaching modes or activities, however. We asked twelve students if there was student-to-student tutoring at the School. All told us there was no structured program, but that occasionally a teacher asked one student to work with another.

In conclusion, we found that the means of encouragement for cognitive learning appear to be healthy in some instances (teachers frequently write comments on papers) and lacking in others (no student we interviewed reported personal contact between his parent and teacher regarding his school work). Of course, balanced against these findings as well is our opinion of the cognitive learning as displayed in the school newspaper. We suspect the journalism teacher at the School gives her class frequent praise for their work (at least she stressed to us how very proud she was of them).

Supervising Teachers

The School is headed by a principal; immediately below him are four assistant principals, each of whom has a different area of responsibility, for example, programming, discipline, and counselors. Then, there are thirty-two department heads, supervising 202 teachers. Department heads receive only modest rewards for taking the position (they may be relieved on some teaching responsibility), and so the positions are largely staffed by volunteers (sometimes persons recruited by the principal) from among the teachers.

We asked the principal what the process is for hiring a teacher. He replied that all teachers are hired by the Chicago Board of Education, which has its own standards, and that he has "absolutely no control" over this matter. Notice that this answer is somewhat different from the procedure presented in the first school description, which was of a Chicago Board of Education elementary school. (The fact is that all Chicago principals are formally expected to take almost whatever they get from downtown, but that some principals are more determined and ingenious, and devise ways of getting around this formalism. The extent to which principals succeed in bending this rule is a critical tool for estimating their general efficacy.)

We then asked the principal if he was required to evaluate newly hired teachers, as well as continuing teachers, on some periodic basis. He replied that, while he makes it a point to visit the classrooms of substitute, temporary, and newly hired teachers, he does not always get the chance to visit every teacher once a semester. But he is required to submit teacher evaluations on all 202 teachers to his immediate superior, the district superintendent, once a year. He added that he pretty much knows "which teachers are doing their job and which aren't." We wanted to ask him *how* he knows this and what his criteria are for "doing the job"—after all, he had only been principal here for six months, and had last worked at the School (before transferring back as principal) several years ago in a subordinate position. However, we were pressed for time in our interview, and he moved to another subject.

But we did find out from him that the only set of guidelines given to a newly hired teacher is the two-page student folder. Hence, we must infer that no general criteria for the performance of one's job are clearly articulated to a newly hired teacher (or any teacher) by the School. That is, the Chicago Board of Education may set systemwide criteria but the School does not supplement these.

The principal told us that at the beginning of the school year each teacher is required to submit a lesson plan for the coming year, but that he does not necessarily expect the teachers to adhere to the plan. "So why are they prepared?" we asked him. He replied that it is a required policy of the Chicago Board of Education and that, for example, the teachers must use special forms provided by the district superintendent for this purpose. One of the teachers we talked to thought the supplied forms were very inadequate and so he also makes up daily plans of his own on "plain ol' paper." He let us see the plans, and we observed that they were very complete and organized, showing objectives, methods, and materials for each day. All of the five said they did prepare and did in fact use lesson plans for their classes.

We also asked the five teachers if they thought it was their responsibility to enforce school rules, for example, the one against smoking. All five again replied affirmatively, although they confirmed the practice the students had told us about whereby the observation of a prohibited behavior warrants, first, a warning to stop, and on the second occasion, a report to the disciplinarian. As one teacher told us, "I try to handle the situation on my own first. Only if that doesn't work do I resort to other actions which would result in the student being disciplined in some way."

We asked them about how many times they were absent during the school year. One replied he had been absent only once in twenty years of teaching. All of the others replied that they were absent about two or three times per year. All also said they were tardy only in extremely bad weather. As one teacher put it, "If there are students who can make it to class all year, why shouldn't I?"

We asked them about how many hours they spent at the school every day. One said she generally arrived at 7:15 and left at 3:45 P.M. Three estimated they put in eight hours a day. One told us that some teachers—for example, those involved with student dramatic productions—put in lots of hours at school. Finally, one teacher, whose only complaint about the School was that she had been sent there to meet faculty desegregation policies promulgated by the Board, stated that she left home at 6:00 to be at school at 8:00 and that if she didn't leave the school at 3:30 in the afternoon, traffic would be so bad that she'd "never get home."

We asked them if they ever contacted parents about a student's work. All said they rarely "had" to do this. Their answer implied that they thought, when we asked the question, we were referring only to children with learning problems; it was as if this was the only time parent/teacher contact was warranted. One teacher did tell us that she thought the School's practice of including the child's home telephone number on the class roster made it very convenient for her to contact parents, although, again, she seldom "had" to do this.

We asked them if they attended PTA meetings and only one had done so "a couple times." All told us they thought there was little parental participation in the School aside from attendance at athletic events, concerts, and plays. All told us that they attend graduation ceremonies and award ceremonies, which are held during the school day, if "invited" (recall the size of the auditorium).

From the answers the teachers gave us, it would appear that their own conception of being a good teacher demands qualities such as diligence (grading papers at home and preparing additional lesson plans), commitment (making it to school despite bad weather), and concern and caring (attending ceremonies).

Because we were able to observe some classes, we were also given an opportunity to assess these criteria as they are translated into the teacher's classroom behavior. One class observed was a mini-course on literature and the supernatural. During our visit, the students were discussing the novel *Dracula*. The class began with a brief written quiz which asked for the recall of factual knowledge. Then the teacher announced that next week they would be seeing an audiovisual presentation on "the horror film" and reminded the students about turning in their money if they wanted to buy tickets for a field trip to see the play *Dracula,* now showing downtown. A discussion of the assigned chapters of the novel then followed.

The students seemed to enjoy the class, the teacher, and the assigned novel. They appeared to be appreciating the techniques, themes, and characterization of the novel. The teacher was excited about the material, and used humor to hold the students' interest. She asked for their opinion and rewarded them for expressing their views and ideas and doubts. The class moved along at a lively pace, and no discipline problems were apparent.

The teacher's behavior in this instance can best be evaluated by considering some alternatives. First, she could have had the students grade their quizzes in class. This would have meant much less time to discuss the novel, but she would have less work to do herself later on. Second, she could have chosen not to bother with "the horror film." Why bother trying to requisition AV equipment? Finally, why plan an outing? It's a lot of extra work for her. Who wants to keep track of everybody's money and be responsible for a bunch of kids going to a play downtown?

We also found in our examination of the school that teaching seemed to be a very individualistic activity at School. Although there is team teaching in a humanities course, the five teachers we interviewed said they had never observed or very seldom observe a colleague in the classroom (one thought doing so would be "highly unethical"), and, moreover, that only occasionally and on an informal basis did they compare teaching techniques and students' work with one another. Also, four reported that their contacts with the principal were very infrequent. In fact, they mentioned that, aside from a few social or chance meetings, his visits to their classrooms about twice a year constituted their main contact with him. However, the fifth teacher, who served as a department chairman, said his contacts with the principal were very frequent. School Bulletins, which are issued about every three days, appear to be the chief means of communication between administration and teachers.

Finally, while four of the five teachers said they often mix socially with other School teachers, only one expressed the opinion that he would like to see more interaction among the faculty concerning instruction, schoolwide policy decisions, and academic and disciplinary concerns.

The principal told us that there are five inservice meetings during the school year which all teachers and administrators are required to attend. Students are dismissed early from school on these meeting days, allowing for about two- to three-hour meetings. In addition, each of the thirty-two departments has a meeting "approximately every six weeks." (Again, no set policy appears to be stated.) The teachers we talked to confirmed these meeting arrangements, although one of them had very irregularly scheduled departmental meetings. The principal also informed us that a meeting is held for newly hired teachers every fall before school begins. For teachers beginning in the middle of the year or at semester break, no such meeting is held and such teachers are "basically on their own."

School Spirit

One element of school spirit is the degree of cohesion and "bondedness" associated with a school. Entering students at the School receive a map, because of its size; and it is our opinion that these maps are needed. Students, who are required to carry identification cards with them, are permitted to leave the School's boundaries for their lunch period. Visitors are required to wear badges while in the School. Security, however, appears moderate. For example, two of our team members entered the School and spent several hours interviewing students in the cafeteria without badges, and were not noticed. Two others were stopped by teacher aides, patroling the cafeteria, who asked to see our passes. Students told us that hall guards consist of both hired personnel and only a few students; they estimated their number at about twenty to twenty-five.

Identifying school pins and badges, worn by students, can serve as another means of generating cohesiveness and boundaries. We asked twenty-three students if they owned a school pin, ring, badge, jacket, and so on, and seventeen replied affirmatively. Visiting the School on a day a pep rally was scheduled, we also noticed that the girls on each athletic team tried to dress similarly so that, as their team was presented to the school body, a "unified look" was apparent.

The School has no academic requirements (other than having passed eighth grade) for admission. Its "rival" local public high school, on the other hand, is a "technical high school." As a result, its entering students must not only pass eighth grade but attain scores on reading and math tests which are above city averages. Therefore, as one newspaper article puts it, "Tech can pick and choose from among the cream of the crop of North Side students clamoring for admission." Visiting the School, we chanced to meet one student who told us she wanted to go to Tech but her test scores weren't high enough, so she "had" to go here instead.

We could not identify a common, publicized purpose for the School. The student folder has no real statement of educational objectives or philosophy. Despite this lack of a common stated objective, there seem to be a few instances where superordinate goals for collective activities have been identified and reached (for example, fundraising to replace the auditorium's sound system). On the other hand, the general impression we reached is that the School is very fragmented, that there are many subcommunities within it, and, while some of these subcommunities have goals, there are few recognized larger community goals. One teacher we spoke to characterized the school as "large and impersonal." Students told us there were lots of "cliques." We return again to the fact that the auditorium isn't even large enough to hold the entire student body. There seems to be no getting around the fact that the School's size is one of its obstacles toward being a truly effective community.

The School does have some expressions of community purpose. Every student we asked could tell us the school colors (purple and gold) and name the school mascot (the bulldog). At the pep rally we observed that, while the students may not know the words to the school song, they recognize it when they hear it. The School is named after an historical figure (who emigrated to America) of some importance during the nineteenth century, and we asked ten students what they knew about the School's namesake. Four did not know who he was other than "probably a famous man" and "who they named the school after." Six knew he was a famous man of German extraction, but only one of these six knew he was a famous statesman of German extraction.

As far as we were able to determine, award ceremonies honoring academic achievement are held during the school day and classes must be "invited" to attend. We were unable to determine how many of these ceremonies are held, but, considering that only three or four pep rallies are probably held during the year, we guess there might be about two academic ceremonies. However, we did learn that many of the subcommunities within the School have their own awards ceremonies or group gatherings; for example, the Football Banquet, the Drama Club Banquet, and so on. Once again, because of the size of the student population, schoolwide assemblies are prohibited.

As for parent-school relations, while there is a Parent-Teacher Association, it generates little interest. The only teacher whom we talked to who attended a few meetings observed that "it was always the same parents who came," and that some parents were active in the organization despite the fact that their sons and daughters had graduated from School. But many parents take an interest in attending activities such as athletic events, plays, and concerts. Eighteen out of twenty students we interviewed said a parent had attended at least one school event this year. On the other hand, there appears to be little additional contact of the parents with the School—except in instances where they must reinstate a barred or suspended son or daughter. Moreover, there is little contact between parents and faculty members.

During our interview with the principal, we asked him what he saw as the major problems facing the School. He replied that he saw the potential problems that gangs can create as being one of his chief concerns. (Earlier a student had given us a list of the major gangs: O-As, Freaks, Latin Kings, Gaylords, Jousters, and Future O-As; we also noticed these names among the graffiti on the outside of the building.) Presently, gang members are not allowed to wear any sort of gang identification, e.g., jackets with gang names, to school. The principal indicated to us that one of his objectives for this and succeeding school years is to "tighten up the rules," since the student folder "has not been revised for years." Asserting that the gangs "can blow up any school," he is concerned about keeping their influence minimal and preventing gang warfare. He told us that just last week a student was "out to get" a rival gang member and entered the school intoxicated. The principal chased him out of the school and, because the student was eighteen years old, he was immediately expelled. The principal made no reference to involving the police in this incident—though it appeared to us that the student's activities described constituted a criminal offense.

We were not able to find out any of the principal's specific programs for "tightening up the rules." It would appear that his assessment of the school as "easy" is apt, considering what students told us about ways to not get caught breaking the rules. Ironically, when we asked teachers if they thought their students cut class often or cheated on exams, they believed that for the most part these things didn't happen. Our interviews with the students, however, indicated otherwise.

The School seems to be an imperfect community. While many good things may be said about it, there remains the feeling that the School's very diversity, and certainly its size, often work against it, that only fragments of communities exist, and that communication lines among all members—students, faculty, and parents—are weak. The School needs to establish clearly stated policies concerning a number of areas, for students, parents, and teachers are often "left in the dark" and "on their own." It also seemed regretable to us that the principal alone was responsible for evaluating some 200 teachers every year. Considering the number of days in a school year, this seems impossible. While it would appear that much power is invested in the principal, we concluded overall that he is subject to much regulation from the Chicago Board of Education, who shape many of the rewards teachers are given for excellent work. Parents and teachers also exercised little authority in the system.

While many students participate in extracurricular activities, a great many more are not "caught up" in any sort of activity—school or even community-sponsored—which helps them develop responsibility, concern for others, pride, and "good character."

3 Student Character Development

Primitive societies, despite their marginal subsistence and the fact that they are frequently close to the starvation point, devote more care and attention, as societies, to the production of good citizens, than to the production of good technicians, and therefore they can be said to value good citizenship more highly than the production of good food producers. Can this be said for modern societies, including our own?[1]

Schools should help students to develop good character. Essentially, good character is constituted of certain forms of conduct, such as the willingness to be affirmatively helpful to others; accept the consequences of one's conduct; and refuse to act wrongly, even if one may get away with it. For the purposes of this book, character can be contrasted with "discipline"; discipline implies not doing wrong things because one is liable to be caught. Schools should both foster good discipline—making students fearful of doing wrong—and good character—making students desirous of being helpful and of avoiding wrong even if they won't get caught.

It is evident that the topic of character development in schools relates to a variety of school operations apart from discipline policy. For example, if school spirit is high, the good feelings engendered among students may stimulate them to treat each other more solicitously. And such solicitude is an aspect of character development. But, as has already been emphasized, to give some focus to this book it was necessary to develop and apply categories to its reporting and analysis—though readers are invited to speculate on the other connections they deem appropriate.

Student-to-Student Tutoring

Student-to-student tutoring is a practice that schools can use to assist students to develop good character. It has this effect because it stimulates the students acting as tutors to learn how to be helpful to others.

1. Several of the students we spoke to felt that student-to-student tutoring would not work at the School. They said that most of the students would be afraid to admit to another student that they were not doing well in a given subject. The only type of tutoring generally accepted by the students is done by members of the faculty (34, P, 9–12).

I have heard similar statements made by various educators and by present and former high-school students. The statements are often used to justify the failure of schools to encourage student-to-student tutoring. The statements are at least partly true. It takes some maturity and courage to admit ignorance and solicit aid. And schools often do not help students cultivate these traits. Similarly, when schools do not stimulate such tutoring efforts, they also fail to help more able students from seeing themselves as transmitters of knowledge, as compared to being only consumers.

2.   Every semester the honor society gives each dean a list of the names of its students who are advanced in particular academic areas. This list includes each member's phone number, grade level, high competency subjects, and the days and times they are available to help. When a student comes to the dean seeking academic help, the dean refers to this list and finds the appropriate honor society member for the student, and makes arrangements at the convenience of both. Students reported that this arrangement is effective and that students make use of it (36, P, 9–12).

3.   At the School student tutoring is an important activity and is the responsibility of students who are members of the National Honor Society. To be a member, a student must have a grade point average of at least 3.5 (out of a possible 4.0 average). Under the auspices of eight counselors and the teaching staff, approximately fifty-five students tutor other students in need. Records are kept of all tutoring. After tutoring, the tutor fills out a form noting his name, the tutee's name, the subject matter, and the time and date of the tutoring activity. The form is filled out in triplicate. One copy goes to the main office, a second copy is retained in the counselor's files, and the third is retained by the Honor Society in a special file (58, R, 9–12).

Perhaps one-third of the schools visited had vigorous student-to-student tutoring programs. In public schools, such programs were more common in elementary schools.

4.   Since 39 percent of the students are Spanish-speaking, with little knowledge of English, each seventh- and eighth-grade English-speaking student is assigned to help two Spanish-speaking students in a lower grade. The three have to spend half an hour a week after school reading and spelling together. Each Spanish-speaking student also has an English-speaking classmate assigned to help with daily language difficulties. Furthermore, in the lower grades (one to four) provisions are made so that the Spanish-speaking students interact as much as possible with English-speaking students in the classroom and during the recess time.

This tutorial program is directly organized and supervised by a teacher of Puerto Rican descent. He[a] told us that, since the School has no bilingual

---

[a] In all the items, in the interest of simplicity, male pronouns will be consistently used to refer to faculty and students, unless such use is obviously inappropriate.

program, because of financial constraints this tutorial program is the only possible way to provide Spanish-speaking students with extra help in order to make them fluent in English.

One older neighborhood girl, who is a Latino, has four brothers in the school. She told us, "My brothers are making excellent progress in English. Before they enrolled in the School, they each had two years in a bilingual program in a public school. At the end, they knew almost no English. They are starting now to speak English, and the two oldest are reading and spelling almost at grade level." The teacher said, "We are proud of this tutorial program that is providing excellent results at no extra cost" (49, R, K–8).

I have never heard of a federally financed bilingual program giving any attention to student-to-student tutoring. I cannot say it has never happened, but the typical thrust of such programs is to hire additional teachers to work with the foreign language students.

5. There is a tutoring program at the School that helps younger students of the community's elementary schools. Students in the School earn one elective credit for assisting a teacher in one of the four public elementary schools. The coordinator of the program feels it provides students with an opportunity to test interests in working with children. It also helps tutors to develop relationships with adults outside of high school and it teaches them to accept close supervision from adults in a work situation (4, P, 9–12).

Logically, it would seem desirable for high-school students to assist students in lower schools, as well as their own schoolmates. Such cross-age helping has been a frequently noticed pattern in most human societies. However, cross-school programs of this sort are rare—partly because of the complexities involved in interschool coordination. And, of course, such helping patterns have been further handicapped by the development of the junior high school, which has increased the segmentation among age groups—when there are junior highs, there are three separate schools covering K–12; without them, there is only one age break. I suspect the above program was facilitated because the high school and the assisted elementary schools formed the entire education system in a smaller suburban community.

Students Advising Younger Students

6. Students from several nearby high schools visited the School on specially designated days to meet with the eighth-grade class and give it a clearer conception of high-school opportunities. A "career" bulletin board was designed to provide visual information (brochures, descriptions, newspapers) about the high schools which were discussed (1, P, K–8).

Helpful student-to-student communication of this sort, which is assisted by school authorities, is very unusual.

7.   To guide students to develop in a Christian manner, the School teaches students to serve each other and be ever conscious of cultural needs and individual differences. Being of service in this respect requires that students engage in cooperation and self-sacrifice. Specifically, each incoming freshman is assigned a senior student who is to act as a "big brother." These senior students are used to inform younger students about upcoming events (dances, games, and concerts, for example), rules and regulations, and matters of concern to the whole school at various times.

Big brothers serve in other capacities as well. They help younger students, for example, in making choices all through their freshman year. Choices sometimes pertain to academic requirements and class subject differences. Other times, however, choices are of a more personal and intimate or moral nature. At times when a big brother is unsure of the direction of guidance, the services of school guidance counselors are recommended to the freshmen in question (58, R, 9–12).

In many public high schools, these supporting responsibilities are left solely to guidance counselors. To my mind, this policy is often unsound. The counselors have too many advisees to attempt serious engagement with many students: a typical ratio is one counselor for every 300 students. Furthermore, it is my impression that there are innumerable benefits to both advisees and advisors in the student-to-student advisement program. Of course, the student-to-student programs do require some staff time for planning and general supervision, but it is probably more profitable to invest time in that than in theoretically allocating an adult to every student. Finally, it is inevitable that students will seek out each other for advice; a faculty assisted and structured program assures that this natural process will be monitored by deliberate adult attention.

8.   The School has a big and little-sister program set up to help freshmen get adjusted to high-school life. Each senior takes a little sister (and even sometimes two) and aids her in problems that may arise. They become friends and exchange gifts and experiences. The seniors even have an induction ceremony for the freshmen wherein they dress them in baby clothes and furnish them with toys and treats as they adopt their little sisters. The big sisters pay for a luncheon as part of the ceremony, to show their appreciation of the freshmen, and entertain them through a program of sing-a-longs, games, and contests (56, R, 9–19).

9.   The spirit of togetherness in the School is fostered through the big sister–little sister program. Senior girls ask freshmen to become their little sisters for the year. Parties are held, gifts are exchanged at Christmas, Valentine's Day, Easter, birthdays, and graduation. There is a close relationship between the big and little sisters throughout the school year (59, R, 9–12).

10. One of the discipline problems in the School is dealing with the freshman class. Most freshmen students who enter the School are not fully prepared for high school. The students feel that they can still play around as they did in grade school. These freshmen must adjust if they are not to become freshmen drop outs. The freshmen must learn to stop playing around in school, to take school more seriously and act more maturely. In classrooms where there are all freshmen, one finds more noise and disorder. In classrooms where there are a variety of grade levels, the freshmen look up to their older, more mature classmates, and they themselves begin to act more maturely (15, P, 9–12).

The preceding episode is a simple and disturbing restatement of a basic problem affecting student character development. As students grow older, they have an increasing capability of showing good (or bad) character traits. A classic means of stimulating better traits was to ask older children to act as "good examples" for younger ones. Such appeals have a powerful logic. The older children are reminded that they have influence—which they see is true—and that, by being "good," they can demonstrate the potential they have acquired through growth. But when schools persistently segregate students into age and ability groups for all school purposes, they lose the power to make such appeals to older students and to help both the younger and older ones.

Of course, some age grouping is necessary for teaching purposes, but the process of grouping is apparently overdone in most schools. There are remedies for this error, some tried and some comparatively ignored. One remedy lies in the mixed age patterns common in extracurricular activities. Big brothers are another method. An alternate device which is rarely tried, but which has possibilities, is forming homeroom classes (in departmentalized schools) so they are comprised of students from all age grades (for example, in a senior high, a twenty-four-student homeroom might have six each of freshmen, sophomores, juniors, and seniors).

The next few items demonstrate occasions where students are assigned to monitor—as well as assist—other students. Such assignments require that they display responsible conduct.

11. The School has patrol guards and hall guards. The patrol guards are boys, and the hall guards are girls. They were organized this way because the neighborhood is a rough one, and it is safer for the girls to be inside the building. Hall guards and patrol guards are selected by the teacher in charge of this activity, based on conduct, scholastic performance, and attitude. They have to be in either the seventh or eighth grade. In interviewing students and the teacher in charge of the guards, we noticed that the kids want to be included in these activities; it's a form of prestige (18, P, K–8).

When we offer visible and significant responsibilities (and authority) to students which requires them to display good character—to stand on street corners in rain or snow, to hold other students accountable in the halls—we assist in the development of desirable traits.

12.   At the School, student hall guards are stationed at every corner of the School, and at each end of every corridor. There is also a hall guard stationed at each washroom, and at each end of the cafeteria as well. Each hall guard usually serves only during one class period per day.

It is the responsibility of the guards to check student passes. Each student walking through the halls during class periods must have a pass. Students without passes are sent back to class. If a teacher is nearby at the time of the confrontation, the teacher usually takes charge—that is, he finds out where the student was coming from, where he is going, and where he is or is not supposed to be. During the time we were observing at the School, we noticed that one hall guard alone checked over fifteen passes in less than a thirty-minute period of time (58, R, 9–12).

Between 20 to 40 percent of the schools studied used students to assist in maintaining safety in and around the school. Such arrangements seem desirable for a variety of reasons: to heighten safety, to cause students actively to identify with the welfare of their schools, and to teach the students constructive character traits. There are many causes for the relative infrequency of these desirable practices: the planning problems of designing and maintaining such programs; lack of faith in the students (a self-confirming prophecy); the fact that federal (and other) funds may make it simple to hire guards; busing programs which lessen the number of students walking to school; the failure of faculty to realize the benefits such programs bring to students who participate; and the philosophical objections of some faculty and administrators to allocating significant authority and responsibility to students.

13.   The School does not need crossing guards because traffic is almost nonexistent on the small side streets around the school. However, it has established well-organized teams of crossing guards as a means of teaching students and their parents the need for cooperation and mutual help on the streets. A team is comprised of sixteen children and four parents. A different team is assigned each week. Each of the four main intersections near the school is handled by one parent, usually a mother, and four children. The children stay one on each corner, and take care of all students who have to cross the street. The parent supervises the guards, and intervenes only when needed (49, R, K–8).

Students Helping Others Away from School

Some schools sponsor students in activities where they are of service to adults and children at locations away from the school.

14.   The School has a social service club. The club tutors inner-city children, works at hospitals, and generally establishes contact with the community. There are approximately fifteen members (30, P, 9-12).

This is the only apparent explicit service club in a large high school in an affluent community. Between 90 and 95 percent of its graduates go on to four-year colleges.

15.   A special-services committee made up of students was designed to devote time and funds to the external community, such as nursing homes and hospitals, but most students lacked interest in this committee, because of required class work and studies (67, S, 9-12).

This is the only away-from-school service activity in a school that sends 95 percent of its students on to four year colleges. The average homework per night for students is about three hours. The average homework per night for the students in the school mentioned in items 3 and 7 (which is also selective) is three to four hours per night. The more significant fact, with respect to Items 14 and 15 is that faculty and administration in the two schools involved do not think it very important that students engage in concrete helping acts—though it is important that they have significant skills in intellectual analysis.

16.   About thirty volunteer student aides help with housekeeping duties at the nursing home near the School, and visit with the patients once a month. The senior religion classes also give the residents birthday parties and make gifts, and have sing-a-longs with them four times yearly (56, R, 9-12).

17.   At least twice a year students engage in some activity which supports the community, for example, community clean-up or fundraising projects, which is noted in the community newspapers (37, P, 8-9).

18.   Our classroom observations revealed that one pattern was very common: teachers praised the students a lot and showed concern for individuals as well as for the whole group. Several of the homerooms in the upper levels have duties charts listing things like paper collector, messenger, pencil sharpener, and housekeeper. In all cases, the positions had been filled with appointments made by the teacher (18, P, 8-9).

These patterns of duty assignment are fairly common in elementary schools; they are much rarer in high schools.

Students Raising Funds for Good Causes

Student fundraising means that the students involved are dedicating time and energy to a constructive end. Sometimes the funds are used for benefits for the students, and sometimes to assist others. But in either case the students are implicitly recognizing, and acting on, a responsibility (to engage in self-help or to assist others).

19.   The Rip-Off bar is a concession stand run by the students who serve as office aides. Soft drinks, candy, and pretzels are sold during the lunch period to the faculty and students. Collection and bookkeeping are done by the students. Profits are used for purchasing special equipment for the school (31, P, 8-9).

Student fundraising, and the subsequent donation of gifts, involves many powerful character-developing activities: commitment to an enterprise that often goes beyond gratifying simple self-interest; acceptance of the emotional demands (as well as satisfaction) that are part of collective efforts; and the testing and maintenance of simple honesty, in handling the funds of others.

20.   The School holds two bake sales a year, one around Christmas and the other in May. Memos are sent home to all parents, and they are asked to make and contribute baked goods. A day is designated for students to bring money for baked goods. The teachers of each class take their classes down one at a time, and children can buy cupcakes and cookies. This is the only time students are allowed to eat in the classrooms. The upper-level students, along with the PTA, sell the baked goods in the cafeteria. The money goes toward funding a special savings bond fund for the eighth-grade honor students.

The School also has an annual smorgasbord which is sponsored and organized by the PTA and the student council. The PTA ask parents (by way of a take-home memo) if they will bring chicken, rolls, potato salad, and the like. The parents who volunteer are assigned what to bring and how much. A PTA parent told me that most of the upper-level children (about thirty) help the parents serve. They get about twelve to twenty parents to help with the food. They charge $5.00 a person. About 100 people attend the smorgasbord. The smorgasbord is held in the spring from 6:00 to 9:00 in the evening. The School took in over $400 last year. This money goes toward the field trip for the eighth grade and also for the savings-bond fund for the eighth-grade honor graduates (6, P, K-8).

21.   There are two annual raffles. Each student is responsible for selling at least twenty tickets. There are prizes for individual students, and for the class that sells the most tickets. The funds collected help pay general school expenses.

A car wash is also organized twice a year by the students. Usually it takes place on Sunday morning. The eighth graders are responsible for the organization. The car-wash money helps finance the annual eighth-grade field trip (49, R, K-8).

Student fundraising is conducted for a variety of legitimate purposes. Each of the purposes (or beneficiaries) has a different constructive significance. For example, when the funds cover school operating expenses, they signify that (1) students owe something to their school, (2) they are capable of beginning repayment (they are givers as well as takers), and (3) by reason of such paying, they "own" part of the school, and should treat it more respectfully since it is their possession. My impression is that the level of student vandalism is low in schools where students raise part of the school costs.

22.   The students work together in many types of fundraising. Members of each class (Class of '77, '78, and so on), when they are freshmen, begin collecting money by sponsoring dances, parties, and so on for a class gift that they will donate to the school upon graduation. The amount collected on the average is between $1,000 and $2,000. The class graduating this year donated a sign which is located on the outside of the field house and says "Home of the Huskies" (the school team) (36, P, 9–12).

When the funds are raised as a "gift" to the school, they are a heightened expression of responsibility and affection. Class gifts, which are often labeled as such, by means of plaques, also represent a contribution from the present to the future—and implicitly represent an acknowledgment that members of the giving class, themselves, have received precious gifts from the past. The social lessons underlying such patterns of giving can obviously enhance the quality of the adult citizens the school is producing. Probably a quarter or less of the schools studied had patterns of annual class giving.

23.   Class gifts are a tradition at the School. Each class since 1966 has donated a gift to the School. Examples are a brick and glass marquee where announcements of events are posted outside the School; a bulletin board in the pool area where names of record holders are posted; and trophy cases for awards presented to the School. Plaques are posted in the halls which list class gifts (31, P, 9–12).

24.   One dance held is a bit different from the other five dances I have mentioned. It is given in the afternoon after lunch about a week before Christmas vacation. This dance is called the Can Dance. The reason why this dance is different from the rest is because the cost to get into the dance is a "can." Everyone in the School is invited to this dance and they must bring at least one container of canned goods. Last year the School took in over 150 cans of food. These canned goods go to a student in the School who has a needy family. The money taken in from other dances goes toward the end-of-the-year eighth-grade field trip (6, P, K–8).

Fundraising for away-from-school causes signifies the obligation of the students (and the school) to show concern for persons beyond their immediate community. Of course, it's nice if, in these activities, large sums of money are raised. However, it is even more important that the activities engage high proportions of students in efforts that are vigorous, sincere, and plausibly successful.

Planning and overseeing such efforts takes some faculty time, but if students in schools are only passive recipients of knowledge, as compared to having active social responsibilities, we may be producing only intelligent parasites. Perhaps we are investing some faculty time in counterproductive directions. And, incidentally, because many students lack a sense of having a stake in their schools, there may be other costs generated, for example, paying for vandalism as school security guards.

Students Practicing Solicitude

25. From a daily bulletin, listing pertinent information for faculty and students and posted at locations throughout the School:

> Ricardo Moreno '80 is in Illinois Masonic Hospital and will probably be there until next Tuesday. He would like to hear from his friends.

The phone listing and room number were then given (60, R, 9–12).

Persons with good character display solicitude for persons around them who are in distress. Students naturally look toward faculty to provide them with clues as to what conduct is appropriate on occasions when members of the school community are hurt, or have had a significant event in their lives. One step in providing such clues is to simply inform students about incidents in the lives of students or faculty that invite supportive attention. The events can represent either "good" or "bad" news—illness, births in faculty families, deaths. Beyond a bare announcement, various forms of appropriate conduct can be suggested. The level of solicitude that prevails in many schools is distressingly low, especially in departmentalized public schools. Of course, students sometimes say, "I don't want others to know about my private business!" But it is the task of adults to see through such adolescent bravado—and self-ignorance. Wise persons share their joys and seek the support of others in their sorrows. If adolescents think things should be otherwise, it is because of the poor "instruction" they receive from the adults around them.

26. Once in a while it is announced over the public address system that one of the priests or teachers, or their relatives, are ill. Students are asked to pray for these people. Whether the students really do pray during five-minute periods of silence reserved for such undertakings is, of course, impossible to measure. Still, the periods of silence do make students think of those less fortunate than themselves (58, R, 9–12).

Developing Self-Control

One measure of character is to see what students do when they act, or initiate policies, on their own. As we will see, sometimes schools cut off students from such challenges and sometimes they give them more authority than they can (or should) handle.

27. A few eighth graders brought beer to a social dance and were caught by a teacher. The childrens' parents were called. The eventual result was that school dances are held right after school at 4:00, as opposed to 7:00 in the evening. Also, the seventh and eighth grades' dances are held separately so as to have more control over the groups. (27, P, K–8).

Successful school efforts to assist character development often require deliberate and vigorous efforts by the faculty. All too often such engagement does not occur. In the incident just described, the faculty opted for a "solution" that (1) made less demands on students and (2) required less work and imagination for faculty. A more responsible and imaginative solution would have recognized that (1) it must be possible to hold a dance at night and still stop eighth graders from bringing beer (that is, teach them self-restraint), and (2) eighth graders can be mixed with seventh graders, and asked to show good examples to them, if they are properly manipulated. And I use that word advisedly.

28.   The School is concerned with changing student values and conduct. It is located in a housing project in a low-income area. The children vandalize and fight, and in general do not get along. The School has been working on these problems for the two years that Mr. B. has been principal. He has been trying to create student pride in attending their school and in living in their community. He has used various activities to try to accomplish this; for example, student-faculty games of basketball, a T-shirt day, a show your school color day, and guidance programs. The School also uses small group guidance sessions to deal with suspension cases. There has been a slow, gradual improvement, but not to the extent he would like to see (6, P, K–8).

Helping students learn responsible and more mature conduct usually requires a deliberate effort on the part of the school administration and teachers. The particular measures applied, and the aims of the campaign, are shaped by a variety of forces. Sometimes such campaigns are not attempted, even when they are probably necessary. And sometimes they are very poorly conceived and executed.

29.   Recently a retreat was organized by the high-school principal. Its purpose was to air student grievances, to gain insight into those grievances, and to enlist the cooperation and suggestions of the students (of this expensive private school). The retreat was conducted by an outside professional organization. It was held on a weekend, at a site about fifty miles from the city. It was attended by seven students, all the members of the governing board, the department heads, other administrators, and the parents of the seven students. The students we interviewed attended. As a group, the students believed their school was not diversified in its racial and economic mix. They wanted a better representation of the general Chicago population. This could be achieved by recruiting students for the available scholarships, increasing the number of scholarships, and publicizing the existence

of the scholarships. All the adults interviewed shared this concern of maintaining greater diversity—without lowering academic achievement. In the past, scholarships were given to inner-city students only to have the students drop out because of adjustment difficulties. Some have worked out, but the number is small.

One of the direct results of the retreat was an elaborate scholarship dinner, organized by the parents. The scholarship fund was greatly enriched, and its availability was advertised through the media (68, S, 9–12).

Presumably, some of the adults involved in the retreat and the resulting scholarship project saw themselves as advancing the "character" of the School's students. However, one might differ with this conclusion. The fact is the students went away for a weekend at the expense of the School and their parents, aired their opinions, and got other people to do the work they prescribed. Of course, if it turns out that the students' scholarship idea doesn't work (that is, the inner-city students still drop out), the students who promoted the idea will probably have graduated before that happens— and anyway, they won't have invested time in arduous fundraising. Activities such as the retreat represent distorted efforts at character development since they reward posturing as compared to commitment. (The School has no significant service programs involving students.)

30.   All the students are required to stay clean. If a student smells bad, he is sent down to the coach and made to take a shower in the gym. This is part of the School's attempt to instill considerate behavior that is not necessarily reinforced by the community (12, P, 8–9).

31.   The School had allowed juniors and seniors the freedom to wander about the campus during the middle of the class day. The idea was that these mature students would not abuse their freedom, while younger students—while not formally assigned to classes—had to be restrained in study halls. Naturally, the younger students began to look forward to attaining similar privileges as they advanced. According to the student paper, it seemed that "a lot of kids go outside and smoke pot during their free time." The administration concluded that the free time plan was undesirable and, in the face of student opposition, abandoned it (36, P, 9–12).

Many school administrators are not this realistic or responsible. Of course, one might wonder if there weren't other ways of constraining the smoking of marijuana, but this is a huge school, and there might be several hundred students milling around in nice weather. It is very hard to police such a large group.

Schools that Do—and Don't—Focus on Character

As the next items show, schools vary considerably in the degree of priority they give to character-related issues.

32.   At the School there is much emphasis on doing things in a Christian way—making others feel good, being kind to others, considering others when acting. Phrases like "Everyone is your brother and sister," and "No act of kindness, however small, is ever wasted" are displayed prominently on the bulletin boards. There are frequent discussions in each classroom about saying the right thing and being considerate to each other. These discussions are usually conducted during religion class, but the attitude is emphasized consistently at the School. School was letting out one day, and we had just arrived to ask the principal some questions. One of the little third-grade students, as his classmates were leaving, was racing around trying to get them to sign a get-well card he had made for a sick friend (49, R, K–8).

Of course, this is a church-related school, but many of the solicitous sentiments articulated in the classrooms would be acceptable to any person of goodwill. It is rare for public schools to prominently display character-related statements.

33.   The booklet published by the School prominently quoted the following remarks by two of its turn-of-the-century founders: "The primary concern of education is character," and "The formation of character and not the acquisition of knowledge *as an end in itself* is the chief purpose of the school."

The report on the School made the following remarks, with implicit reference to the School's focus on fostering character development: "There are virtually no award assemblies, no honors banquets, and the School is very low keyed when it comes to certificates of merit given to individuals or groups. The School believes they can get along much better without these tangible symbols of achievements. Since it is a private school, parents can be said to be the primary motivating factors. The students already know that they are special due to the fact that they are not in an average, gigantic-sized, public school. They know they can get attention, understanding, independence to explore, and most of all love, from anyone at the School. That is why the School works well without the for-being-as-good-as-you-have-been type of awards. Therefore, it can be concluded that, for the students, self-actualization, along with parental motivation, are the major forms of positive reinforcement used" (67, S, K–12).

Developing good character is strenuous business, even when the students concerned come from affluent homes. There is a potential double incongruity in the booklet's quoting the founders' remarks. Does the School really believe that "self-actualization" is synonymous with good character? And, if it does, does it also believe that self-actualization is equivalent to the founders' definitions of good character? It's as if quoting the founders' remarks are a form of fig leaf, to conceal some embarrassing realities.

I suspect the founders believed that character included some elements to excellence: that word is rooted in excel, to be better than many others. But how can excellence be stimulated without identification and recognition of superior virtues?

34. From a prominently displayed statement of purpose in the School; "They search; they discover; they share; they love; they learn, with joy. . . and that is what the School is all about" (68, S, K–12).

35. The School has listed objectives in eight different areas geared toward assisting effective adulthood and citizenship. The objectives pertain to such areas as moral perfection, intellectual development, personal adjustment, physical fitness, social virtue, cultural development, economic literacy, and career development. Consider, for example, the objectives stated in writing by the school in the area of social virtue: (1) students will develop an understanding of American life and the workings of a democracy; (2) students will be willing to make those sacrifices of self-interest that are necessary for living with others in peace and unity; and (3) students will develop an understanding of, and a commitment to, social justice (58, R, 9–12).

36. In 1974, the Chicago Board of Education issued a short flyer, outlining the responsibilities of pupils (and parents) relating to formal education. The foreword said that the "ideas" in the flyer should "suggest specific areas of responsibility," "encourage discussion," and "afford an opportunity for further dialogue." The text said that, among other things, a pupil should

Develop standards of personal conduct that are reflected in socially approved behavior.

Accept responsibility for his own actions.

Respect the rights of others.

Dress appropriately.

Help maintain school property.

In 1978, the board issued a revised flyer on student conduct, of somewhat greater clarity and length. However, it still had provisions such as:

Student responsibilities [include] avoiding abusive, threatening and obscene language in verbal and written expression. . . . Student rights [permit students to] distribute independent publications of students in the school at the places and times established by the school unless school officials can reasonably forecast that the publication and distribution of the publication would substantially disrupt the educational process (no school reference needed).

The language of the 1974 flyer is practically opaque. It "suggests," "aims to encourage discussion" and "promote dialogue"—what should some tenth grader think that means? Then, when it lists possible specific aims, pupils (and others) necessarily have to guess what is meant by "socially approved behavior" and so on. For example, a literal reader would conclude that "help maintain school property" means that students are expected to wash floors, paint walls, and repair broken windows. All this may sound good—but it is done in few or no Chicago public schools. I think that "help maintain" in supposed to mean "do not destroy or deface"; I cannot guess why they said "help maintain" instead of using plain English. There is no suggestion as to what penalties (or rewards), if any, should be applied to students who violate the principles—or who are conspicuously loyal to them.

As for the 1978 flyer, some of its provisions would confuse a constitutional lawyer. I understand that part of the ambiguity is due to the existing conflicts between the common-sense needs of school administration (students shouldn't do, say, or write provocative or obscene things in schools) and the principles involved in some court decisions. And so these divergencies among adults inevitably spill over into the day-to-day life of students.

In about half the Chicago public schools, if visitors ask about the schools' rules or statements defining pupil responsibilities, they will be told, "We apply general board policies." The statements just discussed present the general board policies.

37.   The student newspaper is supported by funds from the student activities fund. In one issue, it published two articles advising students about the uses of contraceptives and abortion. One of the articles described a female student reporter's visit to a planned parenthood center in the community:

> "Do you notify my parents?" I asked the receptionist. I was only there to get a story, but wasn't sure how my mother would react.
>
> "No, never," she reassured me, "even if they call and ask us, we don't give them any information. If for any reason we need to contact you, we call and ask for you. If you aren't home, we say that 'Nancy called," and the 'you should call back.'"

An editorial in the same issue defended the publication of the planned parenthood articles. It noted that the paper had earlier been criticized by faculty by running articles on how students might fake ID cards or evaluate PCP (a new illegal drug). The editorial contended that, in its "activism," the paper was simply acting like any other newspaper, and that its status in the high school was irrelevant. It went on to observe that the information it published could only be helpful, by diminishing ignorance (58, P, 9–12).

Obviously, we have here a complex problem, with a relatively simple answer—and an exhausting one. I will focus on the "simple" answer. If a school is concerned with character development, it should strive to diminish the character-destructive information put before the students with the semi-official approval of the school. Publication in a school-assisted paper is a form of such approval. Skillful, purposeful, and farsighted administrators can do things to make such "incitements" by student papers comparatively unnecessary. Essentially, they can assign sponsorship of the paper to able and responsible faculty members. Such faculty can use careful and subtle pressures to insure that the students who acquire authority on the paper are not puppets, but also not students who self-servingly contend it is "beneficial" for fourteen-year-olds to conspire with private (or public) agencies to keep their sexual activity from the attention of their parents.

If my proposed answer seems repressive we should realize that students always have the "freedom" to try to form (and finance) their own paper, manage it without getting academic credit, publish it in rented space, and sell it to those who choose to buy it outside the school doors, like their competitors. But, if they want the advantages attached to being a "school paper," they must accept certain constraints.

It may also be remarked that my answer subverts the sense of some (possible) court decisions about student rights. The exact import of any such decisions is open to argument. And court decisions are often mutable, if they are vigorously resisted or appealed. But, beyond the (misguided?) letter of some decisions, there is also the practical fact that able and purposeful adults should be capable of shaping the conduct of adolescents in such situations without legal confrontations, if they move toward developing vital relationships with students.

38.   The following are excerpts from the Letters to the Editor column of a high-school paper:

Dear Editor: I'm in bad shape! I stole my best friend's bracelet because I can't afford to buy one of my own. I realize that this is wrong and don't know why I actually took it. She has been searching frantically for it and has been accusing people of this, and I just went along with her. Now I feel guilty about this because others are getting blamed for my misdoings. What should I do?? How can I give it back to her?

"It Takes a Thief"

Dear "It Takes A Thief": It's good that you have enough humility to admit that you have done something terribly wrong as stealing someone else's property. My advice to you is to return the bracelet to the owner. You can do this secretly by placing it on her desk in the morning just before homeroom, or if you would like, you can put it in an envelope and place it in the DEAR EDITOR mailbox in your homeroom, and I'll make sure it's returned. Please put the girl's name on a sheet of paper and seal it in the envelope with the bracelet. Good luck, and remember, best friends are more important than bracelets.

Dear Editor: I'm really in hot water this time! I asked two guys to a really big party in my neighborhood. I don't like the first guy I asked, but I needed a date! Then, the next week, a new guy moved into my neighborhood. Oh! Is he a doll! I couldn't help asking him! The party is in two weeks! What should I do?

"Desperate"

Dear "Desperate": Now you know what you should do. The first guy you asked should be your date whether you like it or not. You will simply have to tell the second guy you already have a date. Then tell him you asked him because you really like him. Ask him if you can make it another time. Next time, T-H-I-N-K!!!

Dear Editor: I have a problem. Well, it isn't exactly my problem, but it's my friend's problem. It's like this. My best friend is going to move out in the summer and live with her boyfriend. I think what she is going to do is really dumb because she has already broken up with him four times. How can I tell her without losing her as a friend that she is making a big mistake?

"A Loss For Words"

Dear "A Loss For Words": The best thing to do is give it to her straight. If you really care about her, you've got to tell her. If she is really your BEST friend, she will listen and thank you for your thoughtfulness.

"Confidential to Me, Honestly":
After reading your letter a few times, I have come up with a solution. Confront the girl and ask her why she had the money. If she can prove that she had it for a good reason, then there is no problem. However, if she denies having it, then it is up to you to bring the matter to the attention of your Homeroom teacher. She will know what to do.

"Editor" (56, R, 9-12)

39. This item is from a similar column in a different school paper:

Dear Editor: I've just decided I should get some advice on a long-lingering situation I'm in. I've been knowing this young man since I've been in eighth grade. It was there that we started to like each other.

After going to separate high schools, we still kept in touch. Sometimes not as much as I'd like to have kept in touch. He never really came out and said that he liked me. But in the beginning he would say things that made me think that he liked me. Of course I never told him that I liked him either. It was sort of a mutual understanding, but nothing ever became of it. And we never told each other.

As time went on there were times when I really liked him and other times when I didn't like him at all—only for a friend.

Now that we are juniors, he still calls me almost every week. But I find him talking more and more about what some other girl did for him or with him. And I really don't want to hear this. It seems as though I've become a very good friend of his (one of the boys).

The problem is that I need to know if he still likes me or if he ever did like me (prom time is coming up). I'd be rather embarrassed just to come out and say, "Do you like me?" And, besides, he's the kind of person who'd say just what he thought I'd want to hear, even if it wasn't what he really felt.

I'm almost at the end of my rope and I'm tired of trying to guess whether or not he likes me. I need to know what the deal is!

"Non-Guesser"

Dear Non-Guesser: If you've been knowing this person personally for that amount of time and haven't been able to talk to him freely, there is definitely a communication gap.

I'm surprised that this young man hasn't been curious enough to ask himself or you about your relationship. Evidently it doesn't bother him.

The only way you're going to find out what the deal is is to ask. Whether you come right out with it or beat around the bush doesn't matter. Just get it out. True, you may not want to come out and say, "Do you like me?" Maybe you could say something like, "How would you describe our relationship?" or "Where has our relationship been and where is it going?" Good luck! (14, P, 9–12)

The difference in tone between the two school papers is significant.

Of course, some or all of the letters involved may have been edited or even made up to keep the paper interesting. But the important thing is that the first column provided students with straightforward answers to thoughtful and clearly stated questions; the second presented a fuzzy answer to a poorly phrased question. The first school enrolls 350 students, and it is not highly college oriented; the second has about 2,000 students, many chosen by selective exams. Presumably, the administration in the first school cares more about what values and writing models are put before students.

40. Part of a detailed set of guidelines issued to all students by the School:

The following guidelines will apply to any activity, home or away, in which students from the School participate:

1. Act like gentlemen at all times, especially since you will be representing the School.
2. When entering and exiting, please drive and park carefully.
3. No alcoholic beverages or drugs of any sort will be tolerated.
4. Do not wander in the parking lot, or sit in cars.
5. Be courteous and respectful towards any adult present at this function.
(60, R, 9–12)

Although these rules do not specify the penalties involved, the students realize, from the other penalties routinely enforced at the School, that these prohibitions will be enforced. Only two or three other schools in the entire study had provisions of this sort.

What Loyalties Should We Inculcate in Students?

Loyalty, in general, is a desirable character trait. But there are occasions where loyalties are directed toward bad ends. Students are sometimes faced with loyalty conflicts between their obligations to their immediate peers who have broken school rules and their loyalties to adults and to law-abiding students. As we will see, schools differ in their means of handling such conflicts.

41.   I was told that the students will generally not turn in one another for in-school conduct such as smoking, drinking, selling drugs, and so on, which are formally prohibited by the School. They do not feel that they are being hurt if someone else engages in these activities. I found out that about twelve years ago there were student monitors who would go into the washrooms and patrol outside of the building to prevent students from undertaking prohibited activities. At that time students were willing to accept such responsibilities, but nowadays "ratting" on a fellow schoolmate is unthinkable (36, P, 9-12).

42.   Generally speaking, students do not report to teachers about significant violations of the rules by other students. I talked to ten students, each from different grades. The main thrust I got was that if a student was doing something that did damage to the School, nine times out of ten he wouldn't be reported to a teacher by any student. But all of the students said that if the student did something specifically to them, they would first try and take care of it themselves and if they couldn't do anything about it, they would tell the teacher (6, P, K-8).

43.   Students usually do not report a violation of the discipline code by another student unless they themselves are hurt in some way. The principal stated that this kind of information is not solicited (39, P, 9-12).

The problem of students reporting on others is complex. But some of the violations involved can be grave (for example, bringing weapons into the school, or drugs to sell to other students), while vandalism destroys the surroundings of all community members. I suspect that some school faculty are unsure of how to discreetly handle the matter of inviting student disclosures (but not encouraging aggravated tale-bearing), while others are afraid of finding out about evils that they have to surpress. But what kind of schools (or society) will we evolve if groups of students can only be trusted if they are watched by adults at every moment!

44.   Five of the students told me of one student whom, they believe, keeps a gun in his locker in school. None of the five would consider informing the faculty about this weapon. The five also mentioned several other students who carry knives with blades over four inches long (14, P, 9-12).

In a discussion with my college class about students informing on weapon bearers, one student told me that, while he was attending high school, he knew of a student who carried a long-bladed knife in school. Other students also knew of the knife, but none of them informed. My student said he later realized the noninformers had all made a mistake; the knife bearer stabbed and killed another youth in a fight. It is the responsibility of adults to try to prevent young persons from acquiring wisdom through such terrible episodes.

45.   Student censoring of others is informally done at the School. A student will suggest to the principal that he should check a certain individual for cigarettes. The students feel secure in telling the principal because he will protect their identity (31, P, 8–9).

46.   The question was raised concerning the monitoring of student behavior. The principal contends that having students report each other's infractions often results in a "tattle-tale" relationship among students. He did mention that each classroom has student line monitors, lunchroom monitors, and bathroom monitors. But he stated that these students must be selected carefully, on a merit basis, and then rotated at intervals to avoid unjust peer pressures and problems. He said that even with the monitors, it is a matter of careful selection (4, P, K–8).

47.   The students share their part of responsibility in order to keep discipline and good manners in the School. In each class there is a student responsible for reporting inappropriate behavior when the teacher is not present. The students take turns at the task. The lay teachers do not like this system (49, R, K–8).

As we see, students will inform on wrong-doers if (1) they have enough trust in the faculty to feel their privacy will be protected (and this can't be assumed in many schools), or (2) if the act of disclosure will be public, the responsibility must be spread among many, and seen as an inescapable duty.

Cheating—or Being Honest—When You're Not Being Watched

48.   We talked to a group of eight graders (without the teacher present) and asked if they ever cheat. They replied, "Of course. Whenever the teacher turns around." The teachers believe the problem is children are too lazy to study (27, P, K–8).

49.   There is no prohibition in the School's rules against cheating. A sixth-grade teacher said that if she catches someone cheating on an exam, she takes ten points off the exam involved. A third-grade teacher said anyone caught cheating in his classroom was given an automatic zero. This teacher said he always reports a student cheating to his parents (6, P, K–8).

50. No written rules refer to cheating. Cheating in the classroom is dealt with by the teachers. I interviewed three teachers, and "cheating on tests" was the basis for their definition of cheating. An older male teacher said that in sixteen years of teaching cheating has never occurred in his classroom. At the beginning of each semester he tells his students that if they are caught cheating during a test, they will receive an F for the course.

Another young male teacher reported that students caught cheating on a test are given an automatic F on the exam. He does not interrupt the class by making a scene or by taking the paper away; he lets them cheat. He returns the exam along with the other exams and does not discuss the event with the student. He has found this method effective. He said, "Teachers develop reputations as well as students. When you repeat this procedure a few times with different students, *making no exceptions,* soon enough the word gets around to the point where the rest of the students don't dare do it in your class." The third teacher, a young female, reported handling the problem in a way very similar to the second teacher. She would be willing to discuss the matter with the student (58, P, 9–12).

Very few schools have clear, general written rules covering cheating. This is part of the reason a high proportion of students admit they occasionally cheat. Among the problems caused by the lack of uniform rules are no consistent definitions (for example, is plagiarism cheating? Is it cheating if you let someone copy from your exam paper?) and inconsistent penalties (for example, some teachers flunk you for the course, others just give an F for the exam, while others may be talked out of it). Incidentally, an F for an exam is only a trivial penalty. There is probably only a 10 percent chance a cheating student will be caught; this means nine out of ten times cheating will increase a student's grade, and the tenth time he or she will flunk the exam—which might have happened anyway!

51. All students who were asked felt that copying homework or letting someone copy off a test was not cheating. There is little trust of the students by parents and teachers in this regard. One mother said, "given the opportunity, they'd probably cheat" (60, R, 9–12).

This school has clear, firmly enforced rules against cheating; it also stimulates an intense pattern of individualistic academic competition among its students. Sometimes this pattern takes primacy over the promotion of moral values.

52. Students are taught to value honesty. Sometimes they even report errors in grading (which errors were to their advantage) to their teachers. When such incidents occur, the students are often still given credit for their original grade (56, R, 9–12).

This school places a high premium on pupil-teacher community and on practicing moral values.

The Role Models Surrounding Students

Student character development is obviously affected by the role models placed before the students in and around the school. The nature of these models is not always under the control of educators, though it often is. But, even when a system of control is not feasible, educators should be conscious of the role-model problem and actively engaged in whatever corrective steps are feasible. The following items present instances of this area of concern.

53.   One street, three blocks from the School, is plagued with prostitutes and drug dealers. Many students walking to the School must walk by these people displaying their wares (15, P, 9–12).

54.   Let me supplement the preceding item with the following story, told to me by a Chicago public school teacher who was a graduate student of mine. She teaches high school in a low-income neighborhood. When one looks out the school windows during good whether, one can usually see a number of students congregated there, hopefully because they are on free periods. There are usually several older males hanging around in these groups. These men are drug peddlers. They are not necessarily trying to market to the students; the crowd around the entrance simply makes the street a convenient place for dealing. Occasionally the police raid the street and make arrests, but the dealers come back. The teacher said the principal has tried to establish a "closed campus," to prevent such exposure of students during school hours. Under the contract with the teachers' union, such a move (which would change the teachers hours—shorten their work day and end their lunch break) required a majority vote of the teachers. The proposal was defeated. My student said she believed it was defeated by the younger teachers, who felt that a closed campus was an undue restriction on the students' freedom. (No school reference necessary.)

55.   Students are allowed to call their teachers by their first names. Many students feel uncomfortable with this because (the young teachers told us) they are looking for authority figures. These students "can't handle it. . . . " He feels frustrated in his class because he wants the students to work on their own, instead of being led around by the nose (20, P, 9–12).

Students are always looking for more mature role models; it is a healthy and inevitable instinct. This searching puts a significant responsibility on teachers. The responsibility is complex, because the teachers must then ask themselves, "What effects might my conduct have on my students?" And sometimes the answer to that question may require the teacher to be more constrained in his conduct than a typical adult. For example, in one of the schools studied, the teachers unanimously voted to give up smoking anywhere in the school; they concluded that such an act would be generally beneficial to their students. One can understand the frustrations teachers must sometimes face at requests for them to be good role models, but if teaching means, in part, an exchange of love and respect, such responses are not transmitted by merely collecting a paycheck and putting in time. The responses are bought through self-discipline.

In many schools, the teachers' responsibilities as role models are obscured by structures which diminish persisting contacts between individual teachers and students, and without some persistance in contact, the effect of any role model is sapped. And, sometimes, the teachers rebuke the students' legitimate demands from irresponsibility or ignorance. In other schools, the teachers—and the school's total value structure—assist healthy contacts.

56. The security guard of the School runs its boy scout troop on a voluntary basis. He promises the boys that, if they are good, he will make them boy scouts (37, P, 8–9).

57. We saw a student hall guard ask a passing teacher if he would watch his station for a moment while he went to the washroom. The teacher didn't hesitate; rather, he went over and sat in the guard's seat and told him to go ahead—that he would watch the hall while the student was away. As the student was leaving the washroom, another teacher engaged him in a fairly long conversation. When the hall guard returned to his post, the substituting teacher did not question his whereabouts for a period of time obviously longer than it would take to use the washroom. The hall guard volunteered an explanation, however. This is how we learned of the circumstances of his rather lengthy departure (58, R, 9–12).

58. Student advisement is built on a dean system; there are sixteen counselor-deans, each having approximately 270 students. The students are alphabetically assigned to deans when they are freshmen; most deans also have responsibilities for disseminating college information, organizing ACT testing, overseeing student activities, and planning PTA programs. We observed that 98 percent of the students see their deans at least once a year and about 60 percent visit them four or more times, especially when personal problems arise. We found that many of the students preferred talking to their dean when a problem arose rather than to their teachers, parents, or relatives. Also, assisting the deans are two special workers, a psychologist and a special-education dean (36, P, 9–12).

This is the form of advisement practiced in some well-organized public high schools. The general pattern of organization in the School tends to encourage students to "rely" on these advisers—teachers are not especially available to many students, and the deans have easy access to much important information. However, one cannot imagine these deans as important adult role models for students; their contacts with students are too tangential.

59. Several times a year, the School brings in former graduates to talk to students about their work, and the steps leading to their careers. The most recent speaker was a dentist who talked about dental care. The students also asked questions about the dental profession, and the requirements for being a dentist. After their meetings, the students in grades six to eight wrote reports about the dental profession, and students in grades one to five drew pictures of a dentist's office. The dentist has hung two of these drawings on the walls of his office. Parents and students consider these meetings valuable.

The School provides the students with books and reading materials that propose historic or fiction role models. Christopher Columbus is one of the student's favorites. Every year for Columbus Day there is a literary contest in which the students of the sixth, seventh, and eighth grades participate (49, R, K–8).

60. I talked to a teacher who was a former student of the School. He told me that sometimes he tells his students what the School was like when he was there as a student. He said that the students looked up to him because he had been at the School and was now a success. He said one of his sixth graders who has always had trouble in school told him that she felt she could get through school, now that she could see what happens when you work hard and apply yourself (6, P, K–8).

61. It is a requirement that the lay teachers be Catholic and behave as such. They have to attend Mass with their class and teach and foster Christian values in their teachings. Parents are required to attend Mass with their children on Sundays (49, R, K–8).

62. The School library contains many novels, biographies, and autobiographies which present constructive role models to students; most of these books were written ten, twenty, or more years ago. The tabs in the back of the books showed that these books were often borrowed by students, until two or three years ago—when borrowing declined significantly. We asked the librarian the cause of the decline. He said that, at that time, the school introduced a new curriculum, which relied on readers (really textbooks) distributed to students; formerly, the teachers had given students many assignments relying on library books. The librarian showed us a set of the new readers. They were attractively designed, and included multicolor pictures and illustrations.

We skimmed several; they seemed to provide few instructive and appropriate role models for students (this was an all-white suburban school). We found the book which encompassed American revolutionary history and discovered that two "heroes" were described—Franklin and Washington. Franklin was presented as an inventor and tinkerer—and such a presentation would, we believe, interest junior-high students. The two themes relating to Washington were largely pictorial. There were three pictures relating to his image on the one-dollar bill, including the basic portrait by Gilbert Stuart. The main point of the text accompanying these pictures was that

Washington was probably grimacing on the dollar bill because his false teeth were hurting at the time he posed for the portrait. The other theme on Washington dealt with Leutze's picture of the crossing the Delaware. That picture was reproduced in a full-color two-page spread. The text was largely dedicated to showing that the picture contained thirteen technical errors; for example, since the crossing was at night, the scene was not actually visible (40, P, 8–9).

As a history buff, I recall another anecdote about the crossing of the Delaware that the text did not transmit to students. After the troops crossed the river, their tracks in the snow (as they marched to attack the enemy) could be identified by the blood which seeped through the rags binding the feet of many of the soldiers. I also remember a Revolutionary soldier's letter—in a collection of readings—describing how Washington, two weeks before the crossing, spoke out to his beaten, unpaid, and poorly clothed troops on the snow-covered parade ground, pleading with them to reenlist (many of them served only three-month terms). Washington spoke twice, boldly but with an undertone of desperation. After each speech, the drums beat for volunteers, but no one stepped out. He spoke a third time, the drums beat, and a few men stepped out, and then more. . . .

63. An annual assembly is held during Brotherhood Week. At this time, the Rev. Martin Luther King is honored. Students contribute compositions and poems to be read at the assembly (1, P, K–8).

64. Through the plays the drama club puts on, students can relate to black heroes of the past. A student can say to himself, "I am black and everything I do reflects on my race." The drama club teacher tells his student members that he wants them to display this in all their actions (6, P, K–8).

65. Each room has a crucifix on the wall and a statue of the Blessed Virgin. Similar symbols are displayed on the corridors and stairwells. Flowers are frequently placed in front of the Virgin's statue (in each classroom) by students. The decoration of the School is done by the students, under the general guidance of the faculty. Numerous religious mottos and banners are displayed in the halls and classrooms to inspire the whole school (56, R, 9–12).

Most societies have assumed that the role models put before the young, through literature, ceremonies, and religion, are profoundly important. I believe Chicago-area public schools, especially high schools, do a miserable job in this respect. I assume this condition prevails nationally—after all, the publisher of the well-illustrated textbook in the Franklin and Washington story was a national concern. One needn't be a psychoanalyst to suspect that our unwillingness to present vital role models to the young partly relates to a form of seize-the-day attitude held by many adult pseudointellectuals. This attitude is reflected (in our curriculum) in an unwillingness to stimulate young people to build a constructive future for themselves or our country. It is as if we do not care what the young will grow up to value, because there is no tomorrow.

Whatever the potential justification for such an attitude, it cannot be excused in the name of "choice." Young persons are compelled to attend schools where adults essentially decide how their time will be spent. If they do not seriously celebrate Columbus Day, or Washington's Birthday, or meet respected graduates, they will be required to spend their time in other activities maintained by adults that "shape" them—for better or worse. (They may even be released during free periods to hang around with drug peddlers outside the school.) Since we must structure time of students, we might as well do it in a wholesome fashion, rather than making them fill it in counting trivial historical errors in a picture. Why do we want them to see the trees, instead of the forest?

66.　The School distributed to parents a list of about 150 books it recommended for its students. The list did not include any books by Cheever, Kesey, Vonnegut or Salinger. The following are the names and authors of twelve books randomly drawn from the list (70, S, 7-10):

Grades 7 and 8
Adamson, Joy　*Born Free*
Cousey, Robert　*Basketball Is My Life*
Forester, C.S.　*Captain Horatio Hornblower*
Nordoff and Hall　*Mutiny on the Bounty*
Shipper, K.B.　*Men, Microscopes and Living Things*
Ullman, James Ramsey　*Banner in the Sky*

Grades 9 and 10
Agee, James　*A Death in the Family*
Costain, Thomas B.　*The Conquering Family*
Hemingway, Ernest　*The Old Man and the Sea*
Miller, William　*A Canticle for Leibowitz*
Roberts, Kenneth　*Northwest Passage*
Tuchman, Barbara　*The Zimmerman Telegram*

How Students Act under Faculty Leadership

The level of character displayed by students varies among schools. It sometimes seems that faculty are indifferent to these interschool differences and accept them as acts of God—as compared to becoming actively engaged in trying to remedy bad situations.

67.　The brick walls of the School's three buildings have been defaced by vandalism. Jars of paint have been thrown against the wall. Glass windows are all boarded up. Spray paint has been used on the covering boards. Five female students were interviewed about the vandalism. All agreed that they would not report anyone trying to deface the buildings; after all, they too, liked writing on the walls, and had put their own nicknames and boy-friends' names on the building. We were not able to identify any significant policy aimed at reducing the vandalism; the administration appeared to accept it as a fact of life. In particular, student fundraising for general school purposes is minimal, or nil (22, P, 9–12).

68.   The metal trades shops is the last shop in the School with an unlocked tool room. One teacher said he felt that this will be the last year they can operate this type of tool room. He is experiencing a loss of tools. This missing tools are not common hammers or wrenches, but some more expensive, high-skill tools. The loss he feels, is due to a general decline in the students' sense of responsibility (34, P, 9–12).

69.   From a comparison of two schools: unlike School A students, who have group pride, School B students take individual pride in being involved in the activity. When being interviewed, they talk in terms of "I," not "we." Their focus is more directed toward who is heading the activity, not the group involved. Unfortunately, lack of respect and regard for one another's abilities is prominent. Teachers state, "It merely reflects the atti-tudes of the community. It is not a matter of us not trying to develop mutual respect and appreciation amongst the students; it's merely a matter of the overwhelming negative reinforcement of the Projects, but we keep working on it" (37, 18, P, 8–9).

70.   One of the English teachers took eighty girls from her senior classes to see *Man of La Mancha* at the Candlelite Theatre. The behavior of these students was excellent (59, R, 9–12).

There are considerable variations in the levels of character displayed among students from (1) different schools, or (2) one era (for example, 1965 versus 1977) compared to another.

71.   I was interested in looking at what the students wrote. An English teacher loaded me up with class anthologies of students' writings, I love creative writing. As I read the samples it seemed there was a melancholy and shroudlike veil to the students' works. I find it very sad that students at the age of sixteen could be so unhappy and overly serious. Two typical titles were "The Lonely Child" and "Death Kept Her Alive." The lengthy first line in the second poem was: "She always had dreams of death. At first, they frightened her but soon they became her friends. Oftener than not she had fantasies of her friends picking her up and taking her away from all her problems. She had of course named them so she could address them prop-erly, there was Susie [short for suicide] and Desi [disease] and Old Man Death [for age and accidents]" (57, R, 9–12).

72.   The students produced an annual anthology of their creative writ-ing. Typical titles from their last issue were "Home Is. . . ," "My Family

Picnic," "An Ice Cube," "A Valentine for My Daddy," "First Date," and "The Last Four Years" (59, R, 9–12).

Obviously, teachers have some power to determine the focus of students' writing interests. And we should assume that such interests can affect conduct. After all, if literature and writing cannot affect our conduct at all, why should students be encouraged to apply themselves to it?

Setting Character-Related Goals for Students

73.   The School assigned a teacher to plan, organize, and conduct a continuing contest among student homerooms. The aim of the contest was to improve student citizenship and leadership, increase homeroom cohesion, and provide homeroom teachers with information to assist student guidance. Periodically all teachers were given fixed numbers of tokens, which they were to distribute to any student(s) they observed practicing significant good conduct. The homerooms whose students accrued the largest number of tokens each week were awarded conspicuous recognition, and all their students also won free ice cream. Homerooms were divided into "leagues" of four each, to increase the proportion of winners. Prizes were also awarded to individual high-scoring students in all homerooms, regardless of the score of their rooms. Homeroom teachers kept tabulations of the attainments of their students, and were expected to counsel "low-scoring" students and to stimulate their rooms, as groups, so students monitored and supported each other. Provision was made for the frequent review of the operation of the program by a representative faculty committee (32, P, 7–8).

74.   The School has several ways to publicize awards and honors. Daily announcements are made over the public address system. Included in these announcements are results of team games, winners of contests, recipients of special awards, and congratulations for those involved in special events. A list of the students who are on the honor roll and dean's list is posted in the student center and released to local newspapers for publication. This year someone has been hired to write press releases for newspapers (38, P, 9–12).

75.   Service letters, which can be worn on sweaters or jackets, are awarded to students who participate in nonathletic activities that are of help to others. Each activity has a certain amount of points assigned to it (a student council member, for example, receives ten service points for his first year on the council, and twenty additional points for his second year). To receive a service letter one must accumulate 100 points. To also receive a pin (in the form of a miniature service letter), fifty extra points must be earned, and fifty more added to that will enable the student to receive a 200 pin. The

credits granted for different service activities were developed largely by the student council (21, P, 9–12).

76.   The most honored award at the School is the Aileen S. Andrew Foundation Scholarship, awarded annually to a senior girl and boy. Recipients are given a $6,000 scholarship, and their names are engraved on a handsome plaque hung near the main office. Above the list of names of previous winners (dating back to 1955) are inscribed the words, "For outstanding potential as a future contributor to human welfare" (39, P, 9–12).

77.   From an information booklet the School distributes to all students:

> Grades are a semester mark, not a semester average. Attitude and improvement play an important role in the evaluation of student progress.

> It is not only for college that one should make a good record. Employers ask for reports on what students did in school, so the high school record is important regardless of what one intends to do. A student can be sure that if he works faithfully and is a good school citizen, the school can stand back of him when he asks for a recommendation (36, R, 9–12).

Official statements of this sort, pointing out to students the connections among class work, conduct in school, and the student's future status, are rare. While the language may seem stern, the fact is that schools can strive to make the status of its students relevant or irrelevant to their postgraduation life. If being a student is relevant, it means one's conduct can effect what happens later. And, of course, such relevance is heightened if information on conduct is kept and made available to appropriate persons. If there are gaps in this chain of information collection and flow, school becomes less relevant.

78.   There is an honor roll and children are awarded for this at the end of the year. To be on the honor roll, you must have no more than one C in a major subject. Points are accumulated for subjects and conduct, which prevents any student from making the honor roll without excellence in both areas (37, P, 7–8).

Recognizing—or Ignoring—Student Conduct That Reveals Good Character

79.   A letter to the editor in a neighborhood paper:

> Letter Lauds the School's Kids
> Letter to students at the School:

> It was a sunny, quiet fall day at the School, the day our students gave blood for the community blood drive. There were no reporters taking pic-

tures; the mayor was not there to shake their hands—and why should there be any fanfare. After all, they were only donating blood. Of course, there should not be any fanfare. Our reward for charitable deeds will come from our Lord.

I just want to take this opportunity to thank each and every student who was able to donate blood so that our community could meet its blood needs. God bless each and every one of you.

A Mom (34, P, 9–12)

While the writer said rewards come from the Lord, she still took the trouble to warmly offer public thanks.

80. From the student handbook:

The School has an established chapter of the Honor Society. The top five percent of the junior class and those seniors in the top 15 percent of the class who have a minimum seven-semester grade index of 3.2, with consistently high academic achievement, are eligible for membership. This is another way of recognizing excellence in scholarship and character. (36, P, 9–12)

While the text refers to scholarship and character, it articulates no standards for assessing character. Its criteria for academic achievement are stated with clarity and vigor.

81. The School has a special program for blind and sight-impaired students. When it began eight years ago, 100 normal students volunteered to assist the blind students as tutors; many volunteers had to be turned down because of oversupply. At this time, only five or six tutors volunteer annually. The teacher who works with the blind students believes classroom teachers could do more to motivate their students to volunteer. The School has no conspicuous program to recognize students who participate in non-athletic service activities. (The student newspaper reported the results of a poll taken of sixty-four students; on the average, the students spend two to five hours a day watching television) (22, P, 9–12).

Most of the elementary schools examined had some sort of program to honor students displaying good character traits; perhaps 50 percent of the high schools had such programs. The quality of these recognition programs varies widely.

82. Up until the early 1970s Chicago public high schools had a grading system which required all teachers to give each student two grades or ratings, one for academic achievement, and the other for character traits. In the early 1970s this system was abandoned. At this time, there is no way high-school faculty can routinely evaluate the character (or character-related conduct) of their students. In effect, only the conduct of students with exceptionally good or bad character may be recognized (through either the discipline system or receiving significant awards). (No school reference needed.)

The pros and cons of the preceding policy decision are complex, and probably the previous procedure was at least in need of revision. However, its abolition implied that it was irrelevant for teachers to consider a student's character-related conduct.

83.   The booklet given to students and parents outlines the provisions of a 1975 Illinois state law on their rights with reference to school records. Essentially the law (1) established two different types of individual student records, permanent and temporary, (2) provided that the permanent records could include very limited, formalistic information (for example, grades, attendance records), while temporary records would contain more qualitative information (for example, disciplinary information, comments of praise of conduct from teachers), (3) required the destruction of information in the temporary files immediately after graduation, (4) gave parents and students the right of access to such files, to monitor and challenge what is inserted, and (5) kept the contents of such files private from most persons, without the consent of the matured student (or, in some circumstances, the parent) (36, P, 9–12).

In effect, the provisions deter the use, in schools of any size, of any routine character-related evaluations on students, since large schools must rely on records (and why keep records that will be quickly destroyed?) and make it less likely that employers will bother to check students' high-school records, except to determine if they did graduate, since such records will contain limited information. The ultimate rationale(s) of the law are not all wrong—however, its form and effect are harmful to students.

One rationale is that students (and their parents) should generally know of their evaluations by teachers. In general, this is wise; students should be informed of faculty opinions, in order to maintain good conduct or abandon wrong practices. "Secret" evaluations are not generally helpful. However, because there are few strong pressures on high-school teachers today to make any such evaluations, the effect of the disclosure provision is only really valuable if teachers are supervised so that they periodically and routinely produce serious evaluations of student conduct (and we saw such a healthy process in operation in the public elementary school described in chapter 1).

Another rationale is that students' mistakes should not be held against them indefinitely. This proposition, too, is to the good. However, the text wipes clear all qualitative records, either for the good or bad. Furthermore, while at some point ex-students (like all of us) should benefit from some form of wiping the slate clean, the law, which operates immediately after graduation, goes much too far. After all, we should probably assume that most adults (for example, future potential employers) should have the common sense to evaluate—and ignore—modest adolescent peccadilloes. And students who are tempted to engage in serious violation should be warned that such violations may look bad on their future record. But there must be a record.

Incidentally, readers may note that the law's text is recited in the same school booklet described in item 77. That booklet also talked of the school's giving good references to students who were good citizens. Obviously the language of the law has vitiated the reference language. Presumably the booklet still contains the conflicting provisions due to inadvertence or the hope that the reference language may still properly motivate "misguided" students. But we should expect that sophisticated students will see that investing energy in good school citizenship now has little clear long-range payoff. After all, in a high school of 4,000 students, written documents are the only way that such citizenship can be "remembered." And now such documents must be quickly destroyed.

I realize that many public high school employees may find my preceding discussion "naive." They know—as I do—that between 1970 and 1980, both before and after the law's passage, most public high school records on students contain little or nothing—either good or bad—about students' character-related conduct. In reality, the law was partly an exaggerated response to a few scattered real (or imagined) abuses. And it also represented a philosophically erroneous public conclusion: that students' school experience—apart from academic grades—should be made irrelevant to future employers. But, the more irrelevant that experience becomes to such employers, the more irrelevant it becomes to students while they are experiencing it! If displays of responsibility and maturity by students in school have irrelevance, logical students may well conclude that their school time might as well be spent in disorder and irresponsibility—after all, what's the difference? And my evaluators have found many students whose conduct and attitudes reflect values such as "Grades are all" or "Who cares?"

Student Councils as Devices to Assist Character Development

84.   The principal told us that early in the year he had met with the student council and promised his cooperation in any activities they choose to promote (excepting only intervention in curriculum or discipline). However, as the year went on, it was evident that the council could not shape itself into an effective body or plan worthwhile programs. This seemed strange, since many of the school's students were competent and energetic, and the principal seemed sincere (60, R, 9–12).

Most schools have student councils. Because councils represent activities where students can assume semiindependent responsibilities inside the school, they can be important devices to assist character development. Unfortunately, in the majority of cases these councils are only moderately effective at best. There are a variety of reasons for this deficiency. Many faculty and students are confused by the (inappropriate) parallels between councils and the legislative bodies which govern our states and nation. They unconsciously assume that the councils should have power and authorities similar to legislatures. The parallel is wrong because students do not have the maturity to exercise such power; legislatures are continuing bodies composed of persons who not only are older, but who usually have been serving for many terms and have learned through such experience; and administrators and faculty—and not students—are delegated to run schools and are the persons legally responsible to parents. And so attempts to apply the parallel are frustrated by these realities.

The other problem is that councils can—and should—be given real and maturing responsibilities. But carving out such responsibilities, and creating a persisting and effective body, takes imagination and energy. Indeed, one part of this imagination is the ability to recognize that (a) the legislative parallel doesn't apply and (b) devising a council role appropriate to the school and students involved. The students can neither be left powerless nor given free rein. Not all educators can find the right mid-point.

85.   The student court of the student council tries minor student offenses, for example, littering or talking in class. In 1976–1977 they heard over 300 cases. They make the final decision in such cases and often levy the small penalties involved. The council is also responsible for cleaning up any graffiti that are discovered on the school premises (21, P, 9-12).

Notice that the administration does not abrogate to the court the authority (and responsibility) to decide matters that vitally affect the health and safety of other students, for example, how to deal with students who bring weapons or drugs into school. And the council, which oversees the court, is also liable for cleaning up the vandalism which may occur if the adjudicative process is not effective. However, within the court's sphere of authority, it has independent power. It can take pride for its effectiveness and suffer for its mistakes.

86.   A student council protest occurred because of the shortage of the time allowed for walking from one class to the next. The council discussed the change with the principal, who remained calm, listened, and calculated with them how long it actually took to walk to their next class. The council agreed with the analysis, and decided to drop the matter.

The council circulated a petition this past week on how to alleviate the problem of adding school days to the year because the School had been closed due to heavy snow. The petition was forwarded by the principal to the Board of Education and reviewed. The outcome was satisfactory to all concerned. The text of the petition follows:

To: Dr. A and members of the board of education. The eighth grade class of the student body of the School hereby submit this petition to elongate all of the school days by twenty minutes for this coming month of February.

This hopefully would eliminate the unwanted process of shortening the Easter Vacation or lengthening the school year and postponing the graduation of the eighth grade students.

We would deeply appreciate it if you would seriously consider our suggestion. (31, P, 7–8)

87.   The booklet distributed to all students provides as follows:

STUDENT COUNCIL

The governing body for all student affairs is the Student Council. Each class elects representatives to this organization. There are ten seniors, ten juniors, ten sophomores, and ten freshmen elected to the Student Council (five boys and five girls from each of the four classes). The freshmen members are not elected until the end of their first semester in school. This brings the total elective membership of the Council to forty. In May of 1974 the Student Council voted to add an additional ten members. These ten are selected in this manner; following the regular May elections, the Student Council announces to the student body that it will accept applications from any student interested in serving on the Council. Before the end of school in June, the officers and committee chairmen of the Council conduct personal interviews with each of the applicants. A maximum of ten are selected on the basis of potential contribution to the Council and the School. A few vacancies are left open in June so the Council may have the option of selecting some of the freshmen in the fall.

CLASS COUNCILS

Approximately every 20 students, alphabetically divided by class levels into "A" or administrative groups, choose a representative Class Councils. These four groups are called Senior Council, Junior Council, Sophomore Council and Freshman Council.

Each Council is organized to provide leadership and direction for the class related activities occuring during the school year. For example, Junior Council organizes and supervises the junior prom, the junior carnival, etc. The other three councils deal with their own class activities. A class sponsor from the faculty is appointed to advise each Council. (36, P, 9–12)

This is a large school, and whether its councils operate ideally is a complex issue. Still, the promulgation of clear, logical procedures for selection of council members helps stimulate student interest.

Offering Choices and Asking Commitments

Learning to make and keep commitments is an important part of character development. A key element in such a learning process is to be provided with choices, since commitment involves some element of volition. Schools occasionally do provide students with moments for choice, though such moments are not always—as we will see—designed to foster learning about commitment.

88. The students who are accepted by my School are randomly selected through a lottery drawn from the total pool of applicants. The lottery attempts to insure that the School's student racial mix approximates that generally prevailing in the city's schools. No other explicit conditions are articulated to applicants (20, P, 9–12).

If we hope to cultivate character, we should try to let students clearly know what they are committing themselves to when they apply to a school that invites applications. Then they can make informed judgments, and be asked to live up to their voluntary commitments. When such information is not transmitted, then students are tempted to plead that their failure to meet some later revealed standards is due to their lack of prior information. (In fact, the operations of this school do make special demands on its students: it "asks" students from different races to fit together harmoniously; unfortunately, there is not much racial harmony in the School.)

89. To attract students to the School, open houses are held each year for future students and their parents to observe the School. They are given a school tour and provided with information about the school and activities. The last open house took place in October and ran from 2:00 to 4:00. It included a slide presentation and the chorus and cheerleaders provided entertainment. Refreshments were also served (56, R, 9–12).

Notice the School's assumption that its current students can appropriately act as its spokesmen.

90. The School's literature for potential students and their families mentions that "we seek students of good character" and "we give homework." There is an open house held annually for seventh and eighth graders, and students who attain the necessary test scores are interviewed by an assistant principal before being accepted (60, R, 9–12).

91. The School is selective and accepts only those who will be able to keep up with its high academic standards. The first step for an applicant is to take an entrance examination. If the applicant passes the exam, he is called in for a private interview; parents are not allowed to participate.

One of the faculty members does the interviewing without seeing any material about the applicant. The interviewer will then get together with the principal and make recommendations on how the personality of the applicant will fit in with the School. The applicant then is required to turn in a writing sample. All the materials are then placed in a file and sent to a group of nine or ten teachers called "folder readers." They read the entire folder and make a recommendation and send it to the principal. It is up to the principal to accept or reject an applicant. The director looks at all the rejected applicants, where he may decide to overrule the principal on borderline cases. The principal tends to be more conservative on accepting applicants because he does not want to accept a student who will have to leave the School at the end of the year (66, S, 9–12).

From other information in the report, it is evident that this careful process is almost solely aimed at screening out undermotivated students—as compared to assessing student character, or informing students of the character-related demands that lie before them. The effect of the screening is to greatly simplify the task of the teachers, and prevent later drop-outs or flunk-outs.

92.   During the first week of school, the principal speaks to all the new students at an assembly. He emphasizes that the School is equipped to handle any educational problem that students have, but the students must assume the initiative, and take the necessary steps to communicate the problem to the staff members who are essential to its solution.

Students cannot decide their problem is insoluble, unless they have been told this in a face-to-face verbal conference with the School's principal. But students must assume the responsibility for making the problem known to the staff. They should never assume that because the staff is there that it knows about all problems (16, P, 9–12).

Obviously, such a "message" makes clear to the students their personal responsibility for their school's success—as well as demonstrating the resources available for help.

93.   Students apply to be accepted by this school and must meet certain academic criteria. When they apply, they receive a four-page detailed outline of the School's various academic programs and its requirements (in terms of earned credits) for graduation. Nine of the ten freshmen students interviewed said they were pleased to be enrolled in the School (21, P, 9–12).

About 10 percent of the pupils in Chicago public high schools have chosen the school they attend; taking the whole Chicago area, and including public and private schools, the figure increases to 20 percent or more. About 75 percent of these schools provide adequate advance information to potential applicants.

Responsible public-school faculty members have spoken critically about the inappropriateness of selective public schools. Essentially their criticism is that such schools draw off able students from regular schools and thus undermine the stability of such schools. On the other hand, if concerned and vigorous parents (and their children) are not offered some options, they may choose private schools, or leave the city. And, as suggested, there are character-related virtues to giving students choice. Perhaps a better solution than the current thrust toward selective public schools is to diversify the variety of separate programs in general high schools, and make such programs vehicles for fostering genuine student choice. There will be more discussion about this possibility in chapter 6.

Discussion

We have just been presented with a large array of data. Explanatory comments were offered intermittently throughout the text. But this is a good place to insert some general interpretive remarks. They will not be exhaustive. The topic of student character development is large and complex. Furthermore, as readers will see, there are elaborate interrelationships among the topics of my chapters. As a result, the succeeding remarks will be relevant in considering future chapters—and the discussions concluding those chapters will add to the significance of this material.

My discussion will present a conceptual outline of the forces that have shaped the patterns of school operation we have been examining. I will preface the discussion with some conclusionary words about these patterns—so that you may know where I stand. Character development is not dead in schools—but it is in a bad way. Some schools are very good at it, many are weak, and some are bad. And some schools, due to family and neighborhood values, are faced with more challenges than others. Bad practices affecting character development seems to be more common in large school districts, in large schools, in public and secular schools, and in high and junior high schools. *But there are obvious exceptions to all of these generalizations.* The underlying causes of these bad practices are both conceptual and operational. At a conceptual level, administrators and teachers often do not know what character-related effects to aim at, or why. And, operationally, when they have some idea as to what they want to achieve, they do not see how to get it done. But now let us consider how we have arrived at this distressing place.

For most of human history, schools—and teachers—have been profoundly concerned with student character development. Socrates, Plato, St. Ignatius Loyola, Matthew Arnold, Horace Mann—to name a few—saw education principally as a device for character development. Indeed, Socrates, who taught when writing was first coming into use, opposed his lectures being copied down. He feared that such copying might lead to his ideas being transmitted to persons who never had personal contact with him. And to Socrates, such direct contact was the core of teaching and learning. After all, contact was essential to character assessment, and the exchange of mutually earned respect.

It is perhaps only in the past 100 years that large numbers of adults have become concerned with teaching and running schools without simultaneously being consciously engaged in character development. This remarkable—practically revolutionary—shift has been due to a variety of factors.

First, as the preceding data demonstrate, schools have not completely abandoned character development. Wise and determined parents can find schools that practice sound policies, and some other parents (and their children) are using character-oriented schools simply by chance.

The fact is there are tremendous practical pressures on faculty members to be concerned with the character of the students around them. Indeed, even today many persons become teachers not just to be technicians at transmitting literacy, but because they actually believe in character shaping.

Second, the role of the schools in character development has never been overtly cast aside. In other words, the revolution has been tacit. Thus, I have never seen an official document issued by any school which said the school was indifferent to student character. It is true that, when character-related terms are used in school documents, the definitions presented are often inconsistent or incomprehensible. However, the general terminology still gives optimistic—or desperate—parents some straws to clutch at. Again, most parents still believe character development is of great importance, and that schools should be deeply engaged in it. At least, that is my interpretation of the persistent concern of parents (reflected in annual Gallup polls on education) with "discipline."[2] Discipline is simply the layman's term for character.

Third, character development has steadily expired as an active educational goal as schools have been enmeshed in the pursuit of efficient cognitive instruction. In other words, as transmitting the school's formal subject matter has grown in importance, character development has been undermined as a goal. This does not mean that intelligence and good character are in conflict; it does signify that the means now applied by schools (supposedly to efficiently increase formal instruction) undermine character development.

These efficient—and character destructive means—are partly hardware, for example, grading machines for impersonal student testing, and computers for class assignments. They are partly the more general outcome of technology—buses that make schools remote from homes; mechanized cafeterias where students can't easily help; and buildings that can only be maintained by skilled technicians, compared to relying on student assistance. But, most profoundly, modern organizational concepts have effected the ways we shape and control the time of students and faculty, and the ways we plan schools and programs for them. We have made schools larger, and more remote from the homes of most pupils. We have tried to focus pupils' time on book-related activities, as compared to more character-oriented affairs (for example, student fundraising, acting as hall guards). We shift pupils and teachers around through each day (and annually) to assist formal instruction, without being deeply concerned with the sense of isolation such shifts foster. We lessen pupil and family choices among schools, to assist planning the flow of students. We increase the influence of modern psychology (and other academic disciplines) on the curriculum, which leads to a decline in the focus on character development. We grade pupils largely (or wholly) on formal academic performance, and thus treat character as irrelevant. And, finally, we establish hiring and promotion criteria that encourage teachers and administrators to see themselves as technicians.

These policies mimic patterns of organization found in our industrial and economic life. In these noneducation spheres, we all can recognize the interest in economies of scale, the appeal of specialization, the depersonalization of work, and the growth of bureaucracy. Perhaps such patterns really are efficient in industrial and economic life. Even so, most large businesses are more decentralized than schools, and research indicates that personal relations issues are (properly, I believe) important in decision-making in efficient businesses. But, even if the patterns "work" away from schools, it is simplistic to assume that children and adolescents should be treated, in schools, as if they were employed by large, bureaucratic businesses. The data about youth alienation suggest that such practices create adults who are too insecure to accept the inevitable pressures incident to all adult life. We are probably moving our youth into impersonality too quickly—it is becoming counterproductive, and thus inefficient.

Fourth, character development has been undermined by the excessive intellectual sympathies of some educators and academics for egalitarian and romantic ideas. There has always been an American tradition of such sympathies—Brook Farm, during the early nineteenth century, was not the last, or the first, American "commune." However, it seems that the apogee of such ideas was reached in the late 1960s and early 1970s. These ideas are hostile to character development. They belittle excellence and distinctions. However, unless distinctions are made, and rewards (and punishments) issued, character development will stagnate. Or the ideas imply that society is so rich that we can all choose to live on air, and that there is no need to engage in the strenuous business of demanding personal improvement from others. Such ideas gained popularity for a variety of reasons. They seem to make the work of teachers and administrators easier. Their low conceptual rigor—"all we need to do is let go of restraints"—facilitates their use as propaganda. And the promise of utopian success is a tempting incentive.

We also cannot ignore the intellectual influence of the ideas of revisionist historians on the school curriculum. After all, suppose we assume our previous national leaders were largely racists, exploiters, and demagogues— as these historians sometimes imply. If they are right, there is little sense in looking to the past for role models for students. Or, if these historians do identify some "good" models, they are often persons who were marginal, angry, and alienated. Such examples do not offer encouraging images to fourteen-year-olds.

Many of these ideas of the 1960s are now declining in their influence. However, it is hard to see what their replacements will be. It seems that neither the "romantics" nor the "technicians" grasp the requirements for managing sound character development. Indeed, it has sometimes appeared as if the technicians have turned to the romantics to supply them with a zeitgeist—a philosophical framework for school management. The technicians attitude seems to have been, "Why don't we let these people [the romantic ideologues] paint the 'big picture'? Then we can reserve for ourselves the significant work in education—managing budgets and improving reading and math learning." Now that the romantics have failed, one cannot have much faith in the technicians who surrendered authority to them.

Finally, over 95 percent of the faculty members in the schools studied were graduates of American colleges. Many of them had done graduate work, and the great majority of the administrators held advanced degrees. The advanced degrees were mostly in education, and the undergraduate degrees were either in education (for teachers in elementary schools) or in various subject areas (for example, math or english) with minors in education. This thoroughgoing process of credentialism is the outcome of laws, salary incentive systems (which give raises for taking education courses), and patterns of professional expectations. The process is supposed to supply faculty with an intellectual framework to deal with the day-to-day problems they confront. But the college work provided these educators gives them little or no useful perspectives relating to character development.

It is not that all American college faculty members are disinterested in character development; it's a big country, with hundreds of thousands of professors. But the school principals my students talk to assume that, if they want to get realistic ideas about how to stop cheating, or give students good role models, they should generally not ask their college professors. And the principals are not cynical just because they have gotten their degrees in "education." Their cynicism is directed at academia in its entirety. I believe it is largely justified. But the lack of procharacter perspective prevailing in higher education has had its impact both on college students and on the prescriptions offered by academics to potential teachers and principals.

To be concrete, on my own campus we have an elaborate, campuswide anticheating rule. It was written by a faculty committee and passed by the academic senate. The rule discloses the campuswide faculty state of mind about an important character issue—student cheating. I read the rule to one of my graduate classes—comprised largely of teachers. One of the rule's most prominent provisions said that the first responsibility of faculty who found students cheating was to foster their "rehabilitation." Neither my students nor I could guess what that meant. The rule also provided six alternative (and progressively more severe) punishments, and three levels of student appeal. After my students and I read the whole text, our only certain conclusion was that wise faculty members should ignore student cheating.

For if a professor caught someone, he would get embroiled in interpreting and carrying out the obscure and elaborate rule. We concluded at the end of this arduous process—regardless of the formal outcome—that the administration, and many of the professor's colleagues, would probably view him as punitive, and a troublemaker, due to the aggravation the necessary procedure would inevitably generate.

On the whole, the professionalization of school teaching and administering (in our era) has probably weakened our responsiveness to character-related problems. This professionalization has made it harder for faculty to rely on simple common sense. Such common sense is not always right in character-related issues. Still, it's probably more useful than the placebos usually prescribed for such matters by contemporary higher education. Perhaps one of the reasons the practices of church-related schools (as presented in this chapter) are so much better for character development is that their faculties have a relatively coherent intellectual doctrine. This doctrine serves to counteract the "do-your-own-thing" or "technology-first" philosophies prescribed in modern colleges of education. Lay teachers in secular schools may also have differences with these "philosophies." However, their personal opinions do not have the intellectual weight of an integrated doctrine. And so the lay persons must often abandon their resistance and go away confused.

There is another important effect to the irrelevance of the training of teachers and administrators to managing character development. Ultimately this irrelevance causes these operators to develop comparatively antiintellectual attitudes. Of course, they usually don't make speeches or write articles articulating their antiintellectual viewpoints. If they did, they would be intellectuals. They just tacitly ignore many academic approaches on a day-to-day basis in their work. They may still subscribe to some periodicals or attend professional conferences or occasionally retool their vocabulary—but they often see their work as almost wholly firefighting. And, in such an environment, ideas are of small consequence. Thus a school principal will almost never consult with a college professor the way a client will with his lawyer, a patient with his doctor, or a businessman with his accountant. But withdrawal from all intellectual engagement is not very helpful, either.

Overseeing character development is partly an intellectual problem. Rules and policies must be written and analyzed. The significance of different role models must be weighed. Activities must be thoughtfully designed. Appeals to virtue must be handled with artistry and grace. And so modern academia may have doubly undermined character development, party by prescribing irrelevant or bad policies and partly by discouraging educators from thinking profoundly about alternatives, or looking to the thoughts of "unmodern" intellectuals.

4 Book Learning

For engendering competence, it is clear that love is not enough, though it matters. Challenge, respect for the child, perhaps some abrasiveness in relations with the child that provokes his assertiveness, good communication with an emphasis on the reasons for directives—these would seem to be important too, and are supported by convergent evidence. [1]

Schools should help students acquire book-related, or cognitive, skills. At lower grade levels, these basically involve reading, writing, and arithmetic. At higher grades, they can extend to physical and social sciences, literature, foreign languages, the arts, and what are termed "communication skills." These communication skills can be subdivided into a great many elements, such as speaking, either one-to-one, in small groups, or before large gatherings; collecting information through interviews (especially from persons of different ages or with different statuses); using the telephone or filling out forms; writing letters (formal and informal), reports, and essays; reading and preparing statistical tables, graphs, diagrams, and maps; and doing library research.

Sometimes persons concerned with evaluating students' cognitive learning in schools pay a great deal of attention to the nature of the school's curriculum, and the instructional theories and methods of specific teachers. Thus they try to determine exactly what information in what form is being taught to different grades, and exactly how teachers are presenting it. These matters are not irrelevant. However, I believe their importance has been overexaggerated. After all, human beings have obviously learned great bodies of skills and information through a variety of methods. There is probably no one right method. But there are other general principles that do apply broadly to cognitive instruction. And persons doing school analyses should focus on these principles, and the effects they produce.

For instance, there is considerable research to the effect that pupils learn more if they are graded on some incremental continuum (for example, they can earn As, Bs, or so forth), compared to only a pass/fail grade. And it is easy for evaluators or administrators to determine the basic grading policies of a teacher or schools, much easier than it is for them to do detailed evaluations of curriculum plans. In effect, this chapter will focus on the important general practices—such as school grading patterns—that affect students' book learning.

One other common way of evaluating schools should also be mentioned at this point. Sometimes evaluators give great emphasis to the school or class average reading or math scores, or to other equivalent data, for example, the proportion of a school's students going to college, or receiving scholarships. Such statistics are not irrelevant, but they have many limitations. Educational research has demonstrated that the performance of groups of students, as measured by these statistics, is usually more affected by the pupils' home background than the quality of their school. In other words, pupils' learning is as much shaped by the educational background and concern of their parents as by the efficiency of their school.

This is not to say that a school's teaching efficiency is irrelevant, or that all children from less educated parents do poorly. It simply means that, in general, schools will tend to do "better" if high proportions of their pupils come from well-educated families. Terms like "generally" and "tend" mean there are inevitably exceptions. However, the overall data do mean that direct comparisons of the average reading scores of pupils in two different schools may be "unfair": one of the two schools could have an excellent book-learning program, but have many students from poorly educated families; the other one may have a relatively inefficient book-learning program, but have a high proportion of students from well-educated families. Because of these family background differences, the first school may look worse than the second in the data, even though, by certain justified criteria, it is doing a "better" job.

Educational researchers have evolved techniques that do permit some defensible interschool comparisons of reading scores. Essentially these techniques require evaluators using the scores to collect additional statistics (about pupils' family background). These statistics can identify schools (or classes in schools) where pupils have essentially the same type of family background. Then the comparisons between scores are made.

But it is not always simple to say when one group of students is "essentially" the same as another for purposes of such comparisons. Some ethnic groups have traditions that give great emphasis to formal education, even when the parents themselves may not be highly educated. And so, merely comparing two or more schools with approximately the same levels of parental education may not be "fair" if they enroll different ethnic groups. Again, some parents with only modest education and income believe education is very important and choose to make economic sacrifices to send their children to private schools. Other parents, with the same income and education, choose publicly supported schools, perhaps because they do not attach such a high value to formal education. Under these circumstances, comparing the learning effects of the two kinds of schools may be difficult; the private-school pupils tend to come from families that are different (by one definition) from those of the children in the public schools.

This discussion is not intended totally to deprecate reading-score comparisons among schools, but to suggest that many such comparisons are oversimplified. For this reason, such comparisons will not be relied on in this chapter.

Another deficiency of these comparisons should also be mentioned. Even when comparisons are appropriately qualified, their usefulness is limited for many purposes. The comparisons rarely tell us what any school is doing, right or wrong. They have been able to identify few (if any) operating measures, which are not inordinately expensive, and which substantially assist cognitive learning. This is not to say there are no such measures. The remainder of this chapter will propose quite a few. But the statistical comparisons have rarely carefully analyzed the effects of many of the measures which will be discussed in this chapter.

The reasons for this inattention are complex. Some of the measures proposed are hard to describe quantitatively (for example, how principals can supervise teachers teaching by watching the interaction between them and their pupils in the school lunchroom and halls). Some are "unglamorous" (for example, how does one run an effective awards assembly for ten-year-olds?). But perhaps the most important reason for this inattention is the surprising fact that the design and operation of systems of cognitive instruction—to a great degree—involves philosophical issues. In other words, the choices among alternative systems are based on views about the nature of man and society. And naturally decisions about whether and how to evaluate alternative systems also are based not only on "technical" issues but on the willingness of evaluators to encourage certain practices they deem philosophically undesirable. For instance, giving greater privileges to students who learn faster than others can be regarded as elitist and ideologically wrong, even if it apparently tends generally to increase cognitive learning. Furthermore, researchers philosophically opposed to such reinforcement techniques may also contend that elitist practices have important undesirable spillovers that will not be identified by simple formalistic evaluation. In any case, from the reports of my observers, a great variety of easily visible school practices are followed which are not analyzed in most research, and which affect pupil cognitive learning.

Homework Policy

Schools apply different forms of homework policies—or nonpolicies. These differences obviously have implications for the level of student cognitive learning.

94.   We interviewed about thirty students, who said they usually got an hour or less of homework per week, and never any on weekends. They were usually given assignments in class, and if they didn't finish them they would do them at home. In my opinion, if more homework were given more learning would take place. Also more time could be available in class for teaching, instead of teachers just watching students do their "homework" (37, P, 7-8).

95.   The fact that classes are on a pass/fail basis generates problems for teachers trying to enforce homework assignments. For instance, one teacher assigned projects to be completed in eight weeks, as part of students' course work. During the eight weeks, she reminded the class frequently about the due date. By the due date, only two of the twelve students in the class had done their work. The teacher could not plan any effective action against the other ten students, since all of them had done enough other course work to warrant their passing the course. As a result, the ten received the same credit as the two diligent students (20, P, 9-12).

96.   The issue of whether to assign daily homework was left to the discretion of the teachers; some gave such assignments, and others did not (6, P, K-8).

The assignment of homework generates work for teachers as well as students. The teachers who assign homework must (should?) plan appropriate assignments, make sure students do them, and collect and grade them. Without some monitoring process, it is possible that both teachers and students may fail to carry out some or all of these responsibilities. Yet it is obvious that well-designed homework can enhance learning.

97.   Out of ten students interviewed, eight said they received homework every night. If the homework was math, it was collected, then returned to them the next day. Incorrectly done problems are circled, and the students had to redo them. English homework was returned one to two weeks after it had been handed in. Composition mistakes were circled or underlined. Failure to do the homework results in a failing grade for the homework, which counts toward the student's final grade (21, P, 9-12).

No more than 25 to 50 percent of the high schools examined gave their students regular homework, which averaged more than four hours a week and was effectively graded by teachers. In considering this matter, I should mention a student survey conducted by a high-school paper; it showed that most of the students in that school watched television from two to five hours a day.

98.   Homework assigned by teachers is well planned and monitored. Students are required to turn in such assignments on time. If it is one day late, credits are subtracted. If it is more than three days late, it is not accepted, and the student thus loses full credit for that particular assignment. The teachers generally agreed that students at the School should put in at least twenty hours a week on homework assignments to receive even passing grades in their subjects. They thus implied that students desiring to get better than average grades would need to put in a minimum of twenty-five to thirty hours per week on assignments (58, R, 9–12).

99. The teachers for the seventh and eighth grades (which are departmentalized) meet weekly to discuss their planned homework assignments, so their pupils will not be overloaded on any one day, and not have enough on other days (29, P, K–8).

100. Next to the door of each classroom we observed charts with each student's name on it. The chart denoted several different areas of student effort—homework on time, homework well done, results of spelling bees (classes often divided in half for this activity—group 1 and group 2). Stars are used to show good work. Better papers are often displayed on the class bulletin boards (49, R, K–8).

101. The School handbook distributed to all parents contained the following language: "There are to be minimal homework assignments in the primary grades; 30 to 45 minutes per day in grades four and five, and 60 to 90 minutes per day in grades six, seven and eight. In grades six, seven and eight the teachers should schedule assignments so pupils will not receive more than 60 to 90 minutes daily" (31, P, K–8).

There is no magically correct level of homework—although one can assume that students should have a fair amount of homework. However, certain other principles regarding such assignments can easily be derived. A uniform policy among the faculty is important; without such a policy, faculty members that assign homework will assume an unfair burden in planning assignments and grading papers (compared to the nonassigners), and also will be subjected to student criticism as "discriminatory." A uniform policy is also important in enlisting parent cooperation. Parents cannot monitor their childrens' assignments unless they can routinely expect such assignments; without such routinization, children will often tell parents (truthfully) that they have no homework tonight, and the parents will have no easy way of checking such statements (especially in departmentalized schools, where one child is "subject" to several teachers). Then, if children later falsely tell their parents they have no homework (when they really have), the parents have no alternative but to take their word. But, if homework is routinely given, and parents are so informed (preferably in writing), children are removed from this temptation. Less than 25 percent of the schools studied provided such clear, written notification to parents. Presumably one reason notification is not given is that such notifications, incidentally, obligate the teachers—in the eyes of parents—to give assignments. Without clear and stated policies, teachers (or administrators) can give or not give homework as they choose, and justify to parents their failure in terms of vague "pedagogical principles." Of course, there sometimes can be legitimate reasons for such flexibility, but the flexibility also significantly deters real parental cooperation.

Attendance Policy

Usually, students are required to attend the schools in which they are enrolled, and show up for the various classes in the school day. However, as we will see, there are differences in the degree of efficiency with which schools monitor their students' attendance. The following items discuss some of these differences.

102.   There is a high rate of absenteeism among students in the School. As a result, teachers have to spend a great deal of their class time reviewing material that was missed by absent students; this review process is often tedious for the students with satisfactory attendance. But, without such reviewing, the absent students might fall even farther behind, and be even more prone to stay out (15, P, 9–12).

103.   One teacher observed that "this school uses the honor system, and it works. There aren't many problems here, except perhaps tardiness and absenteeism." The interviewer asked, "How do you deal with absenteeism?" The teacher said, "Beyond three times a week. . .it's time to talk. I ask the students questions such as 'Do you have an alarm clock?' plus sometimes students are in a state of depression, and I try and get them to talk" (20, P, 9–12).

Theoretically, one might simply say that absent students (in high school) must suffer the penalties that result from missing classes, that is, doing poor work and receiving bad grades. But such a pronouncement is far too theoretical. Students are, by definition, ignorant and need to learn— and part of what they must learn is the necessity for regular application. It is true that their "irregularity" must be punished, to encourage them to learn such application. However, the punishment of low grades (as an indirect by-product of poor attendance) is comparatively remote; and, incidentally, the "reward" of higher grades is even more distant. Thus, in schools where poor student attendance demonstrates the need for greater student learning about application, more systemic and immediate devices must be applied, in contrast to relying on the very indirect punishments and benefits of poor learning and low grades.

104.   The principal has instituted an intensive attendance program for the students. She is attempting to achieve a 90 percent attendance rate. In order to reach this goal, she started a club called the IOE Club, *I*n School, *O*n Time, *E*very day. To gain membership in the club, an individual student or a class has to have perfect attendance for two months in a row. After these two months, one becomes a member of the club after being awarded a certificate at the awards assembly. Members of the IOE Club get to go to movies, have ice-cream parties, and wear a big button in school that says IOE. If students mar a perfect attendance record a first time, they are put on probation. After that, if they are late or absent, they are no longer in the club until they have perfect attendance for another two months. Students and classrooms seemed very proud of their buttons and had them prominently displayed (18, P, 7–8).

Attendance is not a serious problem in all schools; essentially, it is better in schools where parent interest and support are higher. But, among schools where poor attendance is a problem, perhaps only 25 percent of them have instituted unique schoolwide systems of reward and punishment aimed at improving attendance.

School-Fostered Extraclass Learning Activities

Some schools, and their teachers, take steps to encourage students to apply, or display, their learning in away-from-classroom environments. Obviously, such measures can improve cognitive learning. The following items give examples of such activities.

105. Suggestions for school improvement by one teacher: "A teacher should be freed at least part-time to serve as a school-community liaison person. This teacher would get out into the neighborhood, investigate its potential as a learning tool for the students (by talking to residents, checking facilities, encouraging assistance from various agencies) and set up definite programs for the school to involve itself with. As things now stand, the resources of the community are wasted since no school personnel are specifically charged with investigating them or given the time to do so. The proposed change can only increase the understanding and respect that the school and the community have for each other" (3, P, K–8).

106. The seventh- and eighth-grade teachers entered their student art work in a nearby shopping center's art fair. Thirty-two students submitted pictures and the teachers chose fifteen pictures to display at the fair. Of those displayed, four pictures were selected winners, and the students were awarded prizes such as clothing, shoes, or a watch (2, P, K–8).

107. The academic clubs help to encourage student learning through stimulating purposeful student association with other talented students. The spelling club has contests with seven other junior high schools, and the math club took second place in a tournament held at a private high school (31, P, 7–8).

108. The math club meets daily for one hour (ribbons and individual plaques are given to members for excellence). Its members participate in the Joliet Junior College tournament. Sixty to seventy student applicants for the club take written tests in their math classes, and members are selected on the basis of these tests. Eleven students participated last year and won first prize for the school. A large trophy with the School's name and the year written on it is in the display case at the front entrance (59, R, 9–12).

109. The German club's activities begin with soccer and a restaurant outing in the fall, followed by preparation for the *Weihnachtsfest* (Christmas dinner), at which there are folk dancers, singers, and an um pah pah band. Besides producing an annual play in German, members attend the National German Convention and are enrolled in the National Carl Schurz Association (39, P, 9–12).

110. The School holds an annual schoolwide science fair. It is well publicized in the school paper, and visited by many students. Each exhibit was judged by a teacher specializing in the appropriate discipline (for example, chemistry, physics). Where one judge had trouble making a firm conclusion, judges from other disciplines assisted. Exhibits that were recognized were rated as either outstanding, excellent, or honorable mention. Of the thirty-eight exhibits at the most recent fair, six were excellent, nine outstanding, and twenty received honorable mention. The award was a certificate with the year of the fair, the student's name, title of the exhibit, and the level of the award. The certificate also allowed the student to display his exhibit at the annual citywide school science fair (21, P, 9–12).

111. The spelling bee is a big event at the School and it takes place over a period of two months. It is important because of the emphasis put on reading and competition. First every class has contests until the fifth level has its winners, the sixth level, its winners, and so on. These winners go on to the finals in the auditorium, where fifth competes against sixth, sixth against seventh, and seventh against eighth. The winners go on to the districtwide spelling contest. Although the School has not won any of the districtwide contests, most of the students we talked to knew about the spelling bees and thought they were exciting (18, P, 8–9).

The significant common characteristic of the activities just described is that they require planning above the individual classroom level. And, furthermore, at least some of the activities stimulate individual excellence but also put the excelling students forward as representatives of the total school. In other words, excelling students are not engaged in implicitly putting down their costudents, but are essentially enhancing the status of all their peers by demonstrating the excellence of the school on whose behalf they perform. This process of representation should make it easier for students to want to excel, and make all students more willing to encourage the excellence of their peers.

Among the schools studied, there was a wide variety of extraclass learning activities promoted by administrators and teachers. Unfortunately, perhaps only 10 to 20 percent maintained such activities at what could be termed a high level.

Of course, these activities use the time of teachers and administrators, and thus it may be that they add to school operating costs. However, unless persuasive research data to the contrary were developed, I'd assume that such supplementary activities generate more per pupil learning per unit of staff time than most traditional class activities. In other words, it is more "efficient" to dedicate staff time to planning and carrying out such activities than simply increasing, or even maintaining, direct investment in classroom instruction (beyond some minimal level). If this analysis is accepted, many schools should plan to gradually lessen classroom investments (for example, through lessening classroom time for teachers, or shifting pupil-teacher ratios, or giving up some aides) in favor of putting in more staff time in organizing extraclass learning activities.

Grouping Students by Ability

112.   In a number of classes, a constant murmur was present during the session. This background noise was a result of small groups of students conversing in the room as the lesson progressed. As long as this talking did not occupy the direct attention of most of the class, some teachers would accept it. Apparently these teachers place a higher value on class spontaneity, and were willing to tolerate this casual socializing as long as it did not disrupt the learning process. Other teachers run a more controlled classroom situation and demand that everyone pay attention to what they are doing at the front of the room.

It appeared to us that this problem of student disinterest was partly due to the varying ability of levels of the students. This made it inevitable that some students would be considerably ahead of (or behind) the general class level, and would become disengaged from the teacher's basic presentation. Several times we encountered situations where the teacher clearly realized the individual differences among the students, and had broken the class into smaller groups and had them working on separate projects (17, P, 9-12).

Teachers are under practical pressures to group or track students. Many such arrangements are affected by administrative decisions. The issues underlying such practices are complex. As a result they require extended discussion.

It is common for schools to evaluate and label pupils' learning abilities—and sort them according to these labels. Usually, this sorting process is justified as a tool to facilitate teaching and learning. But, at the same time, it is criticized as humiliating to many of the students affected. Unfortunately, many of the discussions that arise about these questions fail to recognize the parallels between in-school sorting and the sorting which is inherent in all adult life. In other words, in adult life, our skills are evaluated and labeled, whether we are surgeons, typists, or taxi drivers. As a result of such labeling, we are then awarded certain benefits or other recognition. It is true that people are often critical of the particular criteria applied to assess adult merit, or believe that the system of judging is not fair. But these criticisms are not objections to the essential process of judging, only at its means of implementation. Thus, while the systems for judgment will always be changing, there will never be an adult world which does not specially reward superior performance in valued activities. In effect, the process of gradation in school is a foretaste of a vital element of adult life. The process adds to the relevance of school for students.

Of course, the processes of labeling in adult life are extremely complicated. Sometimes they are relatively meritocratic (for example, in the cases of computer programmers, or athletes), and sometimes they are greatly affected by considerations going beyond personal virtue (for example, when favor is shown to members of particular families, races, or religions). And so a school whose rating system applied only one criterion (for example, demonstrated learning potential), or always was extremely rigorous in labeling, would be distorting the variegated forms of ratings applied in adult life. Furthermore, the degree of rigor applied in adult labeling varies greatly— almost anyone is permitted to ride a public bus, but few people become state governors. However, in some parts of adult life, cognitive learning ability is a prime criterion and pupils (or their parents) who want to attain adult notability will have to meet rigorous tests.

Actually, many schools do apply a number of varied tests of "entitlement" such as are applied in adult life. Students who are only fair in book learning are often able to excel in athletics, or the band, or equivalent activities. Of course, such gratifications are more common in schools with a rich extracurricular life. And, if the school has a high level of school spirit, even students whose general record is only mediocre may get considerable satisfaction from being part of a vital and admired entity (that is, their school). As a result of such patterns, some schools can comfortably engage in necessary levels of student grouping (to foster book learning) without (1) implicitly abusing students who lack such capabilities, or (2) creating a distorted prestige structure among students which fails to mirror the diversity of virtues rewarded in adult life.

This injection of adult-life relevance into schools through grouping usually occurs incrementally—and this is proper. The learning potentials of young pupils are comparatively unformed, and difficult to assess. And since learning capabilities are partly developmental—children of certain ages are incapable of "learning" certain concepts—young children are often at a common learning level. Thus, in lower grades, it is less necessary to group students on the basis of learning capability. Furthermore, such groupings are more likely to subject these comparatively vulnerable children to invidious tensions.

As pupils grow older, their potentials are more evident and varied, and their emotional capability to withstand implicit comparisons should be stronger. After all, by the time children are (let us say) ten, there are surely areas of activity where they see they are not as able as some peers. Learning to compensate for such inevitable inadequacies is part of the stuff of life. And so, as children grow older (and nearer to adulthood) schools tend to group them by apparent ability level and present them with learning materials appropriate to their capability. Theoretically, such groupings should not be inviolate, but subject to change due to altering circumstances or information. Still, there is no doubt that such labeling is sometimes erroneous, or that it is not changed when it should be. But these errors do not justify the refusing to classify and act on these classifications at an appropriate time. Such a refusal can only lead to either gross classroom disorder and boredom, or covert and unmonitored labeling by harassed and exhausted teachers.

113. The School's reading program is divided into four ten-week periods in a year. Every ten weeks a different reading teacher will teach a new group of students of the same age. The rationale behind this is that every ten-week period will provide students with a new teacher and a fresh, interesting book at the next level. The idea is, the more different materials one reads, the better effective reader one becomes. I personally disagree. Quantity does not replace quality. If students fail to understand the basics (and are still passed on) they will be riding on rickety, wobbly wheels down the ever-increasing incline plane of education. On the other hand, if they understand the basics, they will be able to zoom and fly up toward unending heights. That is to say, when students are able to cope with their material they will be able to advance as far as they can, depending on their inherent abilities and enthusiasm. The basic reading skills must be taught before a student can be come a mature, independent reader and read for the sake of reading. And this takes time and skill, not simply handling many different reading books. In addition, how can one reading teacher be held accountable for his students' deficiencies if three other teachers are teaching the students reading during the same year (5, P, K–8)?

Extensive research has demonstrated that pupils of the same age have different potentials for learning cognitive materials. Sometimes it is contended that these differences may be moderated by providing slower learners with more attention, or more deliberately paced instruction. However, such different "treatments" still constitute recognition of difference in ability.

These differences among pupils place teachers under pressure to group students into categories defined by different learning styles or potentials. With such groupings, the teacher can organize the subject matter into packages appropriate for each separate group. Without groupings, the teacher has the impossible task of shaping fifteen to twenty-five separate learning packages, and of devising plans that keep all other students occupied when he is working with each student one at a time.

It is true that this process can be simplified by various prepackaged learning programs. However, even under such circumstances, as the material becomes more sophisticated (for instance, as pupils grow older) the pressures for some form of homogenizing force increase.

The preceding discussion may seem obvious and comparatively unobjectionable. But it leads to sensitive social questions. The fact is that pupils are usually able to deduce when they are put in the groups of fast or slow learners. And who likes to be labeled "slow"—or whatever other euphemism is employed? Indeed, the school—or teacher—is even under some pressure to create such pejorative labels, and to attribute prestige to the better learners. After all, if the school could actually cause the fast and slow learners to believe either level was equally good, there would be less incentive for pupils to try to become fast learners. For example, suppose "your" child were designated a slow learner, and the teacher made the child satisfied with that designation; would you be pleased if you felt that this satisfaction made the child less willing to try to move up to the fast group?

Almost all of the high schools studied maintained some system of tracking or student ability grouping, at least in mathematics. Many of them applied such systems also to English, foreign languages, and the sciences. Perhaps half the grade schools deliberately followed such policies, and, undoubtedly, many classroom teachers have applied such systems in their rooms without official sponsorship.

114.   Part of the School's academic problem is students enrolling with poor arithmetic and reading skills. Counselors are sent out to the grammar schools to test potential students in these areas. If necessary, the pupil is placed in a low track. Thirty percent of the freshmen are in such programs. Even with these special provisions, problems sometimes arise. A student with poor math skills will have trouble with science and a student with poor reading skills will have trouble learning history (12, P, 9–12).

115.   The students are tested when they enter and are tracked according to ability and interest. Those students who have appropriate abilities are given the advanced courses. I talked with a parent who felt this program was wonderful. Her son was very intelligent but a troublemaker. When he came to the School he was given the advanced courses and no longer caused problems. It turned out he had just been bored and felt unchallenged before (18, P, 7–8).

116.   The *Curriculum Guide* explains that all courses are geared according to their track levels. Level One is designed for the non–college-bound student, while Level Two is a college preparatory level of the non-mathematics-oriented student. Level Three is a college-preparatory level for students with better than average mathematical ability and Level Four is designed to challenge students of outstanding ability in the area of mathematics (58, R, 9–12).

117.   Excerpted from a handbook delivered to all students and parents:

ABILITY GROUPS

For many years it has been the practice of the School to group students according to ability. This is done to better adapt the subject matter content, materials of instruction, and teaching methods to the aptitudes, abilities, and needs of the students. Students are placed in ability groups for specific subjects according to their ability in particular academic areas. For example, a student with superior ability in mathematics and science and typical ability in other academic subjects would be placed in honors sections in mathematics and science and in regular sections in English, history, and foreign languages.

Basic classes are designated with a "B" after the subject title; for example, English B. Regular level classes carry no letter after the title. Honors classes are marked with an "H". Accelerated or Advanced Placement classes, designated by an "A," are academically the most demanding classes.

The following factors are taken into consideration when students are assigned to ability groups:

1. Parent, dean, and teacher recommendations
2. Past performance and achievement
3. Test results
4. Reading ability
5. Personal factors: study habits, motivation, attendance record

Pupils are moved from one ability level to another whenever this seems appropriate. Ability grouping is used in some courses within the following departments:

English	Mathematics
Foreign Language	Science
History	

In accelerated classes increased emphasis is placed upon concepts, abstract relationships, critical thinking, and creative thinking; less emphasis is placed upon drills, examples, and descriptive materials. Students who earn good marks in these courses and in the Advanced Placement Examinations usually receive college credit for the college level work completed in high school. (36, P, 9–12)

Less than a quarter of the high schools studied had clear, written, widely distributed statements of their student grouping policies, and their rationale. And, whatever the shortcomings are to such policies, those deficiencies are aggravated when the policies are implemented covertly, and no one is compelled to publicly justify them.

Adult institutions that give intensive attention to various forms of "ability grouping"—such as businesses with highly competitive job promotion systems—inevitably become concerned with the tensions and devisiveness such patterns generate. And so they simultaneously seek to foster policies which maintain cooperation and individual self-respect among their members (or employees). As already suggested, schools can and sometimes do follow equivalent policies, by stimulating school spirit and providing variegated reward systems. These devices assure that even students with modest academic abilities will have a place in the sun. Another adaptation which is sometimes used—and should be applied more often—is giving better students responsibilities to assist the younger or weaker ones. This approach has already been discussed, and examples presented, in chapter 3. But it should be considered in another perspective in this analysis.

Assigning better students to helping roles (for example, as tutors or advisors) stimulates them to further development—either through causing them to better learn their material through acting as teachers, or causing to learn different (not strictly cognitive) skills, in communication and motivation. And such assignments can increase the social bonds between all students, both those helped and the helpers. In other words, through such assignments the able students are not simply invited to "run" at their fastest, and leave the rest behind; they are also invited to display solicitude, and use their gifts to assist others.

It is possible that such helping arrangements may slow down some able students in the maximum development of their formal academic skills. I say it is possible, and not certain. The fact is we do not have sure knowledge of the intellectual benefits of well-organized tutoring to tutors, compared to having tutors simply continue as passive learners. It is quite likely that teaching responsibilities are a vital part of most learning processes, and that we are now shortchanging our students by usually depriving them of such occasions. In any case, if some students have their formal learning slowed by tutoring responsibilities (assuming their responsibilities have been adequately planned), I'd contend that "cost" is not too high for the many other benefits tutoring renders to tutors. In other words, very few high-school students are going to be much wiser adults cause they took advanced science or accelerated algebra; almost all high-school students will benefit in their adulthood from having met and handled the challenge of causing a less able student to learn a new concept or skill. All of us, in our adult life, must accept the responsibility to instruct others; very few of us will become mathematicians or scientists—and even those specialists must still act as instructors in some contexts.

118. The math department believes a happy teacher gets better results from pupils. To achieve this, each instructor has at least one class in basic mathematics, one regular upper-class course, and one honor class. Each teacher will teach the same course for a least four to five years before a new course is selected. This approach results in each staff member having considerable knowledge of which concepts and skills are required at each level. Furthermore, no teacher is deprived of a chance to teach honors courses—which are usually seen as most desirable (36, P, 9–12).

This ingenious approach would only make sense in a fairly strong department, with able teachers.

Organizing Subject Matter to Assist Learning

119. At least twice each year, each department chair in this high school meets with elementary principals and teachers (from feeder schools) to discuss changing curriculum and course work—in both the high and elementary schools. In one instance, an elementary-school language arts teacher was receiving complaints from freshmen students who had graduated from his school. They stated that English I was a repetition of seventh- and eighth-grade English. As a result of this discussion, students entering the School are given a placement test and those receiving high grades are eligible for Honors English I and Honors English II. The majority of the students in these honors English classes are former students of the teacher who suggested the change (38, P, 9–12).

120. The math department has "social hours" with the eight mathematics teachers of their feeder schools. These meetings are held away from School after the first-quarter grades are sent home. Math teachers in the School attempt to have an alphabetized listing of their freshmen pupils, classified by their pupils' feeder schools. As a result, eighth-grade teachers can find their students from last year, their present high-school teacher, and the grade received in the first six weeks. This provides a common ground for discussion between high school and elementary teachers, in which both can gain knowledge on what each can do to help their pupils. Many suggestions have evolved from these meetings (38, P, 9–12).

Coordinated activities between schools at two levels, such as just described, are obviously more feasible when schools are "fed" pupils from a limited number of lower-level schools. This more typical in a neighborhood school situation.

Inevitably, individual teachers play an important role in organizing their own subject matter. Still, both informal interteacher cooperation and formal planning by administrators can greatly assist such individual activities. Such assistance grows in importance as schools become larger, pupils more transient, and students attend more segmented progressions of schools as they advance (for example, between first grade and twelfth, a student whose family never moves will still often advance through three schools).

121. Reading skills have priority in the School's curriculum. The Chicago Board of Education has recently initiated a program known as Continuous Progress/Mastery Learning which governs the curriculum from kindergarten to eighth grade in all Chicago schools. This program focuses on reading, but is eventually to be expanded to include math, social studies, and science. The program identifies 273 key objectives or skills to be mastered, grouped in levels A through N. The primary cycle includes 167 key objectives in A through H; the intermediate cycle includes an additional seventy-two objectives through L; and the upper cycle includes an additional thirty-four objectives through level N. Eighty percent of the objectives of each cycle should be mastered before the child is promoted to the next grade level at the end of each year. If a child needs additional time to complete the program, it should be provided by the end of the primary or intermediate cycles, rather than at the end of the upper cycle.

The curriculum guide for the program is issued by the board. It is very specific as to the skills to be mastered, and it suggests how a teacher might present the material to the children. Teachers are generally in favor of the program, though they criticize the bulk of its present form, which is time-consuming. Teachers feel the program is a good one because it allows the child and parent to observe the child's progress objectively. The program is sharply defined through testing and evaluation (18, P, 7–8).

There was considerable variation among Chicago schools in the efficiency with which they carried out Continuous Progress. In the schools with less effective programs, the teachers involved were poorly trained and supervised in their new responsibilities, and were not required to keep appropriate records. As we will see later in this chapter, steps were eventually taken which helped correct some of these deficiencies. Incidentally, the program does offer one example of a benefit derived from an educational economy of scale. It would be difficult for a small school district to have the resources to develop—or pay for the development of—such an elaborate program. (Of course, many of the elements of the program were taken from other developers and districts, but the process of acquisition and screening still involved costs.)

122. The goals of the English Department are specified as follows:

1. Students will develop competent written and oral expression: (a) there will be fewer errors in English on papers students write as they progress through a course; (b) students will be made aware of the purpose and usefulness of their writing; (c) students will be aware of the audience for whom they are writing; and (d) as judged by the teacher, students will improve in their written use of conventional English.
2. Students will develop proficiency in language usage: (a) students will be able to avoid diction errors; (b) students will be able to pass a test on the 100 most frequently misspelled words in English; and (c) students will be able to pass a test demonstrating their familiarity with the principal uses of the dictionary.
3. Students will understand the origin, development, structure, and function of the English language: (a) students will know the meaning of Greek and Latin roots and affixes; (b) students will be able to use con-

textual clues to word meaning; (c) students will be aware of when standard and non-standard English usage would be appropriate.

4. Students will develop an appreciation of reading and an interest in literature: (a) students will be provided with examples of famous people for whom reading has been a profound influence; and (b) students will read beyond that which is assigned in class.

5. Students will become familiar with the ideas found in the universe of our literary heritage: (a) students will be familiar with the cycle of English and American literature; (b) students will be able to pass a test demonstrating a facility in the recognition and use of major literary devices; and (c) students will learn representative literary genres. (58, R, 9–12)

I do not have enough information to estimate the frequency with which schools (or departments in schools) maintain and use outlines of objectives, such as the one just presented. I do know that some schools have little or nothing along these lines, and some have relatively clear and thorough materials. Obviously, such outlines are an important resource for teachers. They do not preclude the application of teacher creativity, and they do provide a base for the precise allocation of responsibilities among teachers. Furthermore, when such outlines are available to students and parents, they help these consumers know what to expect students to attain.

123.   One program that should be mentioned is RIF (Reading Is Fundamental). Five times a year the community represented lounge is filled with books arranged by subject matter. The room is decorated with drawings and dangling signs. By turns, the classes come down and get to pick out a free book. The parents are involved in distributing the books. The idea is for the students and their families to start building up libraries. If a family has three children in the school, every year fifteen new books will be added to the household (18, P, 7–8).

124.   When we visited the library, some students were working on a group research project about cancer. There were fourteen students in the library and nine of them were using books from outside libraries in addition to the books from the school library. Five students had books from the neighborhood library, three from the downtown library, and one from a college library. "It means a lot that the eighth graders know how to benefit from any library resources in the community or city," said the librarian (49, R, K–8).

The Role of Teacher Imagination in Stimulating Learning

125.   Many of the courses have catchy new titles, but simply teach the same old things (and sometimes less effectively for lack of discipline). The course

in persuasion is simply a high-school course in logic and debating; Banking is nothing more than Economics; Body Expression is nothing more than a psychology class; Survival English disguises a class which should be called Remedial Reading; and a class called Violence is a study of modern social issues (57, R, 9–12).

It is unfortunately true that the application of imagination by teachers can enhance pupils' learning. I say "unfortunately" because imagination is inevitably a rare talent, and so many dedicated teachers will not be very imaginative. Also, it is unfortunate because novelty and a general lack of discipline are sometimes confused with the display of imagination; as a result, bad teaching practices sometimes win undeserved acceptance because they are misperceived as imaginative.

In sum, imagination among teachers is and will always be scarce, and if it is pursued recklessly, the outcomes for pupils can be disastrous. Schools have adopted a variety of means in dealing with the imagination shortage. One "solution" is the one described above; to make a change—often trivial—and contend that something imaginative has occurred. This may be the worst solution. It presents nothing really new, corrodes the basic subject matter, and eventually increases the cynicism of students.

126. We were not able to obtain evidence of imagination on the part of either the teachers or the administration. It did seem to us, however, that imagination was sacrificed for diligence, reliability, and other measures of application. At the School, in other words, it was not vital for teachers or administrators to complete their work in the most imaginative way possible—rather, it was important for them to complete their work as accurately, diligently, and reliably as possible (58, R, 9–12).

This is another solution to the imagination problem. While it sounds stark and uninviting, anyone studying the other items on this school will recognize that, for a large school, it presents an especially well-organized and humane environment, where pupils are working hard at learning. For example, the English department outline in Item 122 is for this same school. Actually, the most typical "solution" to the shortage-of-imagination problem is for the school neither to be well organized nor to do anything to stimulate teacher imagination.

127. Students in the freshmen English class are required to give five speeches during the first semester. Students are graded on writing, research, and presentation. Students in the freshmen Introduction to Social Studies class are required to complete an opinion poll. They are to interview twenty people of both sexes and different age ranges. They ask questions on current topics, such as gun control, drug usage, open versus closed campus, and violence on TV and in the movies. Specific English classes assign an interview as one important project. This is another opportunity for students to further develop listening, reading, and writing skills (38, P, 9–12).

This is an example of another solution to the imagination shortage—the institutionalization of imagination, by encouraging teachers to exchange good ideas among each other. Through such exchanges, the imagination of one can be made available to others, and halfbaked ideas can be sorted out and either refined or discarded. Perhaps twenty to thirty percent of the schools studied had structures which fostered such exchanges.

128. A creative idea introduced by one of the teachers four years ago is still in operation in the School. He said that he was trying to explain to his students what a bank is and how it functions. He thought that it would be a good idea to open a small bank in his classroom for a period of time. The kids started saving dimes and quarters that they deposited in their own accounts, so they could use them later for field trips and other school-re lated activities. The idea proved so useful that other classes wanted to participate. After four years, the bank is still operating in the School. "Kids are learning not only how a bank functions, but also the benefits of saving money. Most of the kids will pay for the coming field trip with the money saved in the School bank," the teacher said (49, R, K–8).

129. Those classes which deal with subject matter that lends itself to imagination are indeed taught in interesting and imaginative ways. American history classes all work on group projects in which they reproduce a scene from the period in history they're studying. They use any materials they wish. Some projects were forts, log cabins, and wagon trains. They were made from a combination of toothpicks, Popsicle sticks, sugar cubes, and cardboard. These projects are displayed in a showcase in the hall by the lunchroom, where all the students and teachers can see them. The music teacher comes to the American history classes once a week for an hour. The classes are taught to sing songs relating to the material studied. If they were studying the period in which railroads were being built, they would sing "I've Been Working' on the Railroad" (37, P, 7–8).

130. In their history class, one group of students studied the beginning of the American Revolution. Part of the group took the side of the British, and another part that of the Americans. They researched the different positions and staged a vigorous debate. The teacher told us that he feels their understanding of the causes of the Revolution was considerably broadened (66, S, 9–12).

I have already discussed the problem of encouraging imagination versus the dangers of stimulating shallow novelty or undisciplined teaching. But there is another problem in applying imagination: some topics, which can be approached with rigor, and even instructively, are not "fit" for discussion by students of certain ages.

We might start by considering a topic that is an undisputed "No! No!" regardless of its intellectual merits. None of us would probably approve of a teacher of sixth graders asking his students to write papers on whether their parents should get divorced. Yet the students have significant knowledge about the topic, it is important to them, and, at some level, they might benefit from seriously considering its pros and cons.

Whatever the proimagination value of such a topic, it has too many emotional overtones to become a matter of impersonal classroom consideration, like math or spelling. And this leads to the next potential constraint on imaginative teaching. Not all classroom topics are equally "impersonal." And, as topics become more emotional in content, we should become more cautious about approaching them impersonally, as if they were only vehicles for the stimulation of our imagination.

Of course, when students are away from school, their imagination is not inhibited by such formal constraints. And so they can then muse about their parents' potential divorce and equivalent topics. But there is a great difference between private speculations and public statements invited by significant adults. Such public statements assume a special importance. In addition, students in classes are a captive audience, or—even if they are enrolled in electives—they rarely have the maturity to easily reject teachers' discussion topics. Putting it simply, some topics should be approached imaginatively, and some more or less tentatively or even dogmatically. (Note: dogmatically does not mean without sensitivity, or grace or style; it does mean that students should not be stimulated to question the basic premises of certain propositions.)

The statement of this principle leads to complex questions, such as what topics should be sacrosanct, and at what ages (of students) should topics shift from being dogma to becoming subjects for imaginative analysis and criticism? For example, how should matters such as our country's history, the significance of marriage, the appropriateness of premarital sex, or alternative sex roles be portrayed to students of different ages? I believe that some of these things should never be dealt with in formal school classes without the very close involvement of parents. It is not that the current opinions of students about these issues are always informed or right. However, it is also true that the opinions of teachers on such matters are sometimes also often uninformed or wrong—by my lights. And such wrongness will not necessarily be corrected by the teachers' taking one college course or another. Furthermore, the more basic issue is that some topics are never appropriate for general classroom discussion, aimed at some median body of student understanding.

I realize that some of these "private" topics are thrust before the students every day by the media, or through the allusions and phrases of their peers. But teachers are real, mature adults who are in day-to-day contact with students; they possess a special authority, and we should not underestimate the weight of this authority with students. Due to this potency, they should exercise self-restraint, and realize that such restraint finally adds to their impact. It distinguishes their status from the shallow and naive posture of the media.

I am also in favor of teachers' controlling their "imagination" even in such areas of responsibility as history. It seems to me that the literature addressed to American educators is pervaded with a sympathy for trivial fads and ephemeral novelty. Examples that come to mind at this moment include topics such as values eduction, environmental education, sex education, drug education, and multi-cultural education. It appears that the disposition of the intellectual gatekeepers of education is to swarm, like moths, toward the immediate and poorly defined. Given this pattern, I am doubtful of the judgment of teachers who rush to criticize generally accepted traditions in the name of imaginative teaching. My disposition is to give dogma more reverence in education than we now do, and raise adults with deeper emotional roots to their families, communities and society.

My position does not mean that teachers should never talk frankly to students about complex or ambiguous issues. But such discussions are most fruitful if they are truly personal, as compared to general-purpose classroom presentations. In better schools, there are innumerable channels of teacher-student contact beyond formal classroom presentations. These channels arise through extracurricular and service activities, and student-teacher-parent contacts in varied contexts. The meetings on such occasions can provide vital and "natural" channels for essentially personal communications. There, teachers can more appropriately say what is right for the particular student—or, if teachers do not know what to say, they can ask questions, or decide not to say anything. And the students, if really put at ease, can object, or ask their own questions. Furthermore, on some occasions, parents can be present and participate in the dialogue.

Issuing Grades and Reports to Parents about Student Learning

131.   Excerpt from a handbook distributed to students and parents:

GRADING SYSTEM
Grading, though undesirable, is the most widely used means of reporting evaluations of students. An over-emphasis on grades can cause students to focus their energy on achieving grades rather than real learning. Report cards are given quarterly to students in all the grades. (47, R, K-8)

132.   According to the principal, "For grades one to six, three codes are used on report cards: plus, meaning doing very well; zero, meaning making good progress; and a checkmark, meaning needs to improve. In grades seven and eight the codes are different and there are also three: 1

means superior effort, 2 means serious effort, and 3 is given when effort is unsatisfactory. All marking is based on the student's effort in relation to his ability" (47, R, K–8).

133.   A report card from the School is sent home through the students (see figure 4–1). Note that it provides no place for a parent's signature of acknowledgment, and has no request for return of an acknowledgment, and that it fails to list the School's address or phone numbers. This is the only document sent to parents relating to students' grades; thus, it must be considered self-explanatory (14, P, 9–12).

134.   Individual class standing is not recorded on students' report cards. As a result, they are not able to compare their overall performance with that of other classmates. Students would like to see this happen, especially in the upper grades, because they don't know if they rank in the upper third of their class and this question is sometimes found on forms they have to fill out for college or jobs (14, P, 9–12).

135.   There seems to be a definite lack of communication among parents and teachers and the administration. The following story demonstrates this lack: I worked part-time at a camera shop with two students from the School. One of the students, Steve, was a freshman at the time. He used to often come in to work on weekdays between 12:00 P.M. and 1:00 P.M. I couldn't understand why. Robert, the other student, was a sophomore, and said Steve cuts classes, because he doesn't get out of school until, at the earliest, 2:00 P.M. I talked to my boss, and told him to call the School and find out what's going on. But he didn't care because Steve was working for peanuts, and he probably couldn't get cheap help that easily. So I set out to get to know Steve better. He admitted he was cutting classes, flunking a few classes, and was on probation. He said his mother didn't know much since he had a way to prevent this (his mother worked all day). I tried to talk some sense into his head, and for a while he went to his classes, but then he quit work. I know he still attends the School and doesn't seem to have changed much. He told me he was smart where it counted—he knew whose classes he could get away with cutting, and how far he could go. I still don't see how he has avoided getting suspended, but things like that are possible when parents and teachers don't communicate (14, P, 9–12).

136.   A public statement made by a prominent administrator in a church-related Chicago school system: "At one time, we included pupils reading scores on all reports cards. More recently, we have moved away from this, despite objections from many parents. Evidently, there's a communication problem between us and the parents." (No school reference needed.)

"Communication problem" suggests that parents and administrators could agree if we only better understood one another; it also sometimes implies that "we" are right, but "they" do not yet see our correctness. One might question whether there is a true communication problem. The parents

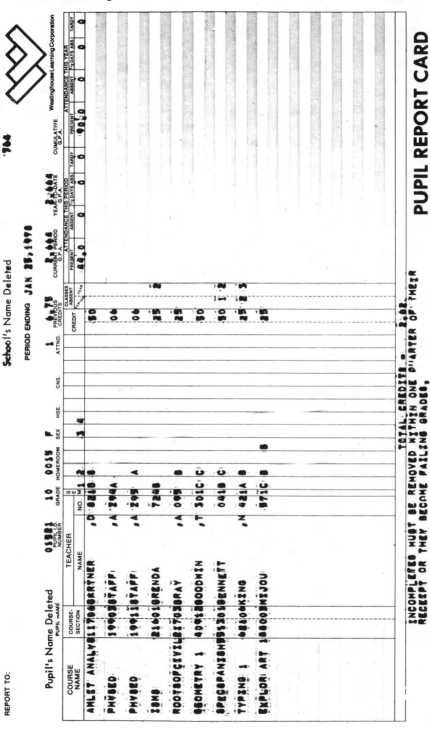

Figure 4-1. Student Report Card

and the schools simply disagree. Another way of stating the dispute is that "we," the schools, possess certain information about our pupils which we do not believe the parents should be told.

No more than half the schools surveyed provided parents and students with timely, reasonably clear and precise information about student performance. The many deficiencies noted in these arrangements included vague grading criteria; infrequent reports; reports of excessively narrow scope; failure to insure that reports were really transmitted to parents; no school contact point designated on the report for parents to utilize; and no efforts to supplement the reports with face-to-face meetings.

It should not be hard for readers to deduce the major reasons for these inadequacies. It takes effort and skill to devise clear and justified grading systems, and to plan ways to reliably communicate this information to parents. And, once the information is communicated, it will often engender tension. Sometimes the "truth" hurts, and parents respond with confusion and anger. Indeed, it is even possible that a teacher may have made a mistake in grading or teaching—and have to admit it. Thus, the teachers involved must be firm, tactful, and articulate—and humans often strive to avoid such tests. Finally, it is true that students can be offended and even scarred by poor grades; and teachers know they are not gods, and that they may make mistakes, or give currently correct grades that do not accurately predict a student's future performance. Because of the potentially harmful effects of grades on students and the possibility of teacher error, teachers may try to avoid developing or communicating clear and honest evaluations.

However, these explanations for fuzzy grading are not adequate excuses. Grades are multi-purpose communication devices. They inform students, parents, and principals, in a summary fashion, as to how teachers evaluate their students. As a result of this information, the persons informed can take corrective measures, or feel secure that no important changes are needed. But grades can only serve their important communication functions if the parties involved speak a common language, and the grades can transmit relatively precise information. For example, if parents are not informed about the school's grading system, or the school only uses pass/fail grades, reports cards or other grade communication devices do not really communicate much. And without clear information, none of the persons involved knows enough to tell what—if anything—to do differently. Furthermore, without informative grades, it is very difficult for anyone to evaluate the performance of teachers. A first step in such an evaluation process is to see whether pupils are learning; once that has been determined, then one can try to decide possible causes for pupil ignorance (which can include poor teaching). But we need informative grading systems before we can talk about measuring learning.

There are several preconditions to the operation of an effective grading system. Teachers must have a good idea of what they are trying to teach, and know how well each of their pupils are learning the necessary material, presumably through applying various formal and informal tests. The "subject matter" graded, and reported to parents, should cover both cognitive material and character-related traits. Next, teachers must have a common understanding how different levels of pupil attainment can be described through letter or numerical grades—and, since pupils of the same age can reach a variety of levels, the grading system should be able to transmit a number of degrees of attainment. Teachers also should have adequate poise to deal tactfully with the questions and complaints of disappointed parents and students (and be appropriately supervised and backed up in such exchanges by administrators). Next, students, parents, and principals must be informed about the levels of attainment represented by different grades. Furthermore, in many cases people want to know not only students' level of absolute knowledge (that is, have they mastered specified skills?), but how a student's attainment compares with others (for example, is the student a better—or worse—writer or mathematician than many others?). Comparative information is significant since excellence, by definition, is a comparative measure—we excel over something. And so, without comparison, we have no way of knowing whether we excel. Of course, the relevance of various systems of comparison can be affected by the pupils' age, and, as a result, comparative gradings increase in appropriateness (and precision) as pupils become older. Next, the grades must be frequently transmitted to parents and others by reliable means, and (usually) be accompanied by explanatory written comments or face-to-face meetings. The meetings and written comments are valuable, but without the framework provided by grades, such exchanges may lack adequate focus and become too diffuse. Where the grading structure shows that students are in danger of ultimately failing, students and parents should be given advance written notice, and corrective steps suggested (or a meeting proposed).

As a final comment, we should recognize that students, like most humans, often have other priorities on their minds than those proposed by their "masters"—their parents and teachers. Thus they may be tempted to give less consideration to learning than adults deem desirable. One means to prevent this rejection of adult priorities is to make students desirous of earning the higher grades that better learning should represent (if the instruction is well planned). But this effect can only be attained if high grades are relatively scarce, and are related to increased student effort. And so efficient grading systems are an important means of teachers and parents stimulating students to give priority to learning. It is true that, in some instances, students are more stimulated by the desire to attain high grades than the "pure" joys of learning; in effect, grades can become a proxy for learning. However, many elements of life are shaped by the pursuit of proxies and other symbols. For instance, in the case of a courtship, gifts of flowers and engagement rings, and displays of evident solicitude, do not really reveal what is in the head of a suitor; but we are prepared to generally assume that a selfish and rude suitor has unloving feelings. And, similarly, we should assume that students who honestly raise their grades have displayed increased interest in learning. Of course, we may be wrong. But it is better to assume interest in a student who has changed his measured learning performance than in one who has simply made the teacher like him better.

137.   The principal stated that students must be made aware of the standards which they are expected to meet. Therefore, students are informed of their reading scores, their level in the Continuous Progress Reading Program, and the skills they must acquire to continue to advance (4, P, K–8).

138.   Grades are used by the School as reinforcement of learning. It is for this reason that the School has established a track system. The track system allows each student, regardless of the level of ability, a chance to earn good grades (58, R, 9–12).

139.   Junior and senior class rank standing are constantly on display in a showcase outside the main office. These standings are updated every semester so that students are always aware of their rank in their class (13, P, 9–12).

140.   Parents receive a variety of documents from the School about their child's academic progress. Each year, there are two quarterly reports, two semester reports, and progress reports as needed. The quarterly reports are termed advisory, and the marks do not count toward final grades. The two semester reports do count—usually 50 percent each. Progress reports are sent home as teachers deem appropriate, typically when students are having problems. They must be returned to school with a parent's signatures.

Grades are given as percents, and not letters. The student's class standing is also included in each year's final report. Separate grades are given in each subject for the student's objective level of learning, and the teacher's estimate of the student's degree of effort. Parents and students are provided with a handbook which provides a clear and thorough four-page discussion of grading criteria, and the procedures for distributing reports. Among the material is a suggested grade distribution for freshmen and sophomores (assuming grades are distributed along a curve).

A copy of a blank progress report (essentially a warning notice) is presented in figure 4–2 (60, R, 9–12).

Pupil Advancement through School

141.   This school does not have a "traditional" grading system. At the end of each nine-week grading cycle, the teacher and student fill out an evalua-

PROGRESS REPORT

School's Name, Address,
and Phone Number are
Deleted.

GRADING SCALES:

95-100	Honors with Distinction
90-94	First Honors
85-89	Second Honors
80-84	Average
75-79	Fair
70-74	Passing
60-69	Failing

ATTITUDES:

In my opinion the student's academic
attitude in general is:
___Exceptional ___Above Average ___Average
___Below Average ___Poor.
In my opinion the student's personal growth
and maturity are:
___Exceptional ___Above Average ___Average
___Below Average ___Immature.

Student's Name:_____

Student Number:_____

Course:_____

Teacher:_____

Counselor:_____

Date:_____

ACADEMIC PERFORMANCE:

1) Currently the student's grade average is _____.
   He is: ___passing, ___failing, ___likely to fail.
2) Major Test Scores:
3) Quiz Scores:
4) Completed Homework Performance: ___satisfactory
                                    ___unsatisfactory.
5) Motivation & Interest: ___Excellent ___Good ___Poor.
6) Achievement: ___Excellent ___Good ___Poor.
7) Class Attention
   (Deportment) ___Excellent ___Good ___Poor.
8) Class Participation: ___Excellent ___Good ___Poor.

Additional Teacher Comments:

Parent's Comments:

Student's Signature:_____   Parent's Signature:_____

                                                 Date:_____

WHITE - PRINCIPAL'S COPY • CANARY - COUNSELOR'S COPY • GREEN - PARENT'S COPY • GOLDENROD - TEACHER'S COPY

Figure 4–2. Sample Student Progress Report

tion of the work. The teacher, after consulting with the student, then gives either credit or no credit (that is, pass/fail) for the cycle. I did not come across any situation where a student was denied credit (20, P, 9–12).

142. The nature of the Chicago public school system Continuous Progress program was briefly described above. Under that program, teachers in grades K through eight were supposedly only to move their pupils on if they had mastered 80 percent of the objectives for their level. But it was difficult for higher administrators to determine if this objective was actually being attained; the basic records on each student kept by the teacher were quite elaborate, and it was hard to insure that the teacher was filling them out correctly or truthfully. (However, principals and other administrators close to the scene could engage in such monitoring via spot checking.)

For a variety of reasons—including lack of clear direction from the top—in the mid 1970s, at least 90 percent (my estimate) of the Chicago public schools graduating eighth graders were disposed to graduate students without insuring that all of them had attained the 80 percent level. This does not mean that most of the graduates were below the 80 percent level (though many were); the point is that the schools would graduate them regardless. In addition to the easy graduation pattern, many elementary schools passed pupils on through the lower grades without assurance that they met the requirements for their level.

The central administration "knew" of these problems, and tried to correct the situation. However, their efforts were undermined through the administration's reluctance to issue clear, uniform rules.

Finally, in July 1977, as a result of growing pressures, the administration issued a promotion policy statement that pupils could not graduate from grade school at the end of a year in eighth grade unless they had mastered 80 percent of the required 273 skills, passed a test demonstrating such mastery, and attained an appropriate score on the Iowa Basic Skills Test (a nationally standardized exam.) In other words, the system articulated relatively precise criteria for promotion and specified how these criteria would be applied. This change has caused some elementary schools to increase their focus on reading instruction and to retain inadequate pupils (often at lower grade levels) so that they received better preparation. (No school reference needed.)

Tensions inevitably arise about the issue of pupil advancement through school. In communities where the level of parent education is comparatively low, the issue begins to appear in elementary schools, where some pupils may already begin to have trouble learning the desired amounts of material in predetermined periods of time. In better-educated communities, all (or almost all) elementary students may attain some minimum standards; however, as students progress to higher grades, there inevitably comes a point where some significant proportion of students perform at levels well below the class room. At that time, pressures arise around the school, and around some students and their families. After all, it has been observed there is a common human tendency to shoot the bearers of "bad news," and it is notorious that many parents have unreasonably high expectations for their children.

Some elements of these tensions have already been discussed, especially under the subject of grouping students—since one way to moderate any problems about advancement of students is to assign pupils into groups which have performance norms appropriate to the apparent potential of their members. But the formation of such groups in themselves often engenders parent and student tensions.

In any case, all the "old" obstacles I have already discussed occur about pupil advancement policies: the desires of faculty members to avoid accountability; the intellectual and administrative difficulties of designing and maintaining and appropriate system; the fears of faculty members of parents' (and students') unjustified displeasure; the emotional discomfort involved in destroying someone's aspirations (albeit unrealistic); and the fact that the school's judgments may ultimately be in error. Unless the school or system involved has a firm grasp on the situation, it is likely that things will begin to slide someplace. As a result, inadequate students will be passed on. Such passing on diminishes both teacher accountability and pupil learning, and corrodes the value of the attainments of able students (since informed persons attribute less worth to degrees and grades earned in diploma mills).

Perhaps half the schools studied had clear, well-understood promotion criteria (which, incidentally, defined who would not be promoted) which were generally applied by all faculty. Whenever a school had an effective policy on promotion, that policy was almost inevitably connected to a program for (1) early identification of potential failures, and (2) well-organized remedial activities. In other words, the existence of effective remedial programs was generally tied to selective promotion policies; where promotion was automatic, there was not enough incentive for the faculties to plan and operate good remedial programs.

143. The School "discriminates" against freshmen, and gives them far less freedom in and around the school than it gives upperclassmen. For example, upperclassmen are allowed to leave the building during their lunch hour, and seniors have the exclusive privilege of using the school gardens during the spring. They also are responsible for maintaining the garden. All of the ten freshmen interviewed expected to stay at the School, and looked forward to attaining the status of upperclassmen (21, P, 9–12).

The creation of significant distinctions—based on years of successful attendance—among different groups of students is the outcome of administrative decisions. Perhaps 25 percent of the high schools studied applied such distinctions. It is true that these distinctions are often overtly revealed through the conduct of students (and sometimes their parents), and not the acts of faculty. But students are a transitory group. Distinctions among students only survive through time if the faculty support them. And so the question arises: should the faculty support such distinctions?

Before considering an explicit answer, we should recognize that the disposition to create distinctions among youth age groups has been identified as a widespread pattern among different cultures. In many cultures, groups of youths of different ages are allocated different statutes and different social responsibilities. Such patterns have been found among the American Plains Indians, many African tribes, and primitive peoples in India and Australia. The cultures making such distinctions designate children, young adults, and even older adults as members of different age groups. For example, they might call those now between twelve and fourteen the "Hawks."

One apparent "reason" for these patterns is that they demarcate the progression of youths to successively higher levels of responsibility as they mature. In other words, increasing physical and emotional capability is reflected in progressively more responsible formal statuses. Of course, as status grows, so does responsibility. More prestige is awarded to those who give more.

In most cultures, these differences in status among youth age groups (where they appear at all) occur in a relatively automatic manner among younger age groups. But, as children become older, the distinctions become more individualized; they depend on the decisions of individual children as to whether they want to accept the burdens of "promotion." But, if they choose not to accept such responsibilities, they are then usually subject to various forms of discriminations and obloquy. In other words, young persons can "choose" not to grow up (and accept the responsibilities allocated to adults), but such choices are not costless. The rejectors are publicly scorned by adults and other young people, both males and females, and relegated to associating with deviates and children. Obviously, in such societies, most children and adolescents do not want to be labeled rejectors. As a result, they apply themselves to satisfying the criteria established for attaining adulthood (or the next step in the progression to adulthood).

This discussion about the patterns of foreign cultures suggests that there is a socially functional value to making obvious distinctions among different classes of students (or among children who demonstrate different achievements). The distinctions increase the incentives among students (and their parents) to strive for advancement. Conversely, if all class levels of students are treated equally, why should a student bother to earn the grades which keep him up with the rest of his peers? Putting it most coarsely, if the school "treats" a seventeen-year-old who has been a high-school freshmen for four years the same as a seventeen-year-old who has steadily moved along, why should a student bother to move along? In sum, when stages of movement in school are demarcated in visible fashions (through awarding significantly different statutes to freshmen, sophomores, and so on), and when movement to each stage is not automatic, students will tend to work harder to stay with their age group. But, if no one who stays around a school all day can tell the difference between freshmen or seniors, the incentive for students to try to win membership in a higher group is diminished.

Obviously, making distinctions between different class groups, and requiring students to earn membership in such groups, is a device to foster social control. It stimulates students to strive to make the efforts required to attain such membership. If the criteria for such membership are determined by adults, then adults shape the goals children and adolescents pursue. If the criteria are not shaped by adults, then young people still will often strive to direct their lives through pursuing conspicuous incremental goals. But their goals may then become attaining membership in the Latin Lords, the Blackstone Rangers, or Satan's Disciples; and the tests for such membership may be far more destructive than passing certain courses, or excelling in extracurricular activities.

144. Seniors receive their ''senior'' buttons in April of their last year. The buttons permit students to go into the school garden, and sign out of study periods (though they must stay on campus). Each senior home room (of about thirty students) distributes buttons to all their students after all members of the room have paid their $20 graduation fee for cap and gown rental, yearbook, and other expenses. Receiving the button is a big event (21, P, 9–12).

As we can see, the School's administrators have ingeniously organized things so as to encourage—or pressure—most graduates to participate in graduation in style. As has been reiterated earlier, when thoughtful and determined adults want something to happen in school, and it is not very expensive or immoral, it usually can be carried off.

145. The School makes an affair of graduation. Students come well dressed, all the faculty attend, and many parents and relatives show up. There are speeches, music, a printed program (with all graduating student names listed), and awards for many types of student achievement. All the graduating students attend, and the lower-grade students (who do not usually attend the graduation) honor the graduates at a preliminary assembly (4, P, K–8).

The conceptual tensions surrounding graduation planning for the faculty are of the same quality as those related to promotion and other gradating devices. In other words, graduation ceremonies are only an example of the problems generated by various systems for making distinctions among student attainments. And, if the faculty has problems with other distinction systems (for example, grades, promotions, student groupings), they will have problems with graduations. Furthermore, if the faculty deprecates graduation activities, they will lower the vitality of the instructional program, since the desire to participate in a dramatic graduation is one motivator for students' efforts; and, if graduations are downplayed and undramatic there will be less incentive for student application to learning.

Superficially, the "drama" of graduation is the outcome of mechanical decisions: how elaborate will the presentation be; will students dress up, or wear robes; will the ceremony be widely publicized; and will pressures be generated to increase attendance? But underlying these decisions is the ultimate question: will all students who merely put in time in school graduate, come what may? It may seem these issues—graduation planning and who will graduate—are unrelated. This is incorrect. If the graduation preparations are elaborate, the question of who is qualified inevitably creeps in. And eventually criteria for graduation are articulated. And some students who have attended school for the prescribed number of years may not qualify for graduation. Then, the formal drama of the presentation is heightened by the covert drama surrounding the question: who will come onto the stage to receive degrees?

Some faculty members have contended to me that graduations lack vitality because of the attitudes of students; they are indifferent and cynical. My observations are that much of this student indifference and cynicism is, as usual, due to decisions made by the faculty. It is the faculty who decide whether graduation represents only putting in time, or whether it also means the student has mastered significant skills. And it is the faculty that establishes the general ceremonial parameters around the ceremony, for example, generating pressures to increase attendance.

If graduation is made a significant occasion, it will heighten student concern with getting satisfactory grades; thus it will enhance pupil learning. Furthermore, as we will see in the discussion on school spirit, ceremonies such as graduation can serve generally to increase student and faculty satisfaction with school life.

Public Recognition of Pupil Learning Achievements

146. There are no awards assemblies at the School. I asked a sixth-grade teacher who is an alumnus of the School, and he said that he had attended this School ten years ago, and taught in it two years, and in all that time he never saw an awards assembly (6, P, K–8).

147. A problem that exists in this School is the lack of recognition of achievement. The School does not have any honor assemblies for the students. The students only receive reinforcements from their individual classroom teachers. Awards are presented only at graduation time, and the only students attending these ceremonies are the graduating eighth graders (2, P, K–8).

About 75 percent of the schools studied had at least one award assembly annually. The quality and frequency of these assemblies varied greatly among these schools. Obviously, such assemblies raise all the issues discussed earlier relating to planning, stimulating, and recognizing student achievement.

148.   The principal said he was opposed to heightening competition among students, or to activities such as assemblies and honors banquets. As a result, the School has no honor rolls, certificates, or ribbons (for achievement), nor does it have awards assemblies. The principal said that the activities took too much time away from classroom learning, and the competition would confuse the children, since everyone would want to be a winner (47, R, K–8).

149.   Honor societies do not stir up too much interest at the School. They exist and are a little more active than before, but there is not much excitement when the honor society elects new members and officers. One of the teachers said that in the seven years he has been there, the honor societies tell their new officers what their responsibilties are, and that ends that (13, P, 9–12).

150.   The National Honor Society sponsor mini-courses for the students and has a turnabout day in which the members act as teachers in the classroom. These girls also tutor students who need help in the academic areas. The criteria for this group are a 3.2 average and a recommendation from the faculty based on twelve quality points: scholarship, leadership, character, participation, and so on. Recognition and pins are given individually to these girls (59, R, 9–12).

Notice the many benefits that flow from such arrangements. The honor society members see their roles as more prestigious. The other students see that also, and want to be members. The School and students are provided with useful services. Good character is fostered in honor society members, and they have a chance to learn valuable skills.

151.   A committee of students and faculty recommended that a new grading system be applied for membership in the honors society. Under the proposed change, students in honors or accelerated classes would receive an extra weighting for their grades in determining eligibility for membership. The recommendation was based on the assumption that students in advanced classes would have to work harder to earn the same grades they would have been awarded in basic classes; unless their grades were weighted upwards, they would have less chance to attain honors than their equally able peers who choose to stay in the basic class. The principal opposed the recommendation, saying that recomputing the top 100 student averages with weighted grades resulted in no significant change in class rank. He said, "An 'A' student will be an 'A' student either in an honors class or a regular class" (39, P, 9–12).

152. Students are assigned to homerooms, and tend to stay in the same homeroom for their entire four years. A separate honor roll is prepared and posted at the end of each grading period for each homeroom (in that homeroom). Some students are in honors or advanced placement courses. The grades received in these courses are weighted, upwards, so students who choose to enroll in such special programs (which involve extra work) are not handicapped in competing with regular students for places on the roll. The weighting system was devised after consultation with the student council (21, P, 9–12).

Note that the procedure just described conflicts with that of the previous paragraph. This school "weighs" the grades awarded from more demanding courses, while the principal in the previous paragraph said that weighting (for the purpose of allocating recognition) would not make a significant difference. This contrast in procedures and conclusions warrants some discussion.

We must recognize that it is important that an award structure have legitimacy in the eyes of students we are trying to inspire. In both schools, it was the opinion of students that weighting was desirable. Such an opinion should practically settle the question. But there is another significance to the first principal's position. Assume he is correct, and that able students apparently get better grades in the advanced classes in his school, while less able students receive lower grades in the basic classes. If this is the case, it suggests that the school's grading policies need revision.

153. Excerpt from a school newspaper (36, P, 9–12):

Forum Held for Student Input

Another area of concern was the proposed introduction of weighted grades. The main point some students made against weighted grades was that they were not necessary, because when a person applies to a college, that school looks at the level of the classes a person takes, as well as a person's grades.

Supporters of weighted grades disagree and say that the present system is not fair when computing a student's grade point average.

The teacher who was Council sponsor brought up that sometimes a student in a basic level class who earns an A does not get one recorded simply because his teacher may think students in basic level classes don't deserve A's. He feels with weighted grades the teacher would feel better about giving the student the A he deserves.

By the end of the meeting, the Council decided that its members would go to a number of classes to solicit reactions from students. A suggestion box will be posted outside the Council office, room 372. Members are hoping to get together a comprehensive report by today.

154. There is an honor roll of the better students in each grade. The honor roll is displayed in the lunchroom where all the students eat. Inclusion in the honor roll depends on both scholastic performance and behavior (18, P, K–8).

155. This discription portrays a school that vigorously rewards achievements in cognitive, extracurricular and character-related activities: About 60 to 65 percent of the students receive either group or individual significant (that is, schoolwide) recognition over the school year. The criterion for academic honors is an A or B in all major subjects, and a C or above in minor ones. The principal "tours" all the classes during the marking periods to determine, with the teacher, whose scholastic averages are high enough to warrant honors. Gold pins are given to the seventh-grade students who get on the A or B honor roll twice a year. If students make the honor roll three or four times a year, they will be awarded a maltese cross at graduation. An honors ribbon is also put on the diploma, and verbal recognition is given at the graduation ceremony.

An awards assembly is held once a year for the seventh-grade students. (The eighth graders' awards are presented at their graduation.) Attendance is mandatory for the faculty and entire student body. Ribbons, pins, and trophies are given for honors, service to the school, good sportsmanship, and excellence in the athletic and band program. Five plaques are given to excelling individual students in memory of the five students from the school who have died. In addition to the individual plaques, one plaque, listing the winners for that year, is permanently mounted on the School wall inside the entrance door.

Service awards are given to students who serve as office aides, members of the student council, lunchroom workers, and concession stand helpers. Band awards are given the students who participate in the regional or state competition. Sports awards are given to members of any athletic team which played in the conference (31, P, 9–12).

From the diversity of awards presented, it is evident that any student who chooses to make a modest effort can attain some recognition, even as a lunchroom aide.

156. From a folder distributed to all students (this school does not have a "track" system, since its enrollment policies are selective):

HONOR ROLL

The honor roll is composed of those students who have a minimum of three A's and the remainder of grades B on their term report card. The student must also maintain A's and B's and 1's and 2's on his conduct and application ratings. The honor roll is announced at the end of each year. All students whose name is on it for four quarters are designated as honor students for the year and receive a certificate (16, P, 9–12).

157. There is an honors breakfast given for all those eighth graders on the honor roll. Their parents are also invited. It is given four weeks before graduation and is sponsored by the local parents' council. It has been going on for five years (64, P, K–8).

From a systemic viewpoint, a major aim of awards is to stimulate other students to strive to attain equivalent recognition. In other words, when one student receives the gratification of public recognition, other students should see that outcome, and want to win it, too. But, if the recognition occurs out of the sight of most students, it may still be pleasurable to the winners—but will not especially inspire their successors. The honors break-fast just described is essentially a device for concealed recognition. Perhaps one reason for the popularity of such systems of concealed recognition is that they enable faculty to offer praise without appearing to humiliate the students who were not winners, or face the resentment of such losers. Thus the process becomes more comfortable (for the faculty and some of the losers). But, if comfort is brought by concealing acts of recognition, we should not be surprised that students in lower grades often appear unmotivated.

These systems of "concealed" recognition are unfortunately all too common in school. One conspicuous example are graduation ceremonies. Awards are often given to students at such occasions, but the award process is frequently invisible to the lower grades. Sometimes the lower grades are absent because of lack of space in the hall, but this problem is not unmanageable. Graduation and awards can be separated. Or the awards can be publicized, through the school paper, or a program distributed to all students. Or plaques or other permanent mementos can be mounted in the hall.

158. A special Mass is held to induct the new members of the National Honor Society. Plaques inscribed with the names of all present and past members are prominently displayed, and a list of the new members is posted outside the principal's office. The group picture of the new members appears in the student paper. Every year the School has a good number of National Merit Scholarship winners. Out of the 196 juniors in 1977, there were thirteen finalists, fifteen semifinalists, and twenty-two letter-of-commendation winners. Their names are listed and posted. Another award given is the National Achievement Award (open only to black students). In the same year, there were fifteen semifinalists and three letter-of-commendation winners for this award. This information is prominently displayed in the college and career counseling office, located on the main hallway of the first floor. Eight-by-ten glossies of each of these boys are hung on one wall of this office.

When a student is awarded a scholarship to a college, it is announced by the principal over the public address system. The winners' names are also posted on one of the display boards on the first floor (60, R, 9–12).

A very significant difference between schools that foster good and not-so-good cognitive achievement is the degree of emphasis they give to recognizing student achievement. Of course, maintaining such an emphasis uses school resources, and this question of allocating resources warrants discussion.

The operation and management of a program of cognitive instruction can be conceived of an economic system. The school has so many resources to dedicate to such an activity, for example, student and faculty time, money to buy materials and equipment. The task of anyone planning such a program is to decide the best way to use those resources. My proposition is that a relatively high proportion of these resources should be used to enhance the values students attribute to achievement—as compared to simply buying and presenting learning materials, and spending the time of students exposing them to those materials. In other words, principals should personally distribute badges and pins, students should go to awards asemblies to see other students being honored (or be honored themselves), money should be spent to buy plaques, and so on. If these activities are well planned and conducted, they can do much to enhance the formal learning process.

159.   The bilingual program in the School publishes an annual booklet of awards, listing the names of students receiving one or more As for the school year, (together with mention of the number of their As). The booklet also separately lists the names of students with "no absences," or "no tardies." Each of the twenty homerooms in the program also designates its outstanding student. Copies of the book are widely distributed to students and parents (22, P, 9–12).

Notice the effort to award a variety of conducts that help learning.

160.   At the end of each marking quarter, honor students are named in the school newspaper, and in the yearbook at the end of the school year. Toward the end of the school year, there is banquet held for the honor students. It was estimated that there were at least two people coming for each honored student. During the banquet, students who were prominent members of clubs or activities are recognized, such as editors of the paper, the prom committee, and members of the student council. Also, students who received awards from outside organizations are recognized, and students who received awards for outstanding achievement in a subject are recognized (36, P, 9–12).

This item invites consideration of another issue related to recognition of achievement. The School is large. One can well imagine a banquet in which quite a bit of the time is spent in inviting different people (who are unknown to many guests) to stand up and receive recognition. While this process sometimes becomes tedious to many guests (who do not know most of the students recognized), the students who stand up generally enjoy their moment in the spotlight.

The problem is that, as schools have become larger, and the recognition list longer, the audience spends increasing amounts of time honoring people they do not know for excelling in activities they do not know about. The process of honoring loses vitality for many of the honorors (and, to some extent, for those honored).

A variety of "solutions" hold promise for remedying this problem. The most basic one is smaller schools, so not so many people need to be recognized. And this plea for a revival of smallness has been offered by others. A different measure that can help vitalize such occasions involves enriched contacts (away from the award occasion) among students and parents in the school; the quality of such contacts is partly a function of school size, but they can also be affected by matters such as proximity between homes and the schools, the average length of school enrollment of students, and the forms of communication used with parents. With such enriched contacts, the audience and the winners know each other, and the occasion is more gratifying for everyone. Another alternative is subassemblies (and, I assume, subbanquets), where lesser achievements can be honored before appropriate audiences (for example, many schools have sports banquets). Finally, there can be subschools or houses, which are semiindependent entities in the school and can maintain their own honors system. Other devices are plaques, certificates, press releases, and published programs, which can list the names of persons honored (and be presented to the honorees), without lengthy lists being read.

But, despite these potential alternatives, we still must accept the constraints generated by the principle of "economy of recognition." The intensity of the winner's gratification at recognition is proportionate to the amount of resources others evidently dedicate to honoring his achievement. And resources can be measured by time, imagination, or money (spent in buying and expensive award). If we seriously sought to recognize everybody, there would be no resources left for other productive activities. Thus, any time we give someone significant honors, we sacrifice resources. But we often purchase precious benefits.

161.   There are academic requirements to participation in athletic activities here, as everywhere. For a student to be eligible, he must have passed three major subjects the preceding year and must be passing three major subjects in the current year. The requirements for eligibility do not seem as strict here as at many other schools. Some schools require a passing grade in all classes, and some require not only a passing grade, but a grade of C or above (17, P, 9–12).

162.   The School rules, distributed to all students, state that the Illinois High School Association requires that participants in athletics and other extracurricular activities shall be doing passing work in at least fifteen hours of high-school work. The rules note that the high academic standards of the School make it very unlikely that any student would stay enrolled and still fail to satisfy the statewide eligibility requirements. Therefore, the rules provide that students' continuing eligibility for participation is to be settled not by the state external criteria, but by discussions involving the students, their teachers, their families, their counselors, and their activity moderators. In other words, the School might very well decide to end the eligibility of a student who is satisfying the statewide standards. A procedure for initiating such discussions is clearly outlined in the rules (60, R, 9-12).

A vital extracurricular program can provide a boost for cognitive learning if participation is related to students' maintaining satisfactory academic performance. In general, there are statewide standards established for such matters; but it seems evident that many schools might do their students more of a service by maintaining higher than minimum standards.

Discussion

Readers may perceive some parallels between the factors affecting cognitive instruction programs and those applying to discipline and character development. In all these activities, success can only be attained if coherent principles are established, and rewards and pressures generated to stimulate students to attain appropriate goals. And the pursuit of these aims can be handicapped by excessive egalitarianism, poor planning, lack of determination, failure to mobilize parent support, and lack of imagination.

This does not mean that all students in schools that apply wrong principles will do poorly. Family support is a powerful stimulus for students, and schools. And, for example, one or two private schools in the studies generally ignored some of the criteria I have just articulated and still produced many cognitively able graduates. But these schools had elaborate screening processes for applicants which excluded all but the most extremely motivated (or parentally assisted) students. They simply "refused" to accept many of the responsibilities routinely allocated to schools. (However, they did accept the responsibility of assuring parents that their children would generally be surrounded with highly motivated, that is, competitive, peers.)

Apart from the one or two exceptions just mentioned, all other schools studied had the implicit task of maintaining systems that stimulated students to pursue academic achievement. Obviously, they succeeded to varying degrees. Many of them managed their responsibilities poorly.

The "solutions" to the problems the chapter has revealed are evident, but also complicated. More common sense. Less utopianism. Greater concern with the effect of the overall school environment on teacher (and classroom) effectiveness. A reallocation of resources to enhance the rewards available for academic achievement. The development of schoolwide strategies to foster pupil learning. Creating student learning teams, or other forms of group learning efforts, and providing appropriate rewards for successful group efforts (however, the teams must have systems of responsibility allocation which pressure undermotivated students to make strong commitments, or leave the team.) Making schools smaller (or forming viable subschools), so more students can receive vital recognition for achievement.

How many of these measures can be carried out, one cannot say. But, until there are more changes of this sort, we will be ignoring the advice of Peter Drucker, prominent writer on business administration. He has said that increasing production is rarely a matter of getting people to try harder and it is more important that they direct their efforts toward the right priorities. And so, without restructured priorities, schools will fail to significantly improve student cognitive learning; more precise thought must supplement—and precede—increased effort.

5 Student Discipline

Multiple choice quizzes were given to groups of students who were then asked to calculate their own grades by checking to see if they had given the correct answers. They cheated (by changing their original answers) about one third of the time. This level of cheating remained unchanged throughout the experiment in a control group which was neither exhorted to honesty nor threatened with punishment. When students were morally exhorted to be honest, the rate of cheating was not reduced. On the contrary, it rose: students took 41 percent of all opportunities to cheat instead of the previous 34 percent. . . . When a threat was made, and was credible, to punish cheaters, the cheating level was reduced from 34 percent to 12 percent. The reduction—nearly two-thirds—was somewhat less when the threat was made less credible.[1]

Children are no more likely to be saints than adults. Thus they should be subject to discipline in school. In other words, they should be prohibited from doing "wrong" acts in or around school, and punished if they do so. Such measures are in the interest of both the potential violators and "law-abiding" students. Potential violators are helped, because effective discipline prevents them from learning ultimately destructive habits. Law-abiding students are helped because most violations are committed against them, for example, their goods are stolen, their buildings are vandalized and made filthy, and their hard-earned grades are depreciated by the grades others attain through cheating.

Apart from the interests students have in good discipline, there are also many other parties who share this concern. There are parents, who want their children to be well-behaved and not victimized by others; teachers, who do not want to be harassed or even endangered; and, finally, the total society, which is paying for the pupil's education and does not want to rear a future generation that disregards the law.

Some readers may object to the implicit proposition—underlying my discussion—that punishment "works." At least, I have met many educators and researchers who have disputed this point. But, once their counter-propositions, or research findings, are analyzed, it turns out that the objectors agree that students—or other wrongdoers—will usually change conduct to avoid vital punishment. Any auto driver who has ever watched cars slow down on an expressway as a police car goes by will recognize this fact. The objectors really mean that punishment, even if it supresses bad conduct, often has other extremely undesirable effects. And so the issue of the value of punishment really moves from research to epistemology. What do we mean when we say punishment "works," or "doesn't work"? And how do we evaluate this process of "working"?

To some degree, the effectiveness of punishment is unprovable. Suppose we are seriously concerned with the remote effects of punishment on some violator, as well as his immediate reaction. To assess these effects, we must compile evidence about the general conduct of the life of the violator before and after punishment, and compare that to equivalent persons who were not punished. We should also be concerned with the self-hate that punishment may generate, or the misdirected aggression that is inspired, and covertly displayed. Furthermore, punishment can effect—and is supposed to effect—persons who see and hear of the punishment, as well as those punished. Thus, serious research must extend to following a variety of persons. In addition, even if punishment seriously "scarred" those punished, it might be justified because of the potential victims that were not victimized (because the punishment might still deter public wrongdoing). Finally, we must recognize that failure to clearly punish wrongdoers will put fear into the minds of law abiders—since they can see that their danger of victimization has been increased through the lack of deterrence. And so on. All this research may be profitable, but it will not immediately tell us what to do in most school discipline cases.

The most important issue involved in assessing the effects of punishment should be its direct effects. After all, when we observe some disruptive act—a rape, a seventeen-year-old selling unlawful drugs to a thirteen-year-old, gross vandalism in a school—our primary response should be to see, and sympathize with, the victim. If we have such sympathy, our second response should be to do what we can to prevent the violator, or other potential violators, from victimizing other persons or places. And, if we want to stop future violations, there is general agreement in the research: fast, unpleasant punishment tends to suppress the conduct which has provoked it. Such punishment is especially effective if it is applied in small doses, for small violations—as compared to being "saved up" for gross misconduct.

What about the problem of the more remote (and possibly undesirable) effects of punishment? We cannot ignore it. But we should not get carried away—or paralyzed—by the possibility that a particular punishment *may* have remote, undesirable, indirect ramifications. If we get too involved in such questions, we take upon ourselves the responsibilities of a god. We may end up ignoring immediate potential victims, or the temptations to other possible violators, on behalf of some ultimate higher good. This is too weighty a responsibility to give people operating in the day-to-day world of teachers and principals. Their first roles should be to stop the violation at the moment, and do it so the violators—and other potential violators—are afraid of being punished in the future. This is what they owe to "lawful" students, their parents, and the general society.

These remarks about discipline have not dealt with the relationship between student discipline and other elements of school operations. For example, there is probably a connection between student discipline and the quality of a school's instructional program. A poor instructional program may aggravate discipline problems.

Despite such relationships, the effectiveness of student discipline systems, in part, must be judged independently. In other words, a poor instructional program cannot be seen as an "excuse" for student misconduct.

The same type of segregation between unlawful conduct and the violator's "excuses" is applied in the society at large—and the principle is sound. Thus, if there is an economic recession crime may increase. And measures should be taken to try to diminish economic hardship. But we do not expect the criminal justice system to stop operating just because times are bad. Nor should we expect schools to ignore discipline because instruction is poor, or because students are surrounded with bad influences and undesirable role models. Naturally, the school should do its best to moderate these harmful forces. Meanwhile, it must try to hold students to desirable standards of conduct. Otherwise, they will victimize other students and grow up unprepared to live in orderly environments. And winking at such destructive activities may be the worst form of discimination schools can visit on students.

Potential Acts of Student Misconduct

163. The School is in a bad neighborhood. Here is a list of social and personal problems which threaten students, or which they will probably witness, in and around the School: physical or verbal abuse by other students outside of school; theft of personal property; enforced gang recruitment of early adolescents by older children; gang, intrapeer, or family fights which continue into the School; parental indifference and brutality; and alcoholism, drug abuse, prostitution, pimping, gun fight, robberies, stabbings, rapes, and shakedowns (18, P, 7–8).

164. A teacher who was a member of the faculty discipline committee told us that the School was especially troubled with discipline problems during the winter, when heavy snows made it difficult for students to hang around outside school between classes, or otherwise stay away from school. Over two winter months, there were eleven incidents of teachers and aides being struck by students, and one student was apprehended in school with a gun. In the first striking incident, the victim required five stitches in her lip. Presumably there were also many fights among students during the same period, though statistics on this matter were not so precisely collected. Our informant does not believe the teacher-student disputes were essentially racial (the student body is all black). However, the students are highly "physical," and faculty members with a "tough neighborhood" background probably have some advantage in handling the student style. Our informant told us that, at the end of each day during the strife, he slumped into a chair when he got home, exhausted from the tension. He had no energy left to think about what to teach the next day (17, P, 9–12).

165.   In 1971, two rival street gangs carried their fights over into the school. Things were especially aggravated when members of both gangs were in the same class. In-school shootings occurred as a result of such fights. In 1975, after the gang was had subsided, two students fought in school, and one of them later returned with a gun and shot the other one to death (15, P, 9–12).

166.   About forty female students become pregnant each year and bear children; there is no information about the frequency of pregnancies which terminate in abortions. Almost all the pregnant girls have their children out of wedlock (12, P, 9–12).

It is not suggested that many (or any) of the pregnancies were consummated in the school. But, as we will see, student male-female intimacy in and around school reinforces relationships which may lead to pregnancies. Furthermore, the intimacies about school obviously involve more than "puppy love."

167.   All of the teachers have heard (or observed) dramatic incidents of sexual intimacy among students during school (39, P, 9–12).

168.   On our visits, we twice saw couples (presumably they were students) engaged in passionate petting in one of the hallways (17, P, 9–12).

169.   I found student conduct in the halls extremely rough (for example, running, pushing, shoving), though the hall guards tried actively to control things.

Outdoor recess was eliminated, due to excessive fighting which spilled over into the classroom (18, P, 7–8).

170.   The principal's office is on the first floor; on the second and third floor, one gets the impression students are free to do as they please (17, P, 9–12).

171.   The students who play "games" in the halls during class time are vexsome. They are chased by the teacher on guard duty, but they run out of their sight into other parts of the corridor and the guards cannot leave their posts to pursue them (17, P, 9–12).

172.   In warmer weather, the students congregate outside the School during class hours, playing softball, talking, drinking, holding hands (or

petting), and smoking pot. Naturally, such activities tempt more engaged students to cut classes and participate in hanging around (15, P, 9–12).

173. The teacher told us that, looking around the school yard and adjourning streets at the end of the day, "I see at least one fight a day between students. Sometimes I see two or three" (4, P, K–8).

174. In one year, the School suspended or expelled 105 students. About forty of them were involved in drugs or alcohol. Those involved in drugs or alcohol represented about 2 percent of the student population (58, P, 9–12).

The last item comes from a large, well-managed school which is relatively selective.

175. Both the administrators and students felt that drugs are a problem, and that there are at least four or five drug dealers on campus. One day as I was leaving the school a group of boys were standing around in a circle outside the door and rolling a joint. They thought nothing of the fact that I was a stranger walking in their direction. When I mentioned this incident to other students, they said the reason why the students continued on with what they were doing was that all the students know who the "narcs" are (that is, plainclothes policemen). One student, Miss C, told me that in the spring the School's lawn is covered with kids passing around joints and pipes, and that no one stops them. She said she felt it was not really dealt with because there are just too many students out there to "single out" just a few.

Miss C told me about the time she and Mr. Z, a fellow student, were on the lawn passing a pipe. A school police officer was watching them from a window upstairs. He came outside and as soon as Miss C saw him she put the pipe into her pocket. The officer then told her to empty her pockets. She emptied everything except the pipe. The officer knew he wouldn't be supported if he closely searched a female student (49, P, 9–12).

176. From time to time, while walking through the School, one smell marijuana (15, P, 9–12).

177. Last year, the School suspended seventy students for drug-related offenses (39, S, 9–12).

178. Students are able to purchase drugs and alcohol from other students in the building; these drugs range from marijuana to LSD (15, P, 9–12).

179. A mother told me there is a large drug store across the street from the School. She had observed some of the younger students stealing candy from the counter after the School was dismissed. She asked the proprietor why he did not station a security guard near the counter to deter such conduct. The proprietor said he had only one guard, and that each day, when school was released, he stationed the guard near the record counter, to stop the older students from stealing records. (39, S, K–12).

180. If a student is absent he must either have a parent call the School, or bring a note to the School. Many students say that forging a note is usually no problem (66, S, 9–12).

181.   The School automatically mails notices of disciplinary actions to parents. The notices are enclosed in easily identifiable envelopes. Eleven of the seventeen students I talked to said they had intercepted such notes at their homes one or more times (38, P, 9–12).

182.   Up until this year, the seniors had a lounge with smoking privileges. This year the privileges were withdrawn, since no students were willing to clean up after themselves (68, S, 9–12).

This item, and those that succeed it, deal with less dramatic problems.

183.   The students are often caught violating the no-smoking rule (56, R, 9–12).

184.   In one class we heard a student quietly talking to another, ridiculing a third student; the teacher saw what was happening and said, "I don't like that," and continued his discussion with the rest of the class. The student reprimanded immediately became silent. (37, P, 7–8).

The entire group of preceding items simply portray, in detail, the general statistical patterns of youth conduct outlined in the National Institute of Education *Safe School Study*, in the Department of Justice's periodic Crime Victimization Surveys, and in Rubel's *The Unruly School.*[2] Essentially, the level of violent crime, crime victimization, and drug use in and around school is higher than almost anywhere else in the society. On the other hand, being law abiding is still the "norm." As a result, most students are safe most of the time, and some students (by reason of their school and neighborhoods in most schools) are safe all of the time. But use of marijuana (and sometimes alcohol) is widespread, even around many safe schools. Exactly how readers respond to the items presented above partly depends on their personal opinion of what is a desirable level of social order—and how many violations of that norm are tolerable.

However, it is likely that some of the schools just described are so disorderly that no readers would want their children to attend them, and few teachers would choose to teach in them regularly.

Now that we see some of the discipline problems that can arise in schools, we should consider how schools go about restraining such misconduct. Obviously, one first step is for the school to write, publish, and circulate rules clearly prohibiting various types of misconduct. Sometimes this happens, and sometimes it does not.

Deciding What to Clearly Prohibit

185.   A discussion with the assistant principal (who is school disciplinarian) reveals that no readily available, specific written rules for student conduct exist. He viewed all problems as a function of a breakdown in relationships. "Rules" were only to be seen as an invisible framework. Since no two people are alike, the assistant principal postulated that no given rule would be adequate in producing the same acceptable behavior from one student to the next.

The assistant principal then explained his system for determining and dealing with student antisocial conduct. This procedure is explained in detail yearly to the teachers and has the full support of the principal.

Procedures for discipline were described as a series of levels. On the first level is the initial student behavior. On this level the teacher only observes the student's behavior in the classroom. Hopefully, the problem will correct itself and the student will form intrinsic values and become more self-actualizing. The assistant principal stated that approximately 60 percent of the school's behavior problems were solved at this level when the child was given latitude.

If the problem persists, the teacher steps in at the second level. Here the teacher relates to and counsels with the child and gives the child clear criticism. If the child fails to correct his or her behavior, the parent is contacted by telephone or letter. On this third level the parent and teacher confer, form an alliance, and work together to help the child correct his or her behavior. When this fails, the assistant principal is called in as a resource and liaison between the School and community. For extreme behavioral problems immediate referral to authority at this level is recommended. The teacher at this point writes a note to the assistant principal explaining the student's misconduct. The assistant principal can channel the child for help from sources as the adjustment teacher, truant officer, nurse, or psychologist. It was stated that most of the students' problems are worked through at this level, and rarely did the need exist for more drastic measures.

At the fifth level, the child is taken to the principal for suspension. During the interview with the assistant principal, three such cases occurred within one hour. On the sixth level action was taken by the district superintendent, and finally, on the seventh level, was the formal authority of the police and court system.

Files were kept on students with chronic behavioral problems for one year and then burned. In effect, rules were set up as the situation demanded. When the subject of fighting was mentioned, it was denied as being a major problem, although one of the teachers described it as a recurring problem. There was a distinct variance between the administration's and teacher's perceptions of antisocial conduct and discipline.

From my observations, it seems that discipline was lax. Children ran noisily through halls, and smiled while being reprimanded by the disciplinarian. There was a steady stream of students in the adjustment room to see the assistant principal with notes from their teachers. These notes mainly involved problems between student who were fighting.

Three teachers interviewed expressed a desire for formal rules prohibiting antisocial conduct. It was their impression that many other teachers held similar views. One teacher expressed frustration of dealing with a myriad of students with behavioral problems without the assurance of full support by the administration. Further investigation did uncover a fifteen-year-old, three-page set of "Discipline Guidelines" for the School, but these were not enforced with any regularity and were not widely distributed to the teachers (1, P, K–8).

The pattern of "discipline policy" just portrayed is found, to some degree, in many schools. It probably persists because it serves the needs of many administrators, and does not produce dramatic harm to students (there is simply a continuing climate of moderate disorder, and a steady tension on the teachers). Administrators follow such patterns because (1) they correctly see them as consistent with many semipopular educational and psychological writings (see, for example, Robert Glasser's *Schools Without Failure*), and the ambiguous signals emitted by some boards of education; and (2) "ad hoc-ing" each case permits administrators to pull back if particular parents (or students—and high-school students can be threatening) choose to fight hard. In other words, administrators often determine their position in discipline cases not by the facts of the alleged violation, but by their estimate of the relative influence (or potential for aggression) of parents, or students. In sum, school rules are often vague or nonexistent because of the desire of administrators to maintain the option to ad hoc.

186. There was a time when the School's rules prohibited boy-girl handholding, but no such provision is in the current handbook. Teachers sometimes see students engaged in excessive intimacies in school and they act to break up their embraces, but they can take no more severe action, since they have no rule to support them (39, P, 9–12).

187. Inappropriate acts of sexual affinity among students were defined by the school's chief guidance counselor as "holding hands, kissing, or any more intimate sexual contact." These acts are supposedly tacitly prohibited in the School (though there is no such rule in the student handbook, which does include an extensive list of clearly written rules). However, the tacit prohibition is not enforced. One observer saw couples holding hands while walking down the hall, and saw a male teacher hugging one female student. The same teacher was also heard making suggestive remarks to other female students, such "When are we going out?" and kissing the hands of others (2, P, 9–12).

In any large school, "unwritten" rules are likely to be "unenforced" rules. One effect of such a vacuum is that neither students nor faculty are left with clear standards. (And, in the distressing incident described above, the female students involved, who are being exploited, cannot even point out to the teacher that such conduct is explicitly prohibited for students— and that such a prohibition would apply doubly to teachers.) When adult policies put adolescents from both sexes together in close proximity for long periods of time (as occurs in schools), adults have the responsibility for exercising realistic control over the students' conduct. Perhaps adolescents, while in schools, should be held to the same standards of conduct as would prevail in almost any paid job, that is, male and female coworkers in an office or store during work hours can't hold hands. After all, if we believe such restraints are needed for adults, they are probably doubly needed for adolescents. About 80 percent of the schools examined do not have any clear prohibitions in their written rules against acts of sexual affinity among students during school hours.

188.   The principal said he and his staff thought it would be desirable to prepare a handbook for teachers and pupils which would promote better communications, improve discipline, and create a better learning environment. I questioned him about what offenses would appear in the planned student handbook. From his answer, I inferred that the following offenses will not be mentioned: stealing, lying, cheating, not doing homework, fighting, swearing, and gum chewing. However, the School's philosophy implies that these are not acceptable behaviors (1, P, K–8).

189.   Excerpt from a student handbook (14, P, 9–12):

We know that as a select group of students from the entire city of Chicago you will be a credit in all respect to yourself, your school and your peers. Should disciplinary cases arise, we want you aware of those areas that will result in immediate suspension. These include:

Fighting

Smoking

Gambling

Profanity

Assault.

Drug vending and use, thievery and students carrying weapons are all problems in this school. However, the rules make no reference to such acts. Omissions of this sort are rather common in school rules. Perhaps administrators are reluctant to refer to such activities in documents which can get in the hands of parents.

190.   Excerpt from a student handbook:

Students are to observe the rights of others who are attempting to learn and achieve. This respect is given by remaining quiet and orderly so as to not hinder the rights of others. This respect is particularly requested at the end of the eight and ninth periods when many classes are still in session as students leave the building. (15, P, 9–12).

The respect is "requested," as compared to required. The rule sounds like a request for a favor. And is it less of a violation if a student is noisy in the fifth period compared to the seventh? And if so, is there any difference in the potential penalty—if any penalty is likely to be levied at all.

191.   My final question to the principal was, "Who makes the rules?" He said that the rules are made by a committee headed by the assistant principal in charge of discipline. This person gets input from the assistant principals in charge of student activities and curriculum, along with the dean of women and the counselors. These is also representation from the teaching staff and the student government organizations. The principal emphasized that, as principal, he reserved the right to make the final determination on what did and did not become a rule; and also the perogative to add rules that he saw necessary for maintaining the qualities of a good school (16, P, 9–12).

Straightforward, clear answers of this type to "Who makes the rules?" are remarkably rare. A survey by the Chicago Teachers Union in 1975 disclosed that half the teachers responding worked in schools that did not even have written rules.[3] And, in the schools with rules, they had often been haphazardly developed. About the only constructive addition that could be suggested to the above answer by the principal is that, in some well-run schools, parent input in rulemaking is sometimes helpful (more typically in elementary schools).

192.   Excerpt from a folder distributed to all students (16, P, 9–12):

STUDENT BEHAVIOR
All teachers have been requested to be on the alert for any student behavior which is in violation of school regulations. Students should behave in a manner that will be a credit to our school.

Students are to refrain from the following:

Smoking in the building or on school grounds.

Fighting on or near school property.

Flagrant disrespect of teachers.

Extreme dress or appearance which is disruptive to class.

Destruction or defacing of school property.

Wearing hats in the building.

Eating or drinking outside the cafeteria.

Loitering in the areas of heavy traffic.

Carrying cigarettes in shirt pockets or any place where they are visible.

Rowdy behavior or running in the building.

Dropping waste paper, candy wrappers, etc., in the building.

Locker misuse.

Gum chewing.

Hand holding and other displays of affection.

Possession or use of alcoholic beverages or narcotics on school property.

Coats in classroom or study hall.

Sitting in cars in the parking lot during lunch period or class time.

Possession or use of anything that might be considered a weapon.

Some schools have thorough, clearly stated rules such as these. Notice the rules include clothing restrictions (for example, no hats), and restraints on displays of affection (for example, holding hands). And observe the obvious thought that has gone into some of the wording (for example, students must refrain from "possession of anything that might be considered a dangerous weapon"). Students can realize that the word "considered" means that realistic toy guns are prohibited. As a result of this clarity, teachers enforcing the rule needn't worry about whether their suspicions are merely being excited by some student prank, which will lead to their own embarrassment. The rule makes it clear the jokes about weapons aren't funny. Perhaps 10 to 20 percent of the public high schools studied had rules with such precision.

Broadcasting the Rules

193. The School has a set of written rules included in a student handbook. This handbook, according to the assistant principals, is distributed to students at freshman orientation. In the case of transfer students, they are given a copy *if* there is one available. I tried to obtain a copy of the student handbook, but there was not one to be found on the entire campus; even the administrators did not have a copy.

Upon questioning seventeen students whether they received a copy of the handbook, twelve stated that they had not. One student said that he didn't know of anyone who has a copy of it. The School now has a student folder (for holding papers) on which are printed the general rules of the school. This folder may be purchased in the supply center for 25 cents. Most students resented the fact that they had to be purchased, and refused to buy them.

I had been told, by the administration, that at the time of freshman orientation parents are required to accompany students. The administration believes that the parents have or at least are aware that there is a student handbook. If the students never received a copy, then it seems logical that their parents have never seen or received one either (15, P, 9–12).

Many schools have rules that are not effectively communicated to parents or students. This policy seems strange; why create rules and then keep them secret? But such "secret" creation can serve various purposes. The principal can then truthfully say the school has rules, if that answer is appropriate in some context. Or, if the existence of rules becomes a bother, it can be said that the rules are nonexistent, or they can be ignored. Furthermore, the publication and periodical dissemination of several thousand set of rules requires some administrative and planning skill; some schools are very short on that form of talent.

194.   The principal told me that the School has a specific written code of what the students may and may not do. He had no copy to show or give me! However, he stated that it was approximately fifteen pages long and dealt with such matters as smoking, study halls, library procedures, hours of every conceivable school facility, procedures to follow in just about every foreseeable eventuality, and so on. This had been worked out over the years by faculty and administration (35, P, 9–12).

If the principal doesn't have a copy of the school rules, it is also unlikely that they are used much by others, either. One of my students told me of questioning a principal about school rules, and being told copies of the rules were in the hands of all teachers. Two days later one of the teachers told him that every teacher—for the first time—had just received a copy of the rules in his in-box.

195.   After the rules were printed, students were given copies to bring home to their parents. No receipts were provided for the parents to sign. When we talked to a group of children, they told us they had not shown the rules to their parents (27, P, K–8).

It is understandable—but unfortunate—that students and administrators sometimes tacitly conspire to keep school rules out of the sight of parents.

196.   Parents are required, along with the students, to sign a receipt for the school handbook, and return the receipt to the school for filing (60, R, 9–12).

Parental involvement generally facilitates discipline at all stages of the process. Parents tend to prodiscipline because they are in direct contacts with the effects (on themselves) or their own children's poor discipline, and their own children suffer from the violations of other wrongdoing students. As a result, parents as a group are usually in favor of stronger discipline than most educators (though individual parents may act defensively if their own child is directly accused). In any case, giving parents copies of the school rules is one step in obtaining parental involvement; but making sure they are delivered takes some forethought. Over two-thirds of the schools examined did not have a reliable means of getting copies of their rules to parents.

197. Compare the following general statements about students discipline taken from student handbooks distributed in two different schools:

DISCIPLINE

One of the most important lessons education should teach is discipline. While it does not appear as a subject, it underlies the whole educational structure. It is the training that developes self-control, character, orderliness, and efficiency. It is the key to good conduct and proper consideration for other people.

With an understanding of the purposes of discipline in a school, you may form a correct attitude toward it, and not only do your part in making your school an effective place of learning, but develop the habit of self-restraint which will make you a better person. (16, P, 9–12)

VIOLATION OF RULES

Rules and regulations are made to help students gain more from their experience at the School. When a student does not abide by these rules and regulations, he is not accepting his responsibilities as a student.

Violation of these rules will result in the loss of provileges and opportunities given students. Violations should be reported to the office and will be handled by the administration. (15, P, 9–12)

The coherence and firmness of the first statement contrasts strongly with the wishy-washyness of the second. Presumably, these matters and style and tone affect the conduct of faculty and students. Incidentally, the general discipline level in the first school (for a vast number of reasons) is incomparably higher than in the second.

198. All rules and policies, along with the School's philosophy, are prominently posted on walls and bulletin boards (and also given to students and parents) as a permanent reminder of their existence and nature (60, R, 9–12).

Conspicuous reiteration—in words and writings—of clear school rules generates pressure for their enforcement. When people know what is prohibited, they tend to pay more attention when the forbidden conduct occurs. And teachers feel more secure—and also under proenforcement presure—to act versus visible violations in their presence. Very few of the schools visited posted their rules.

Providing for Punishment

199. The principal said that "when a pupil is sent to my office to be disciplined, he is reminded of the School's philosophy." The philosophy says that the School's staff "works with the expectations of developing each student through the learning process so that he or she can become: an individual—responsible to himself, his family and his community: and a citizen—useful and productive to his society."

"I ask the student about his conduct in the light of this philosophy and try and help the pupil realize the problem and solution through a process which can lead to 'discovery.'" I then questioned the principal about the use of written punishments and detentions. He responded that he dislikes teachers using the word punishment, for the teachers' job is to teach, not "punish," the children. He suggests that teachers should keep guidance literature on their desks to which pupils can be referred when a problem arises. This way, a student is being disciplined—yet, it is a learning experience. Detentions, he said, are in violation of the Chicago Board rule (1, P, K–8).

I doubt that the principal's statement about detentions being in violation of board rules is correct. I am sure that the board has not provided staff with clear guidance on this issue.

200.   The rules state clearly enough what is prohibited behavior in the School. But they do not say what will happen if they are broken. A student pretty much knows that he can expect a parents' conference, or even be sent to the principal's office. The student doesn't know what will happen when he gets to these conferences, but can only guess what type of punishment he can expect. One eighth grade told me that unless rules tell what the punishment will be, they really cannot be very effective. Students would think twice before they break the rules if they know exactly what the punishment will be (6, P, K–8).

Incidentally, obscure punishment provisions encourage students caught in violations to argue with and harass teachers and administrators engaged in determining what to do with them. If there are alternative punishments, the student can always hope the threat of verbal resistance may pressure the teacher into lowering the punishment. But that threat of resistance must be disclosed—and, even if it fails to work, it may still have to be carried through. An a lot of everyone's time is lost—including the time of "lawful" students, who are deprived of faculty attention because of such distractions.

201.   From a student handbook:

Each student is to have an identification card with his picture, class schedule, and other pertinent information. This card must be carried at all times. . . . By carrying this card at all times, the student is assured his rights and privileges as a student of the School. (15, P, 9–12)

202.   From a student handbook:

HALLS AND PASSES
Absolutely NO student will be permitted to wander. If you are on official business you *must* have an official pass. (14, P, 9–12).

203. From a principal's letter to parents, supposedly announcing a much-needed "get-tough policy":

Cards, dice, radios, tape recorders, cassette players, etc., are to be left at home. They will be confiscated and the parent must come to the School to recover the item.

The wearing of hats by male students is prohibited. Hats will be confiscated and if this is a chronic happening, parents must come to school to pick up the hat and have a conference.

Students are to refrain from verbal assault and/or physical assault on staff members. They are subject to police charges being filed against them and/or being suspended from school. (17, P, 9–12)

The three previous documents are pervaded with a preachiness and ambivalence. Partly, they say, "Please don't do these bad things, or else we will have to think of some way to punish you." But, if the school can't think of any clear punishment to announce in the document, the student is entitled to believe it won't be able to think of one later. Or, when the documents articulate "punishments," they are patently trivial—confiscating dice or cards, so students can buy more and bring them in—or vague—the parents of "chronic" violators must come in to school. Finally, in the case of profound serious violations—physically assaulting teachers—students are "subject" to charges. "Subject" is a qualified word—it means liable to being charged. What about clear English: will be charged and prosecuted to the limit of the law? Actually, the reasons such language was not used was that the school lacked the determination to persecute assaulters (see Item 256). The documents are almost incitements to disorder.

204. Each student was provided with a copy the School's three-page demerit scale. About fifteen types of disapproved conduct were clearly described, and each one allocated a number of demerits (plus information about the likelihood of parents' conferences on the violations). The demerits were cumulated in the student's record, and successively higher amounts of demerits led to progressively more serious penalties. The penalties included detentions after school, parent conferences, loss of club and team privileges, and suspension and expulsion (56, R, 9–12).

205. Excerpt from folder given to all students:

DETENTION

Students may be assigned detention by the Attendance Office or any member of the faculty. This is for those students with undesirable patterns of attendance, tardiness, or conduct as well as other disciplinary problems.

Students assigned to detention are to report to the room designated on the detention notice at the time given and for the number of days assigned.

Each student is to have sufficient materials and books to study for the hour, and is to cooperate with the detention supervisor. Any student who does not abide by the regulations of the detention period may be blocked from school. (16, P, 9–12)

206. The following materials describes the School's detention procedure: If a student receives a detention before 12:00, P.M., the enforcement period begins that very same day. If the detention is received in the afternoon, serving time begins the following day. Detentions involve the student's staying after school up to 5:00 P.M. If the detention period is longer than two hours, it continues the following school day and every school day thereafter until the punishment is completed. Many students take school buses home. When they miss the bus, they must find their own way home. This not only inconvenience the students, but informs the parents that the students are being punished. How many days in a row, or how often each week, can students tell their mothers or fathers that they "accidentally" missed the bus (58, R, 9–12)?

After-school detentions served promptly after the violation are probably the most effective punishment for moderate violations. Many public shools—especially in Chicago—fail to make adequate use of this device. The reasons for this failure are not entirely clear to me. I can make guesses. It means more work for teachers—someone must stay after school. Or schools may assign teachers' aides, or other unmotivated persons, to do the job, and the students just read comics and catch up on their sleep. Perhaps there are also legal questions about restraining students; however, as we'll later note, schools are all too willing to use legality issues as excuses to avoid doing things that are complicated, and so I feel the legality issue is overrated.

207. The School has had a few truancy problems this year. In one situation they are not receiving cooperation from the parents, so they are taking the case to court. They make no exceptions for those who do not comply with the rules. For situations where the child disrupts the class or is fighting a lot, he can be given a suspension. The teacher has the option of giving an in-school or out-of-school suspension.

When an in-school suspension is given the teachers assign work and the student is kept in one room and isolated from all activities for one or more days. This form of punishment eliminates punishments which give the student a "free vacation." Many times this is what students want. In-school suspensions total about twenty-five per year. Out-of-school suspensions are only five per year, and usually are for more serious offenses. They are used until a meeting with the parents is arranged. Suspensions do not occur unless one is a troublemaker, about fifteen students told me. If one is an average student the worst one ends up getting is a detention or two a year (37, P, 7–8).

The following two items point out the inevitable connection between maintaining good discipline and rewarding desirable behavior:

208.   Students in a second-grade class are given stars for their good behavior, such as not talking when the teacher is talking. Different-colored stars have different meanings:

red   fair behavior

blue   bad behavior

silver   good behavior

gold   excellent behavior

In the third-grade classroom there is one bulletin board which is called the behavior bulletin board. All the names of the students are there and the teacher gives them colored stars which have the same definition and colors as above. The students who have the most gold stars in the class will get to go on a field trip with all the other students whose teachers use this system (grades K-6). The stars are given every Friday and the field trip is taken once a year.

The names of the awarded students appear on the bulletin board of their classroom, and on the main bulletin board in the second-floor hallway (47, R, K-8)

209.   Students can participate in a "wooden token" program, in which they will receive tokens for helping with the custodial duties at the School. The principal says he takes the "characters" (that is, potential behavior problems) to help shovel snow, move chairs, sweep sidewalks, and so on. This not only uses up some of their energy, but gives them a sense of belonging. Regarding them in a positive way lessens some of their negative attitudes about the School. The tokens can buy refreshments at the Rip-Off bar or McDonald's certificates. This has been an effective program, according to the principal (31, P, 7-8).

The subject of rewarding desirable behavior is discussed in greater length elsewhere in this book (for example, in chapters 3 and 6). At this point, it can be simply said that almost all the schools that had efficient discipline procedures also had efficient systems of recognizing desirable conduct, and (unfortunately) vice-versa. Evidently, educators who can design and enforce discipline systems can also design systems to reward students—and, perhaps, these efficient educators also realize that discipline, alone, is only a necessary (but not sufficient) condition for a vital institution.

210.   Parents are notified by the dean of boys or by the dean of girls of a suspension or expulsion by telephone. Notices of detentions are sent to the parents in the mail. An average of twenty-five students daily receive detentions and an average of twenty students per week receive in-school or out-of-school suspension. Last year one student was expelled from the school (38, P, 9–12).

Provisions for routinely notifying parents about rule violations are not common.

211. The students had the impression that no matter what it was they had done, they had a choice between being suspended and a work detail. Detentions or staying after school seemed essentially nonexistent. The majority of students took the work detail over the suspension. Probably the main reason for this is that when students chose work detail their parents were not informed of the incidence in most cases. And most students did not mind at all the small tasks in the details. To them it was just volunteer work. It did not serve as punishment, if punishment is meant to deter an individual from doing a particular thing again (17, P, 9–12).

The key test of punishment is whether students dislike it. And usually students are quite frank in giving their feelings about particular punishments.

Enforcing the Rules

212. All of the teachers felt that littering of the School by students was a problem. One stated that he feels the students don't respect school property. The administration doesn't feel there is a problem. I asked an assistant principal if he felt that littering was a problem. He said, "No, we don't have a problem, just take a look for yourself." I looked outside his office door and within five feet of it were several pieces of crumpled paper on the floor. He simply said, "Well it isn't usually like this" (14, P, 9–12).

213. Seventy-five percent of students we interviewed believed that teachers were too lenient with many students. This causes some discipline problems and weakens the standard of fairness in the School (36, P, 9–12).

The majority of students favor clear rules that are evenly and firmly enforced. But, naturally, the students who are punished may make more noise (if they receive adult support).

214. The School has one security officer who seems to be in the wrong place always at the right time. There is a strong smell of alcohol on his breath continuously. Recently, as I passed him in the hall, I heard a teacher tell him that there was a big fight in the playground. He responded by saying he couldn't go, because he was supervising students in the lunchroom. Where are his responsibilities, supervision or security (5, P, K–8)?

215. The teacher said that "looking around school, usually immediately after school, I see at least one fight a day. Sometimes two or three fights. So far nothing has been done to resolve this problem. This is certainly a job for the administration, but they vacate the premises almost before the students" (4, P, K–8).

216. This female teacher was the chair of the School's staff and administration committee (which existed to improve communication among school professionals). She was asked if she would intervene in fights or violent situations involving students. She replied, "I am not here to patrol or act like a policeman, but to teach." She sees the School as a make-believe world, from which she escapes at the end of the day (22, P, 9-12).

In departmentalized schools (essentially, senior and junior high schools), teachers handle several or more groups of students daily. And students often have peripheral contacts with many teachers. Under these circumstances, the impact of any teacher on a pupil's discipline will be modest. Furthermore, each teacher can be tempted to ignore discipline responsibilities, because such ignorance may not directly affect most of the class work. For instance, the student smoking marijuana in the washroom, or swearing in the hall, may never enter the classroom of the teacher who turns away from such conduct. Under these circumstances, school administrations must carefully plan if they hope to enlist broad-scale teacher support for student discipline.

217. During the classroom visits, it was noted that there was good discipline. If a child were to act up the teacher would make him write some lines (1,000) stating what he or she will not do. For example, "I will not talk in class" (49, R, K-8).

Self-contained classrooms tend to foster improved discipline. The teachers get to know the students well, and can estimate whether some act of violation is an ignorable mischance, or part of a pattern of defiance. And if teachers in self-contained classrooms ignore systemic disobedience, they will be eventually personally "punished" for their indifference: they will be harassed by their class. The students can also learn to recognize the teacher's standards, and are less tempted to engage in testing; they have had a chance to discover the limits.

218. The teachers had mixed feelings about enforcing school rules outside of their classrooms. If they have classes the next period, or other work to do, it becomes a hassle to take a child down to the office and file a report. For this reason, they will often simply tell a student to stop the improper conduct (for example, smoking in the washroom, using foul language, angry quarreling) as compared to actually seeing that it is penalized. Teachers believe security personnel or teacher's aides should handle all of washroom discipline (22, P, 9-12).

There are two levels through which discipline is visited on people: the level of mechanical punishment, and the level of social disapproval. Social disapproval is most significant for the young when it is applied by important adults whom they view with respect. It is natural for students to see teachers in this light. But if teachers relegate their adult responsibility of showing disapproval to aides and security guards, they are implicitly saying that they do not seriously care about the misconduct involved. And the discipline process loses some legitimacy. Of course, there are problems for teachers connected with reporting. However, there are remedies that can help. For example, some schools have students carry "demerit cards." Teachers are empowered to take such cards from students for minor offenses, make critical notes on them, and then return them. Those cards are periodically checked out by administrators, and punishments are applied.

219.   The School has attempted to apply a closed-campus policy to freshmen. In other words, freshmen were prohibited from leaving the building during school hours without a special permission. Eleven students were interviewed about this policy. Two students did not know of the existence of the policy. Eight students said that no one enforced it. (None of them had any clear idea why the policy was attempted.) One of the two teachers interviewed felt the policy was an infringement on the rights of the freshmen. A second teacher believed that a closed-campus policy, either for only freshmen or (preferably) for all students, would be very desirable. However, efforts to enforce the policy even for freshmen had been abandoned. The following story was recited by the second teacher: a male student in his class would have a lunch period right before his class, go outside, drink beer, and return intoxicated. The teacher has also witnessed some male students drinking beer on a nearby streetcorner while school was in session. (22, P, 9–12).

Closed-campus policies are applied by schools for a variety of reasons. Some of them are to ensure that large groups of young persons, who have been collected together by the decisions of public authorities, are not left to wander about unsupervised; to shield students from dangers and temptations (for example, drug peddlers, street hoodlums) that may occur about the school; to encourage students to spend their total school time focused on educational concerns; and to make it harder for inappropriate persons to slip into the school by cutting down traffic in and out of school. Not all schools maintain closed campuses. Less than 50 percent of those that tried succeeded. And some of the schools that did not try to maintain closed campuses should have used that procedure (for example, because the teachers could see drug peddlers on the street in front of the school).

220.   There are no hall guards (either faculty or students) in any of the halls. All visitors are supposed to have passes, yet we did not have any. It is possible for anyone to enter the School without being questioned at any time of day. Rules are made but they are not adhered to. Supposedly, only seniors and juniors are allowed off campus for lunch or during a free period. But students from all levels were taking advantage of the policy (66, S, 9–12).

221.   The principal was concerned with student marijuana use in the washrooms. But he had not specifically assigned teachers to washroom

duties. He does not see how their carrying out of that assignment can be monitored in "a school of this size."

On the other hand, one teacher interviewed said that toilet stall doors were redesigned (that is, cut in half) so that students could not stand and smoke marijuana without being observed. Last year faculty were given specific duties in the washrooms and their performance was checked by department chairs. This duty was included in the teachers' contract. However, no definite assignments were made this year, so teachers naturally did not take upon themselves a distasteful duty (39, P, 9–12).

The reasons for the widespread failure of facilities to enforce rules are enormously complex. Some of them are suggested by the previous items and discussion in this chapter, for example, the rules are obscurely written, punishments are awkward, and the rules are not widely disseminated. But there are many other barriers to efficiency. It is harder—but definitely not impossible—to control teachers in larger schools. Administrators who are themselves ambivalent about rules are obviously not going to be good at making others (that is, teachers) enforce them—and this ambivalence among many administrators is evident. The mechanics of supervising teachers—as compared to employees in many other institutions—are complicated. Many administrators also do not clearly invite or require teachers to be fully engaged in the process of rule development and enforcement. And putting it simply, many teachers—and other human beings, too—lack guts.

One of the sad themes in this book is the way many schools (let's say above grade seven) cannot organize things so students usually have privacy and security in washrooms. If robberies, drug dealing, and drug use occur in many washrooms—and this is often the case—then privacy must be restrained. For privacy is really only concurrent with self-discipline. If people use privacy to engage in unlawful acts (or if young people use it for self-destructive acts), there are inevitable pressures for social intrusion. The way people "earn" privacy is by using it responsibly. Obviously, we are less able to teach large proportions of young adults to use their privacy responsibly—and thus systems of observation must be established as a last (desperate) resort.

222. One of the assistant principals had been at the School for eighteen years. He considers himself a "disciplinarian." For instance, he confiscates radios, or hats that are worn in the School by students. The only way they can be gotten back is if the students bring their parents in after a thirty-day wait. He deals with fighting students daily in lunchroom and hall duty. He believes he is not afraid to confront any student doing wrong. Many other teachers ignore such conflicts. He was bitter about some female teachers who ignore potentially violent situations, even though "they are paid as much as the men, and talk a lot about womens' equality" (22, P, 9–12).

The issue of hats and radios needs amplification, though dress will be more fully considered in the chapter on school spirit. During the 1970s it was common for many black pupils to wear hats in school and to carry around transistor radios (sometimes worn over the ears, like headphones). Essentially, these activities signify that, though the pupils were physically in school, they were emotionally "on the streets." And in some schools this meant that the drug and alcohol use, sexual promiscuity, and gang disorder of the streets simply extended into the schools. The "fight" to keep hats and radios out of school was an effort to enforce upon the students a new set of values. The implicit aim was to "help" them escape the isolation and defensiveness of the ghetto, and move toward mainstream society. Naturally, the enforcement of this aim by schools was complicated by many social currents and the general awkwardness of contemporary school rule enforcement (for example, what right do we have to tell a seventeen-year-old that he cannot wear a hat in the building?). Of course, this adult ambivalence has had its reverberations on school rules and student conduct—hence some of the incidents of disorder described at the beginning of this chapter.

223.   The School handbook is made available to students, teachers, and parents. Under the heading "Teachers Policies," it provides:

> Every member of the faculty should consider himself an extension of the dean of discipline. All teachers should insist on good conduct, manners, and order at all times, as spelled out in the students' norms or conduct. Teachers should familiarize themselves with these norms published in the student section of this handbook. Any kind of assigned responsibilities for overseeing students (monitoring lunchrooms, hall guarding) should be considered by the teacher as an assignment distinct from, but just as important as, teaching. Teachers handling such responsibilities should be alert and keep moving. Try to anticipate trouble without looking for it or starting it. (60, R, 9–12)

Precise directions of this sort to teachers about discipline are very rare in the schools studied. And, naturally, without such directions, teachers can object if they are criticized for failure to act "appropriately."

224.   From a statement of school policy distributed by the principal to all teachers:

Prerequisites for Good Discipline
1. The teacher must know that he has the backing of the administration.
2. Every teacher must share in the disciplinary responsibilities of the school.
3. The teachers must make clear to the students what is expected of them.
4. The teacher must insist on the respect of all students at all times. (56, P, 9–12)

225.   All the teachers work together when there is a behavioral problem with a student. They call a staff meeting, where the teachers who have that student during a school day meet to decide how the matter can be rectified. It is rare when a teacher does not enforce discipline. The twenty students I interviewed could only think of 1 or 2 teachers in the School who did not run a well-disciplined class (37, P, 8–9).

Keeping Records

226. The School has a well-organized method of keeping track of student single-period absences (or "cuts"). In order for students to be readmitted to a class from which they were absent, they have to show the teacher an All Purpose Absence slip, obtained from the appropriate office. The slip serves as a control device; in requesting the slip, the students either had to accept a punishment for unauthorized absence, or satisfy the office as to the legitimacy of their excuse. The observer reported:

The All Purpose Slips seem to be easily obtained by the students. While I was in the cafeteria interviewing a student she decided not to go to her next class. She called one of her friends over, who opened her notebook and pulled out a handful of slips. I asked her friend where she got them. She said that the students take them off the secretary's desk in the office, and that some students have stacks of them at home (14, P, 9–12).

227. Excerpts from a handbook distributed to students (15, P, 9–12):

Students who go to class late are marked tardy. If the tardiness persists, the student is to be referred to the attendance office for disposition.

Students who do not present an excuse will have his [sic] absence recorded as a cut from class. The class teacher will then notify the parents of the student.

These provisions are somewhat "extreme," since they explicitly reveal an unsound policy that is only implicitly applied in many schools. This departmentalized school leaves the monitoring of students' lateness (to individual classes) and cutting solely up to teachers—except in aggravated instances. This means that students can play teachers off against each other—by criticizing some teachers as harsh on the ground that other teachers are nicer (they will never criticize the lenient teacher by telling them they are too easy!). The students can also accumulate large numbers of cuts in many classes before they aggravate one teacher to take the step of reporting; and if students are reported, the attendance officer has no idea how they have conducted themselves elsewhere.

"Tardiness" is also another questionable policy. Students are allowed predetermined lengths of time for moving from one class to the next. Some schools (and teachers) allow late students—who exceed the time allowed—to come into class, subject to various penalties, or if they offer good excuses. In other words, tardiness is subject to lesser penalties (or none) compared to cutting classes. The idea sounds humane; the practicality sometimes means that the teacher has to evaluate innumerable hard-luck stories or see many students who go out of their way to "use up" their allocated tardiness. Perhaps the better response is to say all "lates," regardless of their causes, are subject to moderate and real penalties, just as workers who come in late are docked for the time they're not there.

228.   Students who habitually break the rules are brought in with their parents and the whole file on the students is brought out and reviewed. Discipline records are kept up to date on unexcused absences and excessive tardiness. An attendance clerk spends two hours every day calling homes and checking lists. Three times tardy in one class constitutes a one-hour detention (31, P, 9–12).

In any school where absences are at a high level, prompt checking (via phone calls) is an important first corrective step. If the parents both work, some schools even call their place of work. After all, if no one is home, and the absence is "legitimate," it might mean that the child has been injured between school and home; surely this warrants immediate contact with parents.

229.   All teachers maintain an anecdotal record for each student in the student's individual folder. Pink pages are for incidents of bad behavior, and green pages are for good behavior. Every anecdote should be discussed with the student before recording it. In one class we were given the opportunity to check the records: there were an average of a total of four anecdotes on the pink pages, and two on the green pages. Technically, such records are confidential. However, the teacher told us that "there is nothing important to keep secret in them; they are good kids" (49, R, K–8).

230.   The system that monitors students' class attendance also monitors teacher conduct pertaining to record keeping. The attendance officer will reprimand any teacher whose record keeping handicaps the enforcement of the rules (34, P, 9–12).

231.   All detentions, suspensions, and expulsion are recorded in the students' folders. Most reprimands are, in fact, similarly recorded. This record stays with the students throughout their high-school years, whether at the School or at another school to which they may transfer. These records are even kept for five years after the students have graduated (58, R, 9–12).

This is a private school. I assume this is the reason they ignore the Illinois state law (mentioned in chapter 3) requiring the destruction of student conduct records immediately after graduation.

232.   The teachers are expected to make comments (to parents) on the pupils' midterm grade cards. The principal reads all of these cards. He then makes comments to the teachers regarding their comments. He tells them whether the comments to parents are too brief, not clear, or hastily written. The principal receives a copy of every document issued or prepared by the School, especially in regard to discipline. For example, misconduct slips are filled out by the teachers and given to the assistant principal for action. The principal then receives a copy of the slip (37, P, 7–8).

As schools have become larger, record keeping has assumed a more vital role in managing discipline. Records enable the total institution to be informed of students' past activities—to see them as whole persons, compared to just considering the immediate incident in a vacuum. They also permit persons removed from incidents to oversee the conduct of the students and staff involved, and insure that fair procedures are followed.

Sometimes record keeping is a cumbersome process, and—despite its rational and even humane justifications—it has obvious overtones of impersonality. For these reasons, the quality of discipline records in many schools is poor. For instance, many departmentalized schools had no procedure for recording small violations (for example, cheating in class, smoking, rudeness, inappropriate sexual affinity). As a result, persisting levels of low disorder often prevailed, since no one is able to recognize particular students as frequent violators and deserving of serious attention. In smaller or nondepartmentalized schools, such difficulties affecting "institutional memory" are taken care of by the inevitable recurring contacts among limited numbers of students and faculty. But, until we recreate such intimate entities, record keeping must supplement the constrained informal recollection that exists in any large institution.

Determining Guilt and Assessing Penalties

233. From talking to students, it seems that most of the discipline problems occur in the slow-learner classes, and in classrooms where a pattern of misbehavior has set in and the teachers can't reverse it. We heard about one classroom where a student punched the teacher, threw a desk, and other students were rude and used profanity often and freely. A student in the class pointed out that they had had four different teachers since the school year started, and all of them quit in disgust. I asked the student what kind of teacher she thought they needed, and she said someone who could control them and whom they respected (18, P, 7–8).

234. A teacher told us, "A child was suspended for carrying a toy gun that looked real. I can see the implications that this might have for the student body and I can accept this decision. A student was suspended for ditching school. As a result of the suspension, he is doing the same thing he got caught doing, except now he has the stamp of approval from school. A student hits another student in an unmentionable area of his body. A student swears and uses abusive language at a teacher. A student causes havoc everywhere he goes. These students are not suspended. What guidelines do students, teachers, and parents have for possible suspension?" (5, P, K–8).

235. A well-informed teacher reported the following story to me: "A star pitcher of the baseball team got into an argument with a teacher in the

locker room, and grabbed the teacher and began to shake him. A security guard and several other teachers intervened, and broke things up. The next day, in retaliation, two other members of the ball team vandalized the cars (parked in the school parking lot) of two of the teachers involved. The vandals were identified and admitted their acts. The teachers and guard reported the incident to the principal, and asked him to act vigorously to back them up. (All the persons involved in this episode were black.) The principal was obviously reluctant to penalize effective and well-recognized athletes. He refused to go beyond giving the students a verbal reprimand. When the staff objected, he said, "Well, what can you expect from such kids anyway? They come from the projects.'

The guard spoke out indignantly, 'Well, I was raised in the projects, too! Does that license me to be a thug or a vandal?' (17, P, 9–12).

236. The gym teacher had been "cast" into the position of acting principal. He permitted teachers to send pupils to the office for extremely minor offenses, such as gum chewing, getting out of their seats, and so on. It was reported by teachers that ten to fifteen students could be seen sitting and playing in the principal's office at any given time, because he didn't require teachers to send the pupils' assignments to do while they were waiting. In addition to this, he used the pupils who have been sent to the office as his helpers. One might mistake this procedure as an attempt to promote prosocial conduct; however, it appears to me that this only reinforces aversive behavior (1, P, K–8).

243. Most of the complaints from parents about punishments of their children are not considered problems, according to the principal and assistant principal. They are just situations where the student does not go along with the teacher. When this happens, the call from the parent is responded to by the principal. He then acts upon it by transferring the student to another class. The principal believes that if worse comes to worse, he "always sides with the student" (22, P, K–8).

238. Delegation of authority is limited and subjective. For instance (one teacher said), the clerks used to take care of disciplinary problems. Misbehaving students were instructed by their teachers to go to the office, where the clerks would act as disciplinarians and reprimand them accordingly (5, P, K–8).

239. The administrators feel the rules are generally fair. They also said that in some cases they do not always "follow the books" when it comes to administering punishment, and that there are "exceptions to every rule." An example of this would be that the punishment for fighting is ten days' suspension, but the assistant principal usually only suspends the students involved for a maximum of five days.

Upon interviewing six instructors on what their opinion of the students rules was, four of them felt that they should be enforced more firmly (14, P, 9–12).

Inconsistent and feeble adjudication (of student violators) by administrators occurred in 25 ot 50 percent of the schools visited. Such inconsistency is essentially a by-product of the forces which make for vague rule articulation—and which were discussed earlier. In other words, rules are not written, or are poorly drafted by administrators to avoid the demands of being an enforcer; and, if the principals (or other administrator) is still compelled to enforce a rule, they may then try to escape the tension involved in adjudicating student guilt. Or, if they must recognize the student's guilt, they frequently levy a less than appropriate penalty and then say to the student, "Don't get mad at us; we are doing you a favor!"

240.   Rules are enforced up to a certain point. Most students feel that the student adjudication board serves no purpose. When it is time for the board to reach a decision on a violation, many board members do not show up (66, S, 9–12).

241.   Rule violations and other disruptive incidents are handled by the School judicial board, with a mixed composition of students and faculty. The board is supposed to meet weekly, but the recent meeting was the first one in several weeks.

The reasons for this meeting were (1) a student was accused of being a dope peddler, and (2) a student was held up in the School by a man with a gun who was not a member of the School.

After the meeting, to which I as a nonmember was not admitted, we were informed that the first case was dismissed due to lack of evidence. In regard to the second problem, the holdup, tighter security was to be enforced within the building. This meant that the people entering the building through the main door were stopped and questioned by a student. Since I was one of the persons stopped, I found out how easy it was to get past the student at the door. Since no identification was needed, there was no problem of entry for anyone. As long as one mentioned the name of an administrator or staff member, one was allowed to enter. There was no record of visitors coming to the School, and those who did come didn't have to sign in or out. There were also no guards at any door besides the main door. It is true that the doors were locked from the inside, but they were also very easy to open (57, R, 9–12).

Student, and student-teacher boards, are occasionally used as devices to enable administrators (and teachers) to escape the demands of handling student rule violations. Except in very limited situations, they distort the structure of authority in the school. For instance, in the preceding drug-dealing episode, suppose some student later purchases drugs while in school through the released (accused but vindicted) dealer. If the principal is later confronted about this incident, would it be right for him to say, "I always knew the accused dealer was guilty, but I was unable to act due to the decision of the student/teacher board"?

242.   I asked the principal, "How flexible are the rules?" He

responded, "They are inflexible." He then explained that the program for student conduct and behavior is highly structured. There is a committee that functions throughout the school year assessing and evaluating the rules and regulations in effect, and the degree of success the students are experiencing in conforming to them. Those rules and regulations that are found "not needed" are removed. ("Not needed meaning that they serve no purpose in guiding student behavior or conduct and should not be kept just as a means of having quantity in the list.") Also, those rules and regulations that are found to be "not enforceable" are removed. The principal explained the importance of this step. He said that rules that are not enforceable only serve to weaken the other rules that are enforceable, in that we may indirectly communicate some incapability on our part, which can be interpreted by students to mean laxity or some degree of powerlessness. He said the intent is to communicate to the students standards that we have the authority to back up, and strength and power that we will use to back them up (16, P, 9–12).

243.   Punishment will be fair, and in certain instances the rules can be modified. Recently a student entered the School after hours without permission and was caught. He was given a month's detention from a faculty member, and appealed to the principal, explaining that he had gone in to get a forgotten book. The principal discussed the problem with the teacher, and because it was a first offense the teacher changed the punishment to five days of "hard labor." Some custodial duties were given and the student accepted the punishment, considering it to be fair. Each major discipline case is handled by the assistant principal or principal himself. They are totally committed to backing up the teachers, and there is a feeling of faculty trust in the administration (31, P, 9–12).

With reference to the preceding story, it seems strange that the rules would empower a teacher to give (on his own) thirty days' detention. While the principal's moderation of the particular penalty seems understandable, it might be equally desirable to narrow the area of teacher discretion in such matters.

244.   Teachers also stated that they discussed with the principal whatever significant disciplinary measures they thought should be taken. No written communication to parents was sent out without the principal receiving a copy. The teachers said the principal backed them up when they have problems with parents. They stressed how important they felt this was. Without the principal's cooperation, they would not be effective in disciplining a student (37, P, 7–8).

The control just described may not be as constricting as it seems; the communications that are reviewed are often essentially triple carbon forms, where the principal simply routinely receives (and reads) one of the copies.

245.   Offenses such as cheating and swearing and minor fight are punished with a detention. Compositions are often given on various sub-

jects. In case of a detention, a notice that the student is being kept after school is sent home with the student. If a parent indicates an objection to this, the teacher is not permitted to keep the student for the punishment. About fifteen detentions per week are given. The teachers almost never receive interference from the parents. The students I talked with said the punishments are fair. The criterion for behavior is basically common sense. By the time one is in sixth grade, one should know what is proper behavior and what is expected in school. When students misbehave they know they are doing wrong. It is always the same teachers who give detentions out, the students say. "You know what you can get way with after awhile and with whom." I found this to be true while observing in the classrooms.

I saw one group of students act up in one classroom where the teacher had no control. Then the rest of the day, where teachers were stricter and applied punishment, the same group behaved. If a teacher was very strict, they were very good. If a teacher allowed them some freedom they took it. In some classes, a lot of interaction and exchange went on, and a great deal of enthusiasm was allowed, but it was obvious that the teacher had control of the class (37, P, 7–8).

The preceding item reveals some of the fine distinctions involved in drawing a line between healthy enthusiasm, and confusion and disorder. One common prescription for teachers on applying discipline is to come down hard the first few class sessions, and to relax later, once correct principles have been established. Perhaps the students in the relaxed but orderly classes had already seen the iron fist in the velvet glove.

246. If a child strikes another child, he is automatically suspended. The teacher takes the child down to the assistant principal, and she promptly calls the student's parents and tells them that the child is being suspended for fighting. The parent comes and picks up the child, and makes an appointment to see the assistant principal, at which time the child will state his case. When the parent, child, and assistant principal meet, the child gives his side of the story. If the child makes a good case (and, say, apologizes) and doesn't have a previous record for bad behavior, he may be made to wash the blackboard for a week after school. However, if a student has a bad attitude about what he has done, and has a record of misbehavior they will be made to mop the halls of the school or clean up the entire school yard. These rules apply to intermediate and upper-level students. The primary students very seldom fight (6, P, K–8).

247. The School has established a system of probation contracts and meeting. When, in the opinion of the School, a student's misconduct warrants it, he will be given the choice of transferring to another school or accepting a behavior contract. The terms and length of this contract depend upon the nature of the offense(s) that caused the probation. In all cases, one term will deal with the serving of assigned detention, and another will stipulate that the student must attend probation meetings. Violation of any of the agreed-upon conditions will cause the immediate transfer of the student in question from the School to another high school (58, R, 9–12).

248.   Stealing is prohibited by the School rules, and first offenders are referred to the police department (21, P, 9–12).

Written school rules rarely specify what happens to students whose in-school disorder also violates the law. Presumably, administrators are reluctant to report such acts. I suspect one cause of their reluctance is their desire to keep misconduct as concealed as possible (in the interest of simplifying their own work). Unfortunately, this practice may cause students to feel that it is better to steal (from fellow students) or deal in drugs in school, as compared to risking arrest by the police for away-from-school crimes.

249.   The School strictly enforces a requirement that all students must conspicuously wear their ID cards in the building. The badge enables teachers and guards to easily identify unauthorized persons who have slipped into the School, and who may engage in illegal activities, for example, thievery or selling drugs. Faculty and staff also wear such cards. It is pointed out to students that if any of them "worked at the steel mill nearby, and forgot their badge, they would be kept out of the plant and automatically lose a day's pay" (23, P, 9–12).

The growing use of student ID cards is a by-product of the increase in size of schools. The larger the school, the harder it is for faculty to distinguish between students and unauthorized persons. It may be that the "virtues" of size are not great enough to make up for the depersonalization which results from using badges to be known by your teachers. But, until schools are made smaller, the badges are often needed. A substantial proportion of the schools examined had badge-wearing requirement; in about 50 percent of these schools, the requirements were not vigorously enforced. Incidentally, such indifference to enforcing an explicit rule probably gave students the idea that other written rules were equally irrelevant.

250.   Students feel that the rules and regulations are a necessary part of the school's functioning, and that they are enforced in a fair and just manner (60, R, 9–12).

The Police, the Courts, and Discipline

251.   The School has two full-time security guards on duty. They are really city policemen. One is in uniform and the other is dressed in plain clothing. These guards carry service revolvers, and they get full respect from the students. The School also has eight other guards who work in the School from two to four hours per day. These guards receive less respect from the students, because they don't carry guns. Some of these officers are young men who spend a lot of time chasing the young ladies in the School, rather than keeping the building secure (15, P, 9–12).

252. The enlarged role of security forces in schools is a noteworthy phenomenon. In 1975, the Executive Secretary of the National Association of Secondary School Principals estimated that the total number of such employees in American schools had risen from nearly (or actually) zero to 15,000 over the previous ten years. (No school reference needed).

Of course, gross force, and the threat of such force, played a role in schools before the development of uniformed guards. I suspect that the role of "enforcer"—for larger unruly students—was often played in the past by physical education instructors, for example, former football players. However, it seems that (1) the level of disorder has risen so that guns and clubs, as well as muscles, are needed, and (2) the willingness of teachers to be enforcers, and their legitimacy in such roles, have declined.

253. After a period of extreme disorder and stress in the School, about eight plainclothes policemen were stationed throughout the School for several weeks. This strategy, plus an improvement in the weather (which made it easier for bored or restless students to cut classes or stay away from school), brought about a decline in the tension (17, P, 9-12).

Students in disorderly schools tend to respect policemen not only because of their guns, but because they represent the capability of other forms of fast retaliation, for example, arrests, physical punishment for misconduct. Obviously, teachers cannot have all of these capabilities. However, it should not be beyond human ingenuity for schools to devise fast, modest (nonsadistic), and unpleasant punishments.

One adult black college student described to me a discussion with a black security guard in an all-black Chicago high school (not otherwise mentioned in this book). The guard said one of his responsibilities was to physically punish students who broke the rules. The student asked how the guard justified that. He said, "If a student breaks a serious rule, the school has three options: expel him, send him to the police station, or have me punish him. A hard spanking is the best of the three for the student."

In a few moments, while my student was there, four students were ushered in who had been caught playing dice in the stairwell. The guard took his paddle and spanked them with vigor. The students grimaced and winced, but did not cry. They then walked out of the guard's office. My student went out and asked them how they felt about the incident. They said, "We didn't like being paddled; it hurt. But we were playing dice, and did not want to be expelled or sent to the police station."

254. I was very surprised when I questioned the school principal about a dress code. He responded that he couldn't have one. The basis for his reply was a result of an incident that happened last year. A group of students arrived at school wearing identical T-shirts which promoted the smoking of marijuana. His reaction was to send the students home to change into clothing more appropriate to a learning environment. He was advised by the school board attorney not to do that again. He said he "probably would not" after that incident. If the situation came about again, he would request that the students turn the shirts inside out (38, P, 9–12).

Notice the word the principal used, "request". And what can he—or will he—do if his future request is refused?

It is not certain that the lawyer is right, if he says the law prohibits principals from stopping students from wearing marijuana T-shirts. And, indeed, the lawyer may not even be saying that. All he may mean is that the students' parents may sue over the matter, and it is easier to let the shirt be worn as compared to fighting a lawsuit—even if it is eventually won. And there is some logic to that position—after all, one reason we hire lawyers is to avoid lawsuits.

A graduate student of mine (who is also a teacher) told me another anecdote that further illustrates these problems. In her small suburban school district, there are no written rules for student conduct, despite the requests of teachers for such guidelines. The faculty has been told that the school board's lawyer has advised the district to have no such rules, to make it less liable for being sued for having or enforcing "illegal" rules. Presumably, the lawyer expects the school to decide all discipline cases without written records. Such a policy might make it harder for aggrieved students (and parents) to prove a case. Technically, the lawyer's advice may either be good or bad legal tactics; but, as for maintaining student discipline, it is obviously bad.

Of course, a variety of elements underlie the preceding episodes. Parents (or some parents) who might support the "right" of their children to wear provocative shirts. Students who feel emboldened to act this way. Educators who turn to lawyers for opinions about matters that are essentially moral, and not legal, in nature. And courts that have issued some decisions which undercut authority in schools. The wearing of T-shirts advertising marijuana in schools is obviously not all the fault of courts. However, given the already fragile nature of discipline policy in many schools, judicial activism to advance so-called student rights is part of the problem.

255. The teacher was a member of a faculty committee established to improve school discipline during a period of extreme student unrest. He gave us the following report of a meeting between committee members and the district superintendent (who supervises two or three high schools and a dozen elementary schools) to review the situation:

On the question of assaults on teachers by students, the district superintendent mentioned that students have rights. If the teachers initiate the incident, they have no legal backing. "Initiation" can be something like removing a student's hat. He also stated that a student cannot be suspended for more than ten days without a hearing and a hearing officer. This results in a slow process that could take months. In the meantime, the student is free of punishment, and can attend school. After the city hearing, the case can be appealed to the state and the whole process repeats itself if the student loses the city hearing. In effect, the student can postpone decision indefinitely.

One of the teachers struck by a student brought up a practical situation: the teacher is on door duty in the lunchroom with orders to let no one in without and ID. Students come to the door all period long and some attempt to push their way in. What can the teacher do legally? (there are 3,300 students in the School!)

The superintendent replied that the teacher is not to restrain a student physically in any way, but to take note of the student's appearance and notify the dean at a later time (17, P, 9-12).

Note the pattern of generalized, ambiguous statements about the law's provisions. A student is not "licensed" to beat up a teacher because he (ill-advisedly) knocks the student's hat off! However, such situations do make cases more complicated, and require administrators, prosecutors, and judges to make thoughtful—and possibly courageous—decisions. Unfortunately, our systems do not always operate in this fashion. (Remember how, in some earlier items, teachers emphasized that discipline would not work unless their principals backed them up? Perhaps the same principle applies concerning courts and schools: without quick, firm back-up, the people on the firing line begin to stop fighting).

256. This item continues the story of the teacher on the school discipline committee. He told the observer about another meeting of the committee:

One of the security aides attended the meeting to report what happened in the processing of her assault case in criminal court. (The assault by a student resulted in five stitches to her upper lip.) The case is being handled directly through the police. The chair, the assistant principal, explained that all of student assaults on staff cases can be handled either through the School Board or directly through the police. The chair said that three types of criminal charges can be drawn: (1) verbal battery, (2) simple battery, (3) assault and battery. The third charge is the most severe. According to the aide, during case processing, when it became known that the incident happened in school, the charge was reduced to simple battery from assault and battery. The student was released on $25.00 bail. The next day he appeared in the halls of the School. The aide then contacted her lawyer and initiated a civil suit on her own.

The committee then asked the chair about suspension of the student, and she indicated that the School could not do that because that would constitute double jeopardy, and would not be valid under present legal interpretations (17, P, 9-12).

The chair's position about double jeopardy is ridiculous, but real. Possible or actual punishment in a criminal case is one thing; a student's right to hit teachers and stay in school is another matter. However, since the court (or city attorney) reduced the student's charge on finding he only hit a school employee, a layperson might think that courts are not seriously concerned about supporting school discipline (and that they might make such a double jeopardy ruling).

Incidentally, the question of pressing criminal charges against persons who assault school employees on their jobs deserves some comment. At this time, the Chicago schools frequently leave pressing such court actions up to teachers and other employees. In other words, if you're hit on the job, press your own case in court—we may not care enough. This policy probably encourages attacks. Some assailants undoubtedly are not punished due to their victims' lack of funds or time to pursue them, or because the victims fear to press the case on their own and risk further retaliation.

257. The assistant principal related his understanding of a recent incident, where a student was caught and accused of pulling thirty-one (false) fire alarms in the School in one year. He admitted the offenses. He was expelled. A month later, a court ruled that the School had to take the student back, since the expulsion process had not followed the proper formula (22, P, 9–12).

One cannot assume the assistant principal is correct about all the facts in the alarm case. However, he is working in an environment where courts, lawyers, and his superiors have frequently applied the law (or their legal interpretations) to frustrate efficient discipline. His story is either essentially correct, or he has good reason to believe (based on his general experience) that it may be true, and so he and his associates can treat it as true. Thirty-one false alarms have cost the students in the School a great deal of instructional time; perhaps some lawyer will someday sue the School because it has not efficiently applied itself in teaching its students how to read.

Discussion

One of the findings of the 1978 *Safe School Study* of the National Institute of Education can provide a useful backdrop for considering the preceding materials. As part of its data collecting, the study polled a representative national sample of school principals on their priorities regarding school discipline in 1975–1976. Specifically, the principals were asked how urgent were their in-school problems regarding vandalism, theft, and personal attacks. Eight percent of the respondents thought these issues were very or fairly serious, and another 17 percent rated these problems as moderate.

The remaining 75 percent of the respondents thought such issues were of little or not concern.[4]

It seems that many of these professionals do not generally see school discipline as an important issue. The implications of their opinions deserve comment.[5]

We must first recognize the limited nature of the question asked: it does not deal with student drug or alcohol use, cheating, cutting and unauthorized absences, inappropriate sexual affinity, or smoking. On the other hand, it is probably correct that the problems lised in the questionnaire represent the discipline issues most likely to engage principals. In other words, vandalism, assaults, and theft are the forms of misconduct which are most visible to teachers and parents. And principals, for better and worse, will tend to respond to student indiscipline which gets other adults excited.

After all, these other adults can sue, vote, or form pressure groups. And the fact is that, while there is a large body of generalized public dissatisfaction about student discipline, it is rarely focused on any particular school. This lack of focused dissatisfaction partly explains the relatively low priority principals give to discipline issues. The lack of focus is understandable. The indiscipline is relatively pervasive but often muted. It is true there are—as the text shown—some schools with fine levels of discipline. But there are not too many, and there are also some very bad ones. But the great majority are afflicted with a modest level of persisting disorder. Cheating. Drug use. Inappropriate sexual experimentation. Stealing. Cutting classes. But the level of this disorder is just not high enough to focus the collective attention of local parents and adults upon a definite "target." And so the parental frustration just floats off into space and principals give the issue low priority.

The "concealment" of this disorder from the public is partly a matter of coincidence. That is, very few adults who are not teachers have a clear idea of exactly what goes on in contemporary schools (especially high schools) each day. Even if they are parents, and receive reports from their children, they are not always told the truth, or—at best—their children conceal things, since they are not eager to be tale-bearers on themselves and their peers. And, as we can see, teachers often try to avert their own eyes, for a variety of reasons. And so the vision of the outsiders is obscured, unless the student violations are of an aggravated and conspicuous nature.

But the effects of coincidence in muting community complaints are heightened by a variety of school policies. These policies further conceal the in-school reality. For instance, if schools do not publish rules, parents aren't warned about potential forms of student misconduct. Or, if they are published, their provisions may ignore many potential violations (for example, cheating, drug use, sexual indiscretion) or they may not be distributed to students or parents. And, if they are thorough in their scope and distributed to parents (over the resistance and conspiracies of students), they may not be enforced. And, if they are enforced, parents may not be advised by the school of general patterns of violations—or of violations by their own children.

In some ways, these proconcealment policies are caused by—and also extend—the effects of the coincidence discussed above. The coincidence helps cause the policies, because the sudden stark revelation of the (previously concealed) in-school world to many parents might distress them and make them angry at the faculty (even if the faculty had not seriously erred). As a result, the administration makes special efforts to intensify concealment and isolation (since it is hard for the faculty to see how to "tear down" the complex institutional barriers between many schools and their communities).

Due to such factors, many parents do not have appropriate information to stimulate complaints or even thoughful questions about student discipline. Against this background, it is not surprising that many principals are not seriously worried about student discipline; the parents and taxpayers in their communities have other complaints on their agenda.

Of course, a discussion about discipline in schools must also touch on some of the broader American social currents affecting school policy on discipline. During the past fifteen years, the courts have generally tended to increase the rights of criminal defendants, to inhibit the application of more drastic (for example, the death penalty) punishments, and to apply psychological and sociological perspectives in assessing the guilt and punishment due particular defendants. One can have different opinions about the wisdom or justice of these tendencies; however, one cannot fairly dispute that there has been a judicial shift in this direction. At the risk of being oversimplistic, we might say the shift is in the direction of liberalization, focusing on the rights of defendants, or permissiveness.

Since we are a democracy, this judicial shift reflects to some degree a change in the opinions of members of some influential social classes. I do not mean that the shift is universally applauded, but simply that it is not only many judges who now think or act "differently" about punishment and criminality. Or, if one argues that opinions of certain general social classes have remained stable, then I would counter that the shift in judicial opinions, at least, represents a change regarding which social classes (and hence which ideas) have influence.

In any case, many of the discipline policies which modern schools apply—and which seem to handicap discipline enforcement—are congruent with the values shift that has occured in our courts and elsewhere in our society. In part, the schools are just following the shift. Some of this following is due to compulsion (for example, being constrained by restrictive judicial decisions). However, most of this following is due to the normal institutional tendency of schools to reflect the intellectual tone of our society. Of course, the shift and the resulting new tone do not articulate provisions such as "there should not be written school rules" (though there are popular books that say that, too). However, the tone of the shift implies that rules should be drawn with a precision and a persuasive logic that are likely to be beyond the intellectual capabilities of many harried administrators. Or the tone implies that student punishments must be surrounded with elaborate safeguards, and then administrators feel that if they violate such safeguards, they themselves are subject to Draconian punishments.

But the most important thing about the new tone, from the point of view of school discipline, is not its new perspective on the violator—*but its comparative disinterest in the victim!* Student drug dealers are selling drugs to other students. Student drug users are placing temptation before their peers and other students. Students who steal in school are depriving other students. Sexual attractions casually fostered in (and by) schools lead to illegitimate children being born to unprepared mothers. Teachers who become reluctant to enforce discipline (because they are not backed up) are then less able to help and protect law-abiding students. The fact is that, for every significant violator—for example, a fourteen-year-old high-school student whose locker can't be searched for a reputed gun without applying cumbersome safeguards—there are innumerable potential victims—students and faculty who will experience fear, uncertainty, and temptation. Under such circumstances, it is not surprising that increasing proportions of students find disorder attractive. They may receive more "understanding" from the enforcement system as rule breakers than they will as potential rule abiders.

Sensible arguments can always be made about the merits of particular punishments or rules. And some of these discussions can never be clearly settled. But part of this process of settlement—or determination—is deciding what basic presumptions apply.

For most of human history, regarding the discipline systems around children, the first presumption has been that innocent children should be protected from potential victimization and exploitation by others—even if the others were also children. In other words, the key test of a rule or punishment was: are we doing our best to protect the obviously innocent?

A second traditional presumption around child-oriented discipline has been that sporadic reprimands and other rebuffs visited on apparently disobedient children (even if the punishments occasionally are "unjustified") were part of the stuff of life, and they might even benefit the child, by preparing him for some of the inevitable rebuffs of adulthood. In other words, "perfect" justice around children—if it could ever be defined—was an unrealistic and perhaps Chimerical goal. But the current presumption seems to compel principals to endlessly debate the pros and cons of letting students wear T-shirts with marijuana slogans written on them, as compared to saying, "I don't like that shirt. Go home, and take it off, and serve two detentions." Yet, that very evening after the T-shirt episode, the same students may assert himself to attain the proper mode of "dress" to impress some girl—and, five years from now he may be desparately saving money to buy clothes appropriate for his job at selling. Can a student sue his girlfriend for not liking his clothes (and hence, not liking him), or can he sue the customers who refuse to take him seriously because he looks like a slob? When we say schools cannot regulate students' dress without justifying their position via a metaphysical essay, what kind of insulated life are we preparing the students for?

Another perspective on discipline that evolves from the preceding information can best be indicated by a form of line graph which would portray a curve of deterrence. The graph would be plotted from two coordinates. One coordinate would describe what we might call "Burdens" and would represent some statistical assessment of all the inhibitions placed on persons allocating or enforcing punishments. These burdens are obviously varied, and can be psychic (emotional tension) or involve loss of time (serving as a "jailor" or pursuing violators), actual physical injury, or economic liabilities. The burdens are going to be affected by the particular institution where the punisher works, the social climate of the era, and the emotional composition of individual punishers.

The other coordinate would be called "Fear and Injury." It represents the intensity of the actual or potential punishment in the eyes of students. The elements going into a statistical representation of this coordinate would include the unpleasantness of the punishment, the proportion of violations by students which are actually identified and punished, and the level of student knowledge about the proceeding factors. As in the case of the coordinate for "Burdens," the statistic derived for a particular student or school will be determined by many individual, institutional, and social variables.

The concept of the curve of deterrence, and the two coordinates which plot its course, can help us appreciate the many variables under lying the maintenance of an effective school discipline system. When deterrence is very high, we have low burdens on punishers, and violators are subjected to substantial fear and real injury. At some point, such an environment would constitute a despotism. When deterrence is very low, we have tremendous burdens on punishers, and violators are subjected to little fear or injury. Such an environment is brutal and disorderly. Of course, there are other likely of possible mixtures of burdens and fears. Presumably, the optimum mix would provide modest burdens of punishers and would subject students to real, but quite manageable, fears of justified punishments. If some researchers are interested, the preceding propositions might be quantified and tested in operating schools. Meanwhile, we can simply be conscious that placing many burdens on punishers is not a costless process; at some point, such a system of allocation simply stimulated the punishers to resign from their responsibilities as enforcers.

This general discussion about patterns of school discipline should not conclude without mentioning the profound effects of the general institutional patterns that have evolved in American education. I have critically mentioned some of these patterns earlier: economies of scale; teacher specialization; sending students to schools that are often distant (either geographically or emotionally) from their homes and parents; prolonged and compulsory attendance; the frequent grouping and regrouping of students; highly structured and often remote and fluid relationships among faculty; and the granting of raises and promotions to teachers and principals on criteria not related to a common-sense definition of performance. And, not too surprisingly, these patterns strongly reinforce the destructive effects of our current ideologies about punishment and rules.

The handicaps these patterns impose on school discipline are not insurmountable. In a number of the previous items about discipline, we can see exceptional people (or schools) who have maintained both orderly and humane environments. But an analysis of these orderly situations reveals that often these schools, and their leaders, have been assisted by intitutional elements that conflict with the patterns just listed. Some of the good-discipline schools have unusual staff stability. Or—even if they are public schools—they have been deliberately chosen by their pupils and their parents, and this act of choice (as compare to compulsion) has assisted their faculties in devising constructive policies. Or the shools are geographically—or emotionally—close to the childrens' homes. Or the community seems unusually stable. Or—and this is the final exception—the principal seems such a powerful and vital administrator that one is curious why he or she chose a career which began with spending five years with thirty children in a classroom (and, in essence, all public school principals are required to begin that way). This last matter of the career path of principals needs some expansion.

The fact is that the talents and style needed to be an effective principal in a large high shool are sharply different from those involved in classroom teaching. Such a principal needs to understand children and adolescents, but they also need to deal with a great deal of paper, write clearly, hold adults accountable, enjoy exercising authority, know how to delegate, and have facility at thinking in systemic—or broad-scale—terms. People with characteristics such as this probably don't often seek degrees in education, or want to become teachers. Thus the present system for hiring and promoting staff seems designed to keep away many potential principals who might improve school discipline.

In sum, the systemic patterns of modern schools frustrate the maintenance of good student discipline. The effects of these systemic flaws are immensely aggravated by the general ideologic climate (relating to order and discipline) which has evolved over the past ten to twenty years. And, finally, the lack of coherent information to parents about student indiscipline has left schools—and school policymakers—prone to respond to other more publicized and focused issues. As a result, in the last quarter of the twentieth century, the level of discipline in our schools may be at the lowest point in our history.

6 School Spirit

Take us singly, and what are we? The prey of all creatures, their victims, whose blood is most delectable and most easily secured. For, while other creatures possess a strength that is adequate for their self-protection, and those that are born to be wanderers and lead an isolated life have been given weapons, the covering of man is a frail skin; no might of claws or of teeth makes him a terror to others, naked and weak as he is, his safety lies in fellowship. Fellowship has given man dominion over all creatures;. . .it is this that has checked the assaults of disease, has made supports for old age, has provided solace for sorrow; it is this that makes us brave, this that we may invoke as a help against fortune. Take away this fellowship and you will sever the unity of the human race on which its very existence depends.[1]

The term "school spirit" is typically perceived as a topic of interest to some students, and to adults who have failed to grow up. However, it is more appropriate to treat it as a layman's way to describe the level of community in and around a school. The substitution of "community" for "school spirit" can have more than semantic implications.

Community is a word with substantial connotative and intellectual overtones. And, if we recognize that community is, for many purposes, synonymous with school spirit, we can be emboldened to dedicate attention to the analysis of school spirit.

School spirit is synonymous with community because most of the concepts associated with the analysis of the concept of community are applicable to the study of school spirit. Typically, communities are characterized as bounded environments whose inhabitants share common values, symbols, and ceremonies. And sometimes all the inhabitants work to attain collective goals. Thus, when we say that the students and faculty in a school have a high level of school spirit, we are saying they have a strong sense of community. They are more a group of "we's," compared to a collection of disparate "I's."

If one accepts the parallels between school spirit and community, one may still question the importance of school spirit as an educational issue. You might say, "Yes, most people, for much of their lives, do live in communities. But school is essentially a transitory environment. Why should it be desirable that school spirit be high, when students each day go home to their families, and when they will all move on to other—perhaps more communal—environments?"

157

Schools should have spirit, or be communities, partly because they are largely inhabited by the young. And, since the young are more emotionally vulnerable than adults, it is important that they spend much of their time in sharing and supportive environments; and such environments will naturally have the essential characteristics of communities. In-school community is also important because we are not born inherently possessing all the complex skills and attitudes needed to make communities work. We must learn how to live in, and help make, communities. And, if we do not learn these skills and attitudes when we are young, it will be harder for us to participate in adult communities when we are mature. But how can children or adolescents learn community-related conduct unless they participates in community life in their school?

To be concrete, let us identify a community-related skill: the ability to differ with someone, and to still care for and regard them, and to practice such care and regard. Children first learn and test this skill in their families, where interpersonal tension and frustration are inevitable. But in a vital family these difficulties are generally overridden, as family members ultimately mute individual differences in the interests of attaining mutual goals. Similarly, in schools with high levels of school spirit, interstudent and student-teacher conflicts are still normal; however, the disputants learn how to smooth things over, and resume more supportive relationships.

Community is especially important in schools due to the uniquely isolating nature of the environment of typical schools. I say uniquely isolating because the inhabitants of most schools—both students and faculty—are more emotionally isolated from each other than the inhabitants of many other environments, such as offices, factories, and families. This isolation is due to a variety of factors.

Faculty members are isolated partly because many of them work as individuals, in classrooms that are usually physically cut off from other faculty. Most workers and family members do not operate in such isolation. Furthermore, the day-to-day work efforts of teachers are often not highly coordinated with each other; thus, fourth-grade teachers, or math or English teachers in a high school, largely perceive themselves as working along with their students, as compared to working as part of an integrated team (as is common in work and home environments). I realize that coordination among teachers is important, but (1) such coordination often does not occur, and (2) when it does occur, it usually occurs at a less intense level than the coordination practiced in many other jobs. In sum, the level of isolation among faculty members is usually higher than that among adults in most other environments. Unless steps are taken to intensify community in a school, this isolation can have debilitating effects on school operations. After all, a lack of community can result in a decline in trust and security, and the heightening of anxiety and loneliness. Such effects are bad both for teachers and for their students.

Students are even more emotionally isolated from each other in typical school activities than faculty members. Of course, students spend most of their time sitting near one another, but physical proximity does not necessarily insure collective emotional cohesion. All of us can imagine traveling on a crowded subway train, being surrounded by other people, and still maintaining a profound emotional distance from those around us. The development of emotional sharing requires relative proximity, plus factors that stimulate shared interests and common identification. This sharing and community does not usually occur in subway trains. Often, it does not exist in schools.

It is true that many students have the same self-interest: to get good grades. But this self-interest is like the self-interest of most subway riders, to see that the train keeps going and to avoid embarrassing contacts with fellow passengers. And many students, like subway riders, discover that their self-interests are best advanced by keeping their attention on their work, and not becoming seriously concerned with those around them.

The characterization of studenthood just presented represents a model, or abstraction, of the process of being a student. Like most abstractions, it is subject to qualifications. For instance, most subway riders have run across exceptional coriders—deviants—who try to generate engagement with other riders, either through hostility, ignorance, or extraordinary good fellowship. Still, we all realize we can characterize typical subway riders patterns as stressing withdrawal. Similarly, in some schools, there are important variations in student conduct—and, unlike subway trains, some schools do have systems for stimulating engagement among their inhabitants (that is, they may have school spirit; there would almost never be a subway with "car spirit"). But, despite these exceptions, we can still identify certain general forces operating on students that stimulate isolation. And, incidentally, as we identify these forces, we can see how schools are (or can be) managed as to fight these influences and raise the level of community.

Probably the most important anticommunity force affecting students is the pressure of the grading systems typically applied in efficient American schools; in other words, effective grading systems stimulate students to do their best, and not be too concerned with the performance of those around them (just like subway riders). Indeed, it is "inefficient" for students to put time in helping others, unless such others are nearly at their level of performance, and they're then engaged in a form of cooperative studying.[2] Otherwise, helping others just serves to (1) make less study time available for the helper, and (2) raise the performance of the student helped, and thus tends to heighten curve-based grading competition. We may criticize these effects of grades. But we should realize that grades themselves simply reflect a more basic human condition: human learning abilities are innately unequal, and any institution aimed at stimulating such abilities must partially aggravate and intensify such inequalities. Conversely, the schools where grades and learning are not important can be schools where differences in academic ability are not divisive. But such schools are also places where learning is low.

Due to these complex factors, there is a dichotomous challenge facing educators. They have to maintain an adequate level of individual grading pressure, so cognitive learning occurs and excellence is stimulated, and must simultaneously support a vital level of school spirit. As we will see, the tactics followed in stimulating school spirit are varied, and the level of success is also mixed.

One of the first means applied to cultivate school community is to identify and heighten the physical boundaries of the school community. This process helps delineate community members (those who belong within the boundaries) from nonmembers (those outside of the boundaries). After such delineation, the members, during the time they are in the boundaries, can assume that all the others around them are also community members. The assumptions permit a level of easy acceptance to prevail. Schools vary in their ability to develop such impermeable boundaries.

Maintaining Physical Boundaries for the School Community

258.   One entrance door remains unlocked during the whole school day. There are no hall guards, door monitors, or officials posted to challenge any visitor's entry. This might be an understandable situation in the heart of a quiet suburban community. However, it poses many problems in a ghetto setting. It is entirely feasible for a person to walk throughout the School without having to pass by the School's office, where there is a secretary seated at a desk outside the door. For this reason, all of the teachers keep their class doors locked throughout the day. The extraordinary permeability was a potential threat rather than an asset (2, P, K–8).

This item reveals an aggravated, but real, effect of too permeable boundaries. Because of the appropriate fears of the teachers and students of attack by nonmembers of the community (within their "own" school), each class has locked itself away from the others. Inevitably, this sealing off handicaps interclass communication among students or teachers. Thus the level of school spirit is lowered, since communication is a condition to emotional sharing.

259.   The doors of the School are supposedly locked after 11:00 A.M., except for the main entrance, where there is a hall monitor. However, students told us that they can easily get in some of the doors, and they know

which ones are the "safest" to leave from and enter during hours when school is in session (36, P, 9–12).

260. A teacher's suggestion as how a principal could heighten school security: "The principal must first make certain that the safety needs of his school are adequately met. Equally important, these needs must be perceived by all factions in the school as important, if the school is to then operate effectively. This recognition can be achieved by setting up a committee charged with safety to be composed of representatives from the faculty, student body, parents, custodial staff, and community residents. This group would determine the security needs of their school, and then examine ways to meet these needs. For example, how many school doors will be kept unlocked, and is there a need for a guard at those doors, and who shall these guards be? Once this committee has acted and their actions have been publicized, the level of anxiety within the school schould decrease" (3, P, K–8).

The quality of security measures in the schools studied varied widely. Sometimes they were lax, in communities where the effects of inefficiency were not too important, and sometimes they were poor in very harmful situations. Very few schools applied the thoughtful procedures suggested in the preceding item.

One purpose of delineating school boundaries is to establish a distinction between the school and the extraschool environment. Such patterns of distinction can be used to achieve educational purposes, as the following item shows.

261. The inside of the School has many lively murals done by the children. There are murals in the entrance lobby, and in the cafeteria, the teachers' room, the main office, and on the second and third floors. On Halloween there were decorations in all the halls, as well as in the classrooms. After being inside the School for ten minutes, one forgets what is outside—a disorderly and fear-ridden environment. This effect was consciously planned by the principal. The idea was to make the School a learning sanctuary, where the problems and distractions of the surrounding community would not penetrate (18, P, 7–8).

Sometimes the immediate environment around the school can be supportive and reassuring, and then there is less need to maintain boundaries around the school. The following description portrays such a situation:

262. Although this neighborhood is in the city, there exists an intimate feeling around the School. There is a sense of small-townness or community. Everything is within walking distance in the area, including a small grocery, an Italian bakery, several Italian restaurants, a hardware store, a laundromat, a barber shop, and a funeral home, among others. Most of the parents live close to the School (49, R, K–8).

Incidentally, there is a high level of parental support for the School. And so its community encompasses not only students and teachers, but also their families.

Student Dress

Communities are defined by a variety of boundaries; the boundaries are not only physical and immovable, like walls and doors, but also visible and mobile, such as people who are members of an athletic team and who demonstrate their commonality by wearing uniforms. Thus various patterns of dress help define school community membership. And, as the next item about a ghetto school shows, they can also be used by students to declare that they are not, in any vital sense, students, but. . . .

263.   Many of the male students try to dress like the neighborhood pimps and playboys. These students wear dress suits to school, and many have their hair processed. Many of the students also wear large mod-styled sunglasses while they are in the School. The female students wear high-fashion dresses, high heels, and large-brimmed hats to school. Apparently they are trying to mimic the dress of the prostitutes they may pass on the way to school (15, P, 9–12).

264.   The following item presents the dress code provision issued by the School in the previous item, where many students try and dress like pimps and prostitutes:

CLOTHING

Students are expected to show respect for themselves and to the School's student body, faculty, and staff members by dressing in fashions that are appropriate and comfortable for school wear. Young men are expected to remove hats and scarves as they enter the building. The Board of Education passed this regulation, and everyone must follow this regulation. Those who fail to respond will have their hats and scarves taken by teachers, security officers, and administrators. The property may be picked up by parents. (15, P, 9–12)

The language is ambiguous, preachy, and tentative. The rule, insofar as it is capable of being defined, is not usually enforced; male students routinely continue to wear hats. Also, since the rule contains no penalty except the threat to confiscate hats and scarves, it is not clear what would happen if a teacher decided that a student who came in dressed like a pimp or prostitute should be vigorously corrected. And this lack of clarity of penalty must inevitably deter teacher action.

I understand that some school administrators may excuse such lax policies on referring to court decisions about students rights. But my earlier criticisms of such excuses still apply. I doubt that any higher court, in an appropriately argued case, would uphold the rights of students to dress like pimps or prostitutes in school. But clearly raising such issues takes imagination and vigor. Now, it is true that courts bear some responsibility for this distressing situation; their "support" for the authority of school administrators has been highly qualified, and this restraint has had its foreseeable effect. Still, both administrators and the courts share responsibility for the current situation.

Incidentally, we should not ignore the connection between dress codes and simple school physical security. If a school adopts and maintains a dress code that seriously constrains student dress, it becomes comparatively easy to identify nonstudents wandering through the school; the intruders will usually not be dressed like students (but, perhaps, like pimps or prostitutes). Of course, it may be technically possible for intruders to buy and wear the prescribed student dress. However, the practical fact is that most intrusions are relatively spontaneous, and thus the intruders are unlikely to choose to buy student clothes so they can wander around in school. But, as school dress codes have declined in vitality, it has become important to have other immediate means of sorting students from intruders, so we have moved on to student ID cards, which often have to be worn. This substitute serves some useful purposes, but has far less associative power than some common mode of dress.

The following two items are excerpted from school rules. They show there are differences in the amount of determination public schools dedicate to dress code enforcement.

DRESS
265. We take pride in the appearance of our students. Your dress reflects the quality of the school, of your conduct and of your school work.

All students are expected to dress and groom themselves neatly in clothes that are suitable for school activities. (14, P, 9–12)

DRESS
266. There appears to be a definite relationship between good dress habits, good work habits, and proper school behavior. Any type of attire which attracts undue attention to the wearer, and thus causes a disturbance in the school, is in bad taste and not acceptable. However certain hairdos and clothing should not be worn in shops because of safety hazards. (16, P, 9–12)

The school that provided the second of these two items enforces, in practice, a much more restrictive dress code than the first school. Perhaps 50 percent of the public schools studied had rule patterns which significantly inhibited student dress habits.

As the following item shows, some private schools (both elementary and secondary) go beyond restricting student dress, and prescribe uniforms to be worn by students.

267. Juniors and seniors wear brown blazers, cream-colored blouses, brown plaid uniform skirts, solid dark brown knee socks, and uniform shoes of the Hush Puppies or Earth Shoe style. Sophomores and freshmen wear green blazers, mint green blouses, green plaid skirt uniforms, solid dark green socks, and uniform shoes which can have a heel no more than two inches high and must be of soft soles. One demerit point will be given for each article out of uniform, and the student must visibly wear an out-of-uniform excuse slip pinned to her uniform (56, R, 9–12).

One should note that not only are uniforms prescribed, but that the uniforms make distinctions between students enrolled in upper and lower classes. The concept of such distinctions was mentioned earlier (see Item 143) as one means of stimulating student interest in advancement through school. Later in this chapter, we will generally consider systems of intra-school student grouping, as a device for creating wholesome (or harmful) subcommunities. Obviously, different dress requirements between or among student groups or classes can help advance this end.

The uniform requirements in the School are relatively precise, even among church-related schools. (About 30 percent of such schools have uniform requirements, and another 50 percent have relatively strict dress codes.) In general, the schools that have uniform requirements tend to have high levels of school spirit.

Another effect of uniforms is that they permit adults in the neighborhood to easily identify students (by their school) going to and from school. This process of identification simplifies adult control. If School X has a uniform requirement, and its students engage in vandalism on the way to school, a complaint can be made to the School, and some action taken. Likewise, if students of School X conduct themselves responsibly while coming and going to school, complimentary remarks can be transmitted back to the school. And students can begin to think of their school as a place that they identify with, and should (therefore) care about.

While the idea of uniform requirements may seem abnormal to Americans, we should realize that most of the other public school systems in the world, including those in the Western democracies, usually have affirmative dress requirements for students. It is also interesting to realize that one of the recent annual Gallup polls on public attitudes on education revealed that the majority of adults questioned favored schools that had dress codes for students.[3] Presumably the adults were partly recognizing a fact of adult work life; most adults work at jobs where their dress is constrained by the nature of their work and the demands of their superiors or customers, for example, salesmen, doctors, plumbers, politicians. Children and adolescents may be the only group in the society who are supposed to be doing something public and significant and who are often exempted from dress requirements. Perhaps we have doubts about the significance of their activities.

Symbols of the School Community

Sometimes, various objects take on emotional or symbolic value in the eyes of the members of the school community. Such symbolic weight is typically the outcome of some combination of coincidence and deliberate decisions. When vital symbols exist, or are cultivated, they can enrich the sense of sharing among students and faculty. In some cases the school building itself can be an effective symbol.

268. The main school building is 108 years old. It is very imposing. A double set of huge steps leads up to the heavy, twenty-foot-tall wooden doors. Once inside, visitors check with a friendly elderly receptionist, not a guard. If one looks up, one sees that the ceilings in the halls and rooms are the same height as the outer doors (60, R, 9–12).

269. The name of the School is a combination of the names of the two communities it serves. There is a School seal which symbolically spells out the name of these two communities. For example, there are trees drawn on the seal to symbolize a forest. The School motto, written in Greek, is written across the middle of the seal. The seal appears on all correspondence, stationary, handbooks, and so on of the School. It was designed in 1908 by a teacher of the School, and has been used ever since. This can be regarded as an excellent link between the past heritage of the School and its new community members. The seal is displayed on a wall in the School's student center, which is on the main floor and is the first area that one walks into when entering the School through the main entrance (36, P, 9–12).

270. The symbols and practices evident in this Catholic school articulate the ties among students and teachers (who are Catholics), and between the school community and the students families. The awards given to students for success in activities (spelling bees, for example) are small luminous religious statues. Small Catholic medals are also given as prizes for academic achievement and good citizenship. There is a crucifix in every classroom and a large statue of St. Mary outside of the principal's office. Prayers are said twice daily (49, R, K–8).

When we say that particular objects or words have a symbolic value, we are saying that they communicate certain things to persons who understand the applicable symbolic code. For instance, a school seal doesn't mean much unless the observer knows something about the school involved, and religious medals acquire greater significance when one understands the traditions and beliefs involved.

One of the important things symbols communicate is information about relationships; and they transmit this information to members of the community that revere the symbol. The varieties of relationships portrayed by symbols are infinite. For instance, in the case of the preceding three items, the symbols all "tell" community members how they should regard the school's past—and future. The past is presented as determined, far-sighted, respectful of its own past, and committed to building for the future: and that is why they constructed large buildings, designed elaborate seals, used Greek inscriptions, and maintained a historic religion. Implicitly, if the members of the contemporary school community want to be respected and revered by the future, they must mimic the conduct of their predecessors. And thus the symbols described "tell" students and faculty about their shared relationships with their past and future. If this message is accepted by members of the school, then they hold important common values. They become more of a community. In effect, the relationships portrayed by powerful symbols increase the sense of community among students and faculty.

The ways in which a school uses symbols to "create" a tradition are largely the product of human determination. In other words, we always have tradition-building materials around us. We must be wise enough to seek and use them.

I recall a graduate student (and teacher) telling me about his public school, a new building in a ghetto community. It was named after the first black astronaut. Obviously, the persons who chose the name had a motive in mind. My student said none of the School's students knew who its namesake was. The School did have a picture of him hanging near the principal's office, but there was no legend near the picture—so the picture was meaningless to students. My student and I developed grand plans for a school rededication, with a black poet writing a poem or text to be mounted near the picture and perhaps an annual ceremony memorializing the School's namesake—and suggesting to the students what was possible for them. I do not know the outcome of our well-intentioned plans.

Another teacher-student told me that his public school was named after a late nineteenth century industrialist who had donated the school site to the public. He jokingly (cynically?) remarked that the teachers thought the donor probably had a guilty conscience. I asked my student if he had any evidence of this point. Did he know if the donor had, in fact, done anything wrong? He said, "Of course not!" I wondered whether it wouldn't be better to take the donation at its face value—the donor loved children and wanted to help them learn. If one operates on this level, the students might feel that their school exists because people cared about them before they were born, and other people are capable of doing the same thing now.

271.   The School prominently displays its link with the past. Pictures of all its past presidents and principals, from 1870 to the present, and of all its graduating classes, from 1922 forward, hang in its halls (60, R, 9–12).

These symbols say to the administrators and students that (1) there is a past that helped create you and surmounted challenges such as you face, and (2) you should conduct yourself so you may similarly help to form and inspire a future. Very few schools spend money and wall space on creating and displaying such momentos.

272. The School is one of several Chicago area schools named after Carl Sandburg, a prominent Illinois citizen and poet. Sandburg was alive when he was designated, and the school superintendent wrote him, asking his consent. His handwritten reply was sent on the stationary of the Southern Railway Company. He said, "Both proudly and humbly consent to your naming school as undersigned. With profound regard, Carl Sandburg." The letter, with a lithograph of Sandburg, is displayed on the wall in the principal's office. The office is comparatively inaccessible to students and most faculty. (No school reference needed.)

273. Last year there was a dedication ceremony when a mosaic portrait of the School's namesake was completed and mounted in a main hall. The library also has a glass display case where mementoes, photographs, and books about his activities are displayed (14, P, 9–12).

274. The School's symbol is a picture of a muscular discus thrower. He is termed the "Mighty Man." The symbol is reiterated throughout the School—on a sign out front and on the folders (with school rules and other information) distributed to students (16, P, 9–12).

275. There is an eight-foot-high statue erected in a small public square across from the School. The statue symbolizes the Iron Man, whose determination will enable him to remake the ghetto, and contribute to the reinvigoration of society. The theme of the Iron Man is reiterated in many of the activities for adults sponsored by local community agencies. Even in the preschool run by the community, the children have a song—or chant—about the Iron Man and his significance. The two-year-olds in the School enjoy singing the song, though they know the rhythm and not the words (69, S, K).

The analysis of symbols in schools gradually moves into a consideration of words which interpret and intensify the effect of the symbols. And, also, the analysis must consider ceremonies which honor and further explain the symbols.

276. The School has a song that was written especially for it, both the music and lyrics. This group was unable to obtain a copy of this song. None of the students who were asked knew the words of the song. Two freshmen students who were asked about the song said, "You have to learn it when you're a freshman and after that everyone forgets the words." It is only sung during commencement. For this ceremony the students must be given copies of the words (60, R, 9–12).

277. The School has two songs, one sung by all students in assembly, and one sung only by seniors. The School has a schoolwide assembly each week. All students know the School song, and the seniors know "their" song. A student said, "At one time, the School song was going to be revised and brought 'up to date,' which might make sense. But we couldn't change it because it was a tradition, and part of the School" (56, R, 9–12).

In about 50 percent of the schools studied, 50 percent of the students or more knew the school song. This knowledge is a proxy measure of various elements of school spirit such as the frequency with which students are brought together (in assemblies) to assert common values and the energy the administration devotes to building school spirit. I recall a conversation with one school principal who told me that, when he first came to his school, no one in the assembly stood up when the school song was sung. He told the faculty that he wanted all of them to stand at the singing; in a couple of years, the whole audience was standing.

278.   Students receiving athletic awards must attend the appropriate school award dinner. An unexcused absence can jeopardize their award (39, P, 9–12).

A subtle line needs to be drawn between compulsion and persuasion in fostering respect for symbols and ceremonies. A viable community must have symbols and ceremonies that are widely respected, and that are ultimately protected from desecration (the term desecration is rooted in desacralization). And such protection must sometimes mean that potential desecrators fear significant punishments. But the protecting system must rest on a judicious mix of affection and fear. Excessive reliance on fear implies that the vitality of the symbols and ceremonies is weak (and, conversely, an inability to ever punish desecrators can also be a sign of weakness). The pressure on athletes described in the preceding item is relatively subtle. The adolescents involved are "told" that if they want to display their bravado by not showing up at the award ceremony (where their presence not only honors themselves, but also the other attendees), they can do without their award. This pressure represents only one of the many potential forms of compulsion that schools may and do apply. The story following the previous item—about the teachers standing in the assembly—represents another example of such pressure in operation. Exactly when, if, and how pressure should be applied by schools to support symbols and ceremonies can never be simply prescribed. But, from my contacts with educators, it seems that too many of them philosophically question the propriety of such pressure in the first place.

279.   Rings are worn by the juniors after they receive them, and by the most of the seniors. Some alumni still wear their rings to show pride in the School. Rings are either silver, gold, or white gold, depending on the girls' choice and the price (which goes higher accordingly). Girls aren't forced to buy a ring, but everyone does. There is a blue stone in the middle because it is the School's color, with the class year on one side and whatever words the class decides upon on the other (56, R, 9–12).

280.   School rings are purchased by 99 percent of the junior class and are given out by the principal at a special ring ceremony. A rose is given each girl when she receives her ring. Parents are invited to attend, and the faculty and student body are present. A ring dance is also held that evening for the juniors and their dates (59, R, 9–12).

281.   The principal organizes an annual luncheon for parents of the high achievers and their children. A Chicago celebrity is invited to speak. The School attempts to have a prominent figure from the black community, to instill pride and aspirations in the students. Aspirations and careers are emphasized heavily at the School. In the classrooms we saw pictures of famous black scientists, politicians, athletes, inventors, and so on. February is going to be Black Awareness Month, and each month has an achievement theme that is followed up in the classroom and at assemblies (18, P, 8–9).

282.   Many of the students are proud to wear the badges and pins they have received from School. A lot of them said that their pins were for attendance. The saying was "In School On Time Everyday (IOE Club). A few of the children were also wearing pins for academic performance. There is one for good academic performance for all four marking periods, and a different one for making the honor roll three out of four marking periods. The pins and badges are made by the teachers themselves. So many are given out that it is just too costly to have them professionally made (18, P, 8–9).

We can recognize from the preceding items how wise administrators have woven symbolism and ceremony so as to assist the aims of their schools. For instance, receiving an attractive ring, as a junior, in a ceremony or accompanied by a dance, is naturally gratifying. As a result, it provides lower-level students with an achievement to "shoot for" and attain before achieving seniorhood. Thus it enriches their progression through school. And, in the instance of the black school, we can see how the principal uses various occasions as vehicles for ceremonies and symbolism to intensify student pursuit of desirable goals. Finally, we can sense that symbols and ceremonies, because they are often inclusive—*all* juniors receive rings—create a form of countervailing cohesion in an environment that often can be segmented and disjointed.

283.   At least 50 percent of the students buy and wear jackets prominently displaying the School's symbol. Many of them also carry their books in books bags bearing the same symbol (60, R, 9–12).

There were symbols prominently associated with perhaps 50 percent of the schools studied. Of course, the prominence of such symbols is partly a matter of administrative determination. A student of mine told me that students in the high school studied would not wear their school jackets in or around the School, but would wear them when they got back to their home neighborhoods. Evidently, such jackets had become low status symbols in the School; I suspect there are measures an imaginative administration could take to correct this, since the basic fact is that students want to show off their school.

Cohesion between Students and Faculty

284. Most students felt that only about one-third of the faculty evinced any interest in after-school activities or students' personal welfare. One student did recall that a teacher telephoned her when she was absent for two weeks, and inquired about her health. Others said they had no personal contact with their classroom teachers. Coaches and club moderators were regarded in a more familiar light (39, P, 9–12).

285. The School decided to change the nature of its student advising program. Instead of allocating students to counselors, it now requires each teacher to act as advisor to a small number of students—about thirteen per teacher. Inevitably, the teachers will not be as informed about the details of advisement as were the traditional counselors (who were full-time specialists). Therefore the School has prepared a thorough outline of the formal advisement process, stating the typical problems and aims of each year's advisement, as a student progresses through school. This written plan has been disseminated to students, parents, and faculty. A few counselors are still used, but only for special situations. The aim of the plan is to create more intense relationships among students and faculty (38, P, 9–12).

A small number of schools follow procedures of this sort. Up until about twenty years ago, such procedures were much more common in high schools. The older procedure began to change when federal funds were made available to encourage specialized guidance services; it was assumed that such services would provide students with more informed help than they received from a teacher-generalist. As a result of the encouragement, most schools shifted advising and counseling responsibilities from teachers to their enlarging counseling departments.

Obviously, not all educators believe the shift was a sound idea. The current typical situation in schools is that several hundred students are assigned to a counselor, who may be well qualified but who can only "know" a small fraction of his or her charges. Furthermore, many teachers feel disengaged from their students, since they are in effect told to leave their students' personal problems to the counselors. Thus the teachers, the adults with whom the students spend most of their in-school time, often become indifferent to the personal and emotional life of their students. And the counselors, who are supposed to worry about such things, never have the time.

Perhaps one assumption underlying the current counseling process is that only a small fraction of students should require professional attention. To a certain degree, this is correct—if, by professional attention, we mean psychotherapeutic help. But it is wrong to assume that most students do not need—or want—significant, day-to-day engagement with out-of-the-family adults. We must remember that the adolescents in our schools are undoubt-edly forming opinions (and feelings) about their careers, the relationships with members of the other sex, how to tie together school and work, what's going on in their parents' marriage (or divorce), and so on. It is obviously healthy for adolescents considering such matters to be encouraged to talk them over with responsible nonfamily adults. And those adults don't neces-sarily need academic certifications in "how to talk to young people."

286. The principal does not believe that assemblies in and of them-selves have any great community-building value. In fact, he said that "stu-dents at the secondary level can see right through attempts to bring them together in such a corny way and usually balk, thus destroying what you were trying to accomplish" (35, P, 9–12).

287. My reporter concluded that "I would say that about half of the student body identifies only with themselves, and not the problems of this innovative school. The other half of the students actively participate in school life." Rita, a junior, said, "It's the same people all the time who volunteer to help out in raising money, or putting on a show. The other kids just don't pitch in, because they know that the same ones are gonna do the work. They have a bad attitude about free schools, because they expect someone to tell them what to do all the time, and no one does! It's too hard for them to deal with responsibility! They can't handle it! There's no pres-sure here. The kids who don't volunteer are the ones who complain about the School" (57, R, 9–12).

As we can see, some educators attribute student and faculty indiffer-ence to school spirit to the nature of the times, or the attitudes of modern youth. Other, more perceptive administrators recognize that an important variable in determining school spirit is the policies of the school. Indeed, if there is any predisposition regarding school spirit in human beings, their tendency is probably to pursue and value factors that provide community. And so, when faculty or students display low interest in school spirit, we should probably assume that there are school policies which actively frus-trate the attainment of such spirit. To be concrete, take a "mundane" topic like school assemblies. No matter how much students and faculty may want assemblies, only administrators can bring them about. Administrators establish class schedules, allocate meeting space, design buildings, and pro-vide incentives and disincentives for attendance.

288. Another area of expression of cohesion are assemblies. On the average there are four to five large assemblies held at the School each year, and numerous smaller ones held by different clubs. The assemblies usually last one class period (forty minutes). Due to the large number of students, there is only one all-school assembly on Memorial Day each year. The other large assemblies are attended by all the School, but the students go in different shifts.

The Memorial Day assembly is held in the football stadium. It is a tradition of this school that goes back many years. Parents are notified about this assembly and invited to attend. There are war veterans who present the colors of the flag and then various speakers. It is generally well received by all (36, P, 9–12).

Incidentally, the Memorial Day ceremony portrays relationships: among students, faculty, veterans, and American war dead. And, really, our "relationships" with the dead are very important. How do we feel about the people who preceded us in our school, city, family, or country? We can feel affection, indifference, or even scorn. Our feelings toward the past, and the people who lived in the past, are a prototype of how we imagine future generations will regard us. And, if we do not know how to (hopefully) win the regard of the future, or if we feel sure they will despise us, then it is harder for us to coherently manage our contemporary lives. Such a lack of certitude makes the school community unstable and diffuse. In sum, ceremonies and symbols honoring the attainments of the past show us (1) the kind of conduct that will attain remembrance (for example, being an astronaut, a soldier, a social reformer, a businessman who contributes land for a school) and (2) that appropriate conduct will be remembered. The ceremonies and symbols thus shape the conduct and feelings of the inhabitants of a school.

289.   Students complained that they had little opportunity to attend performances by fellow students. Only once each year were they allowed to purchase tickets for a band concert, although the music department sponsors a concert band, an orchestra, a string quartet, a jazz band, a chorale, and a concert choir. The only schoolwide assemblies are three pep assemblies and an annual appearance by the Navy Band (3, P, K–8).

290.   Club moderators pointed out that the prime obstacle to student performance is the lack of a theater. All of the high schools in the district have cafetoriums, a combined lunchroom and auditorium. A recent program sponsored by the French Department had to be scheduled for 8:15 A.M.; attendance had to be limited to certain French and history classes. A conflict with the lunch periods had to be avoided. Using the gym would require rescheduling or canceling gym classes, and 2,651 students must eat lunch in four shifts in a cafetorium that seats between 500 and 600 students.

Moderators must schedule programs one year in advance to obtain an evening date in the cafetorium; sometimes they are forced to use facilities in nearby elementary schools. The gym has no stage and therefore is inappropriate for some programs (39, P, 9–12).

One selling point for our modern large high schools was the economies of scale they permit. However, an auditorium that can hold all the students in a large school may be a very expensive investment. But, if the school cannot afford such an auditorium, it may have to accept some costs for the resulting lack of "wholesomeness" in their school.

Later in this chapter I will discuss the creation of subschools or other intraschool communities as a means of assisting school spirit. If techniques of this type are applied, smaller auditoriums may serve for many spirit-related purposes.

291. Suggestions from a teacher being interviewed: "To insure a good emotional environment within his school, the principal must work diligently to develop and to maintain a strong sense of community. How? There should be lots of faculty get-togethers: formal faculty meetings, grade-level meetings, department meetings, meetings of those with a particular problem, seasonal social activities both within and without the school building. There should be lots of meetings for students: assemblies for entertainment, assemblies to honor outstanding students, pep rallies, and school parties" (3, P, K-8).

292. If a student is not doing well in the School, he or she receives as much extra help as needed to improve. Two teachers spend one hour daily after school helping students. Seven students from the fifth grade, eight from the sixth, four from the seventh, and two from the eighth (9 percent of the school population) are receiving such extra help. The principal said, "Teachers are requested to remain after school if some of their students need extra help. Of course lay teachers have some other duties, and it is difficult for them to dedicate extra hours. However, every now and then they are willing to provide extra help to their students. There is a sense of pride in the School, and none of the teachers wants to have students who do not learn." The students usually appreciate such dedication (49, R, K-8).

293. The commitment of teachers at the School can be measured by their willingness to do more than is required of them. Most of the teachers—approximately 94 percent—are sponsors of service clubs and organizations, or other extracurricular activities, such as serving on committees for in-service days (58, R, 9-12).

One of my graduate students (who was a teacher) interviewed a principal and teacher in a church-related school two blocks from her own ghetto school. Neither of the interviewees was clergy. She was surprised to discover them routinely working in their school at about 4:30 on a weekday. Both the principal and the teacher had formerly worked in public schools, and were now working for less salary than before. They told my student they had taken their current jobs (with more work for less pay) because of the gratification they received from being in a small, vital, essentially independent school, where they could expect support from administration, parents and their colleagues.

294. Among the important ceremonies celebrated during the year in this church-related school are Mardi Gras and the May Crowning.

For the Mardi Gras, members of each homeroom select one student as their candidate for the Mardi Gras Queen. The homeroom which raises the most money for the missions has its candidate designated queen. (Usually the winner comes from a senior homeroom.) The homerooms raise their missions money through a variety of sales and other activities.

The queen is crowned on Ash Wednesday, in the early Spring. She has a "court" made up of members from each class level. She leads a procession through the School to the hall, where each class has set up a booth for a bazaar. Students also bring along small children to enjoy the festivities. There is usually a dress theme to the occasion, and the best costumes receive prizes. The festivities conclude with a film and a dance.

May Crowning is held on a Wednesday in May. The seniors, in caps and gowns, lead a procession, and one senior is designated to crown the large statue of the Blessed Virgin in the convent garden beside the School. At the crowning, officers from various student divisions present flowers to the statue, and songs are sung and speeches made in honor of the Virgin.

The School also has a studentwide assembly every Wednesday, and each morning the president of the student council leads the School in prayer over the School public address system. In the prayer, each student offers to God "my prayers, works, joys and sufferings of this day" (56, R, 9–12).

Again, we see that ceremonies and symbols are about relationships: between the School and people in foreign countries (that is, the "missions"); between the School and the shared religious beliefs of the students and faculty; and among the various subgroups in the School (that is, each homeroom, and the seniors and the rest of the students). The relationships are portrayed as largely supportive, but also demanding, and sometimes competitive.

I should mention that, among the pool of reports by my students, are two which portray schools with many of the characteristics presented in the preceding item. For various reasons, it was not appropriate to include these reports in the book. Both of these schools were Hebrew day schools, that is, schools for Jewish students, which ran for the typical school day, 9:00 to 3:00, and where traditional Orthodox Jewish observances were followed.

295.   The student who prepared the report containing the preceding item was a former student at the School. She concluded her complete report with the following pertinent comment: "The School is warm and supportive, and has a personal, friendly atmosphere. I would like my children to attend such a school. However, there is one drawback to the School: if a student wishes to continue her education through college, they have to make a huge adjustment to the impersonal, numbing environments found in many universities" (56, R, 9–12).

I have heard educators contend that schools should be bureaucratic and unsupportive, since that is the way the adult world (or college) is. The student's comment directly relates to this issue. Putting it bluntly, one might ask: in general, do supportive schools make students better—or less adequately—prepared for adult life or for the pressures of college?

Before answering, we should realize that there is a great deal of competition in the School. The students aren't just sitting around giving and receiving love, but are engaged in many demanding activities (in item 307, we'll see how the School won a school spirit prize through extraordinary application). But it is significant that these activities involved collective efforts, as well as individual ones. And so students worked hard, but felt they were not alone.

Perhaps 20 percent of the students in my own undergraduate classes came from schools that tend to have some of these supportive characteristics. My impression is that, while they are dissatisfied with the impersonality of my university, they are purposeful and essentially quite secure, and they learn to get on with things. In particular, they relate to college faculty in a comfortable and nondefensive manner. On the whole they adjust much better than the students from comparatively chaotic and bureaucratic schools, who often lack the emotional resiliance to deal with the impersonality of a large institution. In other words, some foundation of stability may be necessary for us to learn to deal with disorder.

296. The community supporting the School holds collective "feasts" on many holidays. The feasts are partly designed as community-building devices. There are about eight such occasions a year. Elaborate meals are prepared, and various entertainments performed. The preschoolers play a large part in these celebrations: they help make decorations, prepare some of the food, and put on a program of songs and other actitivies (69, S, K).

297. We now shift to another aspect of cohesion: "Every morning, all the classes, in their rooms, sing the 'Star Spangled Banner' and 'My Country 'Tis of Thee,' and recite the Pledge of Allegiance to the American flag" (2, P, K–8).

I do not have sufficient information to estimate the frequency of this practice in the schools studied, though I understand that it is required by many school boards (I do not mean to imply that, because it is "required," it is always carried out). The ceremony described, and the symbol involved—the flag—articulate the relationship between the School (and its inhabitants) and American society. The words and gestures portray this relationship as constructive, persisting, and noble. The aim of the ceremony is to communicate to the students that their fellow citizens care about them; that their country has persisted and will persist; and that the goals of the country were, are, and should be admirable.

Since students are young people growing up in America, it is inevitable that they wonder about their relationship to "their country"—just as they might wonder about their relationship with their career, their religion, or with their ethnic group. The ceremony just described is a means of answering this implicit question. Furthermore, since the ceremony is collective, it also informs them that "everyone else" in the school feels that way, too.

We all understand that not everyone in our country is proud of America, or wants children to love it essentially as it is or to admire its past. And so there are naturally mixed responses among adults to the concept of this starting ceremony. This is not the place to air or settle these complex disputes. But criticism of the ceremony (and what it communicates) must recognize that children do need to be told something about their country; they especially need to be told how to value it. This need is especially significant in a large, ethnically heterogeneous nation like America, with its comparatively brief historical existence (for instance, most European countries, by many definitions, are about 1,500 years old). If we decide not to vigorously encourage Pledge of Allegience ceremonies in our schools, we should then direct ourselves to determining what will take their place, and what the new activities will teach. If the activities do not affirmatively teach students to love their country, then what should they love, and how should they feel about America? Finally, if we practice a little historical wisdom, we will realize that values are more often taught by persisting and powerful ceremonies than by books and lectures. If we do not ask students to salute the flag about 1,000 times during eight school years, what other vital collective system of teaching about our country will we use? What will be taught? And what effects should such teachings have?

Writings That Foster School Spirit

Press releases, school newspapers, and other documents can be important in assisting school spirit—or they can be neglected opportunities.

298.   The principal said that the information about the money raised for the Forgotten Children's Fund by the School's students was reported to the local newspapers, but the story only received three lines. It seems the school district has been receiving mostly bad press these days. The district employed a public-relations person in the past, but the position was eliminated with budget cuts. The principal now relies on department chairs to report news to the local papers, but "some people find it difficult to write a news story." Students interviewed said they themselves contacted the local newspapers about club activities but had some difficulty getting coverage (39, P, 9–12).

299.   The school employs a public-relations person who does an excellent job of getting press releases in the community paper. This can be substantiated by perusing this week's issue of the community newspaper. Almost three pages are devoted to sports at the School. Special mention is also made of various other achievements by student groups (36, P, 9–12).

300. The School's successes are publicized in many different places and ways. The display cases on the first-floor hallways are one place. Other means are the School's newspaper; a quarterly magazine to parents, alumni, and friends; releases to the Chicago media; and announcements over the loudspeaker in homeroom each day. These successes are portrayed so that both individual students and the students as a whole can be proud of themselves. The successes are also compared to those of other schools in many ways: the sports standings are listed on the bulletin board and in daily announcements, and the math league and debate team standings were listed in the latest issue of the school paper (60, R, 9–12).

About one-third of the schools studied made effective use of local papers to publicize school achievements. Such efforts are easier in suburban communities, with strong local news traditions. But many ingenious city schools find outlets in the neighborhood press. External publicity leads a special validity to the activities of a school; the students can see that their school, and its achievements, are broadly recognized. Furthermore, lists of achieving students publicized in the local press can serve as a valuable stimulant to greater student efforts.

Another factor to consider in publicity is the extent to which student achievements highlight the "whole school," as compared to only the achieving student. Such matters of portrayal can have important effects on school spirit. Thus there is considerable difference in the tone of a headline saying, "Jane Smith Wins Award," compared to "Jane Smith, Another Outstanding West High Student, Wins Award." The latter headline may be just as true as the first, but it is different. It invites all West High students to share the winner's place in the sun.

Obviously, another important source of school image is the student paper (which typically is only found in senior high schools).

301. The School newspaper is published twelve times a year, with each issue consisting of six pages. It has had the same faculty sponsor for thirteen years. It is popular with students. The annual cost per student is $4.00, which is included in student fees. About half of the paper's expenses are paid through the same of advertisements.

The staff of approximately thirty comes from all classes—freshmen, sophomores, juniors and seniors. Many students take newspaper as a class. They get one credit a year, and it may be repeated for up to four years. This credit does not fulfill their English requirement, but is merely an elective. All students are invited to submit letters, feature stories, poetry, and all other items (34, P, 9–12).

302. The School newspaper is issued weekly and is published by the students. The basic purpose of the paper is to publish news for and about the student body. Its hope is to reflect student life in as many facets as possible. There is an emphasis on training students on its staff in professional journalism. Approximately 2,000 copies of the paper are issued each Friday. Roughly forty to fifty students serve the paper in different capacities (58, R, 9-12).

303. The School maintained a tutoring program for students from several nearby elementary schools. Some students working on the School paper believed the faculty was not giving the program sufficient backing, and published an editorial clearly and politely raising some questions about this. The principal looked into the matter, and arrangements were made to give the program more effective support (60, R, 9-12).

As mentioned earlier, the problem for an administrator is to maintain a student paper that is informative and interesting, but that does not adopt an adversary posture toward school life. I suspect the essential step is the designation and retention of an able faculty sponsor. There is obviously a wide range in the quality of school papers.

The Identification and Pursuit of Collective Goals

304.   From a text on a folder distributed to all students:

WHO OWNS THIS SCHOOL
Surprisingly YOU do! Your parents and all taxpayers are legally required to pay taxes that build and maintain the Public School system. Everyone pays taxes in one form or another. Therefore, any damage done to this building, equipment, buses or books must be paid for with your own family's money! It is not enough that you should refrain from doing anything to increase this cost to your parents, neighbors and yourself, but you must help protect the school by discouraging or reporting such activity by any others. REMEMBER, *most trouble starts as fun!* (16, P, 9-12)

305.   The area in and around the School is very clean. Perhaps part of the reason is that students are responsible for sweeping up after school, and know what it is to pick up trash left by others. I have often seen students pick up papers discarded by others. There certainly is pride in school appearance here (56, R, 9-12).

306.   While many schools try to promote a communal life, we found that the School was lacking in this area. The principal claims that the faculty do a good job preparing the students for college. He feels that they do not prepare students that will socially take their places in the adult community (66, S, 9-12).

This is a commendably frank, but remarkable, statement. And it is consonant with the evidence gathered by my students. The School is racially integrated. Most of the people associated with it would be characterized as liberals. It has an adequate level of resources, and deliberately chose its teachers. The parents involved all have agreed to pay relatively high tuition, and care about the education of their children.

Despite these assets, the School is highly cognitive in its orientation, and engenders an intense sense of covert competition among its students. Furthermore, its extremely rationalistic and individualistic atmosphere has made it impossible for the School to have a vital symbolic and ceremonial life. The faculty and students are trained to take things apart and to criticize every side of an issue; as a result, they find it hard to engage in simply admiring, caring, and enjoying together. Such simple acts of release are antithetical to their values. My belief is that the dis-integration which pervades the School is the outcome of these factors. To go back to the principal's comment, we might wonder what will happen to the School's "well-prepared" students when they finally graduate from college, and have to live their lives outside of school. Of course, they may then go to graduate school, but perhaps someday they will have to live closely with others.

307. In this school, the student council is vigorously used to stimulate the identification and pursuit of corporate goals:

The student council has forty-three members and is assisted by a faculty moderator. The council also has an executive board, composed of its five top officers. The general membership of the council is made up of representatives from each homeroom, the heads of numerous clubs, the officers of each of the four student divisions (one for each year group), and the traffic court and hall guard captains. Most of the members have been elected to the various offices which entitle them to council membership, and the top council officers are elected by the whole school.

The council's motto is: "Learning, Developing, and Understanding." The members go through an induction ceremony and are pinned with council pins by previous members, and take an oath of office. The activities they have planned in a typical year include dances, skating parties, splash parties, a mother-daughter breakfast, a father-daughter dance, a Thanksgiving donation for needy families, food service for every Tuesday and Thursday, and hotdog and hamburger days. They also sponsor walk-a-thons and bike-a-thons to raise funds for cancer and muscular dystrophy research.

A recent major activity of the council was to organize a campaign so the School could first place in a school spirit contest sponsored by a local radio station. The School won the contest by collecting more signatures from outsiders attesting to its merits than any other competing school. Its students collected over 108,000 signatures. The student collecting the highest number of signatures of any individual contestant also came from the School; she collected over 7,000 names. The prizes included a $15,000 customized passenger van (presented to the School), the complimentary publication of the annual issue of the School's yearbook, and a free concert by a rock group (56, R, 9-12).

I have already suggested that communities in schools teach us how to live in communities in adult life. I think I can safely contend that the students who attend this school learn how to work with others, and get things done. (Remember, the School's total enrollment is 356; that is, it is a very small high school; they averaged over 300 signatures per student.)

It also sounds like the students have a good time, which is part of what community is about. Incidentally, we can see that the council found plenty of difficult and worthwhile things to do without intruding into academic issues beyond their competence.

Sometimes the collective goals which students (and their schools) pursue are inherently unsound. Then awkward conflicts arise between the need for collective goals and the effects of pursuing ones that are inherently destructive. This item illustrates the problem:

308. Many of the students take the subway to the School. The head office of the subway decided to close an entrance/exit close to the School, because (it was said) the students were jumping over the gate and not paying, and creating other disturbances at the gate. An article criticizing this decision appeared in the student paper, and students, teachers, administrators, and parents protested the decision. Finally, as a result of these pressures, the plan was abandoned (14, P, 9–12).

From other evidence available to me, I know that there was much merit to the subway's position: the students were extremely unruly, and tried to slip by without paying. Of course, the city could station a policeman at the entrance, or attempt other forms of deterrence. And, if the station was kept open, perhaps such measures were applied. However, the more significant thing is that there is no evidence of serious public discussion in the School community about the basic issue: the students' arrogant irresponsibility! Of course, not all students acted irresponsibly. But communities must have a sense of corporate responsibility. If there is a "we," then the members share both authority and responsibility over one another. But, if there is no "we," there is no caring, no pride, no authority, and very little constructive learning.

Community Members Engage in Giving

Members of a community give to each other, and also give collective gifts (or contributions) to others in and outside of the community. The gifts signify and reaffirm relationships. Most of the gifts are intangible (for example, courtesy, tact). This section will be concerned with the tangible ones.

309. Private schools usually have their own fundraising activities, which are carried out by students and their parents. However, the School has very little fundraising done by the students. The principal said the PTA raises almost all of the funds for scholarships (66, S, 9–12).

In modern urban societies, it is often difficult for schools to devise ways students can make concrete contributions to the operation of school. The most obvious means of such contributions, giving money, is sometimes degraded because students (may) have much less earning power than their parents. Thus it can seem foolish for students to put their time into (let us say) washing cars, instead of studying, when their parents can earn so much more per hour.

In contrast, in more primitive environments, manual labor was important. As a result, the value of the labor contributed by a student might begin to approximate the value of a parent's help. Thus, the student could perform a self-evident service. But this is not so much the case at this time. And so there is less for students to give to their schools, and less ways giving can be used to portray and demonstrate procommunity relationships—at least this is the conventional wisdom.

First of all, the wisdom is wrong because we often do not really try to use students enough around many schools. Some of their potential roles have already been listed: crossing guards, hall guards, tutors, library aides, organizers and presenters of entertainment. Others are not so common but deserve exploration: preparing the noon meal, cleaning the lunchroom, keeping the school clean, and maintaining the school grounds. These can all be "gifts" from students.

Second, if we look directly at money, the issue is not so much the amount of dollars raised but the amount of student effort expended in the pursuit. It is the act of helping that is the learning effort—just as students at the School in item 307 learned a lot from simply collecting 108,000 signatures, so well-designed student fundraising contests can have many beneficial effects beyond the mere total of dollars raised, if we want to generate such student effects.

310. At the end of each year, the student council presents the School with a monetary gift, composed of the money raised by the council in its activities during the past year. The last gift totaled over $1,000. The gift is used to improve the School. Individual gifts are exchanged among students and teachers on holidays and birthdays. And each year, big and little sisters exchange gifts with each other (56, R, 9–12).

The concept of gift exchanges among students and teachers warrants some discussion. Such practices are rare in public schools beyond the lower elementary grades.

Giving is discouraged in public schools partly by the schools' bureaucratic structure: in larger schools, where students have transitory relations with many teachers, it is not exactly clear how and when to give appropriately. Furthermore, formal and informal school policies often discourage such patterns to prevent the "exploitation" of students, or the encouragement of favoritism among teachers.

Ironically, the giving of gifts by students is partly due to the students' natural desire to have power over their environment. In other words, when we give through a relatively free decision, and people accept our gifts, we subconsciously assume that the receivers accrue some reciprocal obligation to us. Therefore, giving provides us with reassurance. (Thing how disturbing it would be to children if parents refused their gifts!)

According to my analysis, students should actually be more at ease in schools where patterns of student giving are common. Of course, these patterns are subject to abuse, either by teachers or students. And this danger is one reason why some schools try to foreclose all giving and keep all relationships on strictly "professional" bases. Perhaps a more valid vision of education professionalism would be based on school policies which fostered mutual exchanges of gifts, and sensitively monitored them so as to prevent abuses.

311.   The School has maintained a tradition of each graduating class donating a conspicuous gift to the School. The nature of these gifts vary, for example, a display case for awards, a flagpole outside the building, a special collection of books for the library. Each gift is labeled with a plaque designating the year of the donating class, for example, Graduating Class of 1919 (36, P, 9–12).

312.   On one or two occasions graduating classes have given gifts to the School, but it is not a common practice. One teacher mentioned that the students in the garden club had recently donated their time to plant trees on the School grounds, but there was no plaque or other device designating their "contribution." A former dean of students said that whether a gift is given depends on the decision of the graduating class. When six students were asked about this matter, they said they had heard no discussions about class gifts (60, R, 9–12).

Perhaps 10 to 15 percent of the schools visited had regular patterns of class gift-giving to the school. Class gifts demonstrate a variety of symbolic relationships. Gifts from previous classes, which become part of the school property, and are labeled as gifts, show students that "the past" cared about the school and its future, since the gifts do not help the givers, but future students. They also show that the past was capable of gratitude, a valuable characteristics for students to learn.

When a particular class gives a gift, that act demonstrates the class has attained a certain level of collective cohesion: money must be raised, and a decision reached about what to give. The act also shows that the class knows about gratitude, cares about the future, feels an obligation to adopt the responsible practices of the past, and has left the status of studenthood (and students are largely takers), and moved into adulthood, where more giving is required.

When administrators say the matter of class gifts is left to the decision of the graduating class, they are saying that adults do not care whether students learn the characteristics listed above. After all, it is unrealistic to believe that the perspectives associated with class giving will arise in the heads of seventeen-year-olds without some adult stimulation.

Interscholastic Sports

Interscholastic sports are a well-established and significant means of encouraging school spirit.

313.   The School has a variety of teams that compete in interscholastic meets. The relationship between the teams and the general student body (and the faculty) is unusual. The teams are relatively successful, but receive little support from the students, or most of the faculty. There are no pep rallies, and cheerleading is usually lacking. Some teams are supported by small groups of students who do attend games or meets, but these groups are little more than cliques. Some athletes say they also feel handicapped by the School's stress on academic achievement, and its high level of homework. However, I personally believe the problem is not so much the homework, but the lack of systematic School support for the teams that discourages the athletes (66, S, 9–12).

Patterns such as that just described exist in some highly academic schools which, incidentally, do not generally stimulate student collective activities.

314.   This item describes a school which also has a high academic focus, but which also supports group spirit: Roughly, 800 or more students—about 30 percent of the student body—can be found at any major game, whether the team in question is in first place or not. It would seem, then, that the School supports team games, regardless of the record of the teams. Although there are only a few minority-group students on most teams (with the exception of the basketball team, which is comprised mainly of black students), audience participants represent a cross-section of students (including minority students) and friends and family members (58, R, 9–12).

We should note how school spirit—or community—is encompassing, and brings together students of different races in a common cause, and heightens ties among students and their families.

315.   The athletes program is a credit to the School. The students and teachers support their teams. In the classes we visited there were reminders for an important girls' swim meet (which, by the way, they lost by one point to the conference champs). This support shown by the teachers and students gave me a sense of community. This attitude was new to me because, when I went to high school, the only people who knew there was a swim meet were on the swimming team. The School also had a pep rally for *all* the teams during all the lunch periods, so everyone could attend. This impressed upon me the concern the teachers and the administrators had for the students. My own high school wasn't like that; they had one pep rally (for football) and only certain classes could go (36, P, 9–12).

316.   The School offers track, baseball, and basketball for both girls' and boys' teams. They also have a coeducational volleyball team. Sixth graders are not allowed to join team sports because the principal feels they need the first year in junior high to adjust to the curriculum. Out of forty students I talked to, all but two had tried out for some sport. They said it was fun, even if they didn't make it. They all said they attended the games as often as possible. The teams usually finished in first through third place, but that wasn't the main reason they attended. They felt they had lots of school spirit, enjoyed cheering, and it was "the thing to do." Cheerleaders were chosen from the seventh- and eighth-grade girls. A panel of three teachers chose them. One member of the panel is the gym teacher. They have sixteen cheerleaders, eight from each grade. I talked with one new cheerleader, and she said that girls are chosen by gymnastic ability. She said that this year seventy girls tried out. Everyone wants to be a cheerleader, but some just aren't good enough (37, P, 6–8).

Of course, we should not ignore the traditional learnings associated with athletic participation: the ability to decide to voluntarily enlist in a rigorous regime of physical training and skill learning, and carry it through; mastering the emotional stress of team competition, which inevitably involves supportive and competitive tensions among team members; furthermore, there are always occasions when the team loses, and athletes must know how to adapt to, and rise above, conspicuous defeats.

I remember discussing the nature of modern colleges with the president of a large corporation. He said he felt obligated to make gifts to his alma mater but had little faith in most of its academic programs. He did not believe these programs prepared the graduates for vital adult roles. He said, "The only activities I can comfortably support are those connected with competitive athletics." His tone was a mixture of frustration and apology. Of course, his judgment may be wrong; still, it represents the opinion of someone who may know more about competency in adult life than many academics.

About half of the high schools visited maintained effective athletic programs that mobilized both the players and the other students.

The Faculty Routinely Socialize among Themselves

317.   There are some social interactions among teachers, but not many. The principal does hold informal gatherings a few times a year so the teachers can get to know one another. And the rate of staff turnover is very

low. Despite these facts, the principal says there are still a lot of teachers who do not know each other (66, S, 9–12).

318. There is only one social function (occurring away from the building) each year for the staff. The rationale for this limited activity is supposedly legal: the fewer outside functions that occur, the less potential legal liabilities the School assumes (for injuries people might suffer while having fun at a gathering) (5, P, K–8).

One of my students provided me with the following anecdote about a public school that is not otherwise described in this text:

"I asked the administrator if there was anything he might do to heighten the feeling of community in the school. He said there was probably more he could do, but felt there was no more he *should* do. Community, he said, is something that should evolve on its own, perhaps as a partial result of other policies, but a community is not 'true' if it is forced. He seemed to feel I was overly preoccupied with the question of community.

We talked about staff social activities. He said there are a few such occasions, but not many. I asked if that revealed a low level of community in the school. He said it simply reflected the busy times in which we live. Here, again, he seemed a little defensive."

I believe the content of this exchange speaks for itself.

319. There is a teachers' lounge in which the teachers see each other before and after school, and during lunch. There are two groups of teachers who interact socially with each other. The division is by age (that is, the young and old) although a few do cross over. Some younger teachers are settled, and so they join the older teachers. On the other hand, the older teachers who are "young at heart" join the "swingers," as the principal describes to them. Some of their activities are volleyball teams, softball teams, bowling, and going out to dinner (37, P, 6–8).

320. Teachers are invited to visit with the principal at any time. His secretary greets visitors with a warm, informal approach, which he states has been requested by the principal. The secretary said, "I am here to accommodate the teachers, parents, visitors as much as possible. It is part of my responsibility to create an inviting atmosphere to all who enter the main office, making it known that if the principal isn't busy, he will be more than happy to see you." When our group arrived the first day we were immediately greeted with consideration by the secretary, and then by the principal.

On Halloween, which was also the principal's birthday, the office was elaborately decorated. Donuts, cookies, fruits, punch, and candy were offered to us to help celebrate the occasion. Presents were stacked on a desk, with the principal sitting in the middle opening them. A classroom of students stopped by with their teacher to wish him a happy birthday. A large banner was placed in the entrance hall of the School wishing him a happy birthday with his name on it.

The principal, over the past two years, had engaged in a deliberate campaign to encourage faculty, students, and parents to relate more socially with one another. Because of the instability in the community, the School is trying to say, "We care about you, and each other. Our doors are open, we'll help, if you'll help us." A teacher said to us, "Little by little, parents, teachers, students, and administrators are communicating and working together, instead of against each other" (18, P, 8–9).

The degree of socialization among school faculty varied widely among schools. Perhaps one-third of the schools visited had a high level, one-third were indifferent, and one-third were poor.

The attitude of the principal can obviously be an important factor in this area. There are innumerable real and imaginary barriers to such socialization—and I count the issue of legal liability as an imaginary one. It takes determination, imagination, and a certain social flair to overcome these barriers. It is unrealistic to expect that someone will possess these talents just because he has an M.A. degree, or has passed some exam, or served many years as a satisfactory teacher.

Having Fun Together

321.   During one of the weeks we visited the School, we observed the events of Activity Week, planned by the student council. Various special days were designated: Baby Day, Marriage Day, Nostalgia Day, and Hobo Day. Students were invited to participate by dressing appropriately. Leaflets were passed out advertising the occasions. Many of the costumes were ingenious and amusing (14, P, 9–12).

322.   The council organizes various fun-promoting activities. On School Spirit Day, students compete for prizes, given for the students who wear the most clothing items using the School colors. There is also a slave day, in which seventh-grade students sign up as eighth graders' slaves for the day (with their parents' written permission). Slaves are asked to carry books, hold doors, and so on. The slave who helps the most wins a prize (31, P, 8–9).

323.   Item from a student paper:

Parade to Highlight Spirit Week Festivities
Every year just before Homecoming, the School has a Spirit Week.

On Tuesday, the Freshman class sponsored "The Matchmaker Game." During the lunch hours each person picked a number out of a bowl. They had to find the person with the same number. The first three couples to find each other won.

On Wednesday, the Sophomore class sponsored a day when everyone had to wear something from Disneland. Students wore everything from Mickey

Mouse T-shirts to Mickey Mouse ears. During the change of classes, the halls were filled with music from Disneyland.

On Thursday, the Junior class sponsored a "Mummy Wrap." During the lunch hours, there were contests to see who could wrap up like a mummy the fastest.

On Friday, the Senior class sponsored "The Inside-out Day." Many students walked around the whole day with their clothes inside out.

Tomorrow, there will be the Homecoming parade which assembles at 10:00 and starts at 11:00. The parade starts at the Park, goes west on 97th to Central Park. From Central Park, the parade proceeds to 95th and goes east to Main. The parade then continues down Main to the south parking lot at the School.

All four classes and various clubs have entered a float for this year's parade. Each float picked a theme from past Homecomings.

The Freshman class picked "The Roaring Twenties." The Sophomore class selected "Night in Disneyland." The Junior class picked "Color My World," and the Senior class chose "Stairway to the Stars."

The Swim Guards also have a float this year. Their theme is "Rock Around the Clock." The Foreign language clubs chose "When Knights Were Bold."

Spirit Cars include: "Memories," Spirit Boosters, "Somewhere Over the Rainbow," Business Club and "Isle of Golden Dream" SBI.

"We hope we get a big turnout for the parade because much work has been put into it," stated the Special Events Commissioner.

Floats will be judged for originality, neatness, theme, and design. Awards will be given.

After the game, which starts at 2:00, there will be an alumni Koffee Klatch in the School at 4:30. (34, P, 9–12)

324. Each year, a picked team of students between grades five and eight competes against the faculty in a volleyball game. The event takes place before the whole School, and generates great excitement and amusement (2, P, K–8).

325. About four plays are held a year. The one I attended was in the afternoon for the sixth graders. It was presented by the seventh grade. About fifteen parents attended (37, P, 7–9).

326. The School has a small chorus and band, comprised of twenty-one singers and four guitar players. Its main function is to perform at Sunday Masses (49, R, K–8).

327. The upper grade School band performs at assemblies. At each assembly, they first present the "Star-Spangled Banner" and then go on to the Black National Anthem, "Lift Every Voice and Sing," which is considered the School song (6, P, K–8).

Perhaps half the schools visted maintained a good level of engaging, fun-promoting activities. The activities are obviously valuable in themselves, and incidentally are an important general gauge of school efficiency. People can't really have fun together unless they possess a good degree of self-discipline; otherwise, the stimulation of high spirits may be transformed into disorderly conduct. And so if a school lacks a well-run fun program, one may wonder about the degree of self-discipline possessed by its students.

Maintaining Constructive Intraschool Groups

328. In most high schools, the school community is subdivided into smaller subcommunities, or cliques. The School seemed to have a normal, or even higher, proportion of these cliques. Essentially, they were along racial or ethnic lines. Students feel their peers put them under pressure if they try to make friends outside the predetermined clique. Despite these groupings, students agreed that the faculty exercised no discrimination in grading or in organizing sports activities (66, S, 9–12).

No schoolwide community can persist unless students are simultaneously assisted to form smaller subgroups within the whole. Indeed, the vitality and nature of these subgroups is probably the chief determinant of the school spirit in any total school.

These subgroups form because (1) the total school is too large an entity to easily provide students with networks of close relationships, and (2) groups of students (for example, members of clubs, or teams, or one class) have common concerns which they need to share with each other. To offer a simple analogy, in any large nuclear family, it is "natural" for the children to see themselves as an entity partly separate from their parents. This does not mean they routinely oppose their parents. However, the children have certain common experiences different from those of their parents and have more contacts with each other than with their parents. It is healthy when the children group to share their concerns. Thus a nuclear family may become a two-part entity, composed of parents and children. And so a school with school spirit will be an entity composed of many vital components.

The essential task for larger communities, whether they are schools or families, is for them to insure that the components maintain a supportive relationship with each other, and their umbrella entity. When such integrated relationships prevail in a school, one has school spirit. But, if the school does not actively try to create and shape such groups, they will tend to form spontaneously. And the resulting relationships may lead to gangs and cliques that become vehicles for the release of childish or adolescent aggression.

One of the first measures applied by skillful administrators in fighting such centrifugal tendencies is to encourage the formation of vital subgroups which are under general adult governance, and which act as part of the total school system.

329. The following item is from a school newspaper:

213 Wins School Volleyball Title
The Freshmen of Homeroom 213 defeated the Seniors of Homeroom 215 by a score of 21–19 on January 10, 1979.

Homeroom 213 received a trophy for their homeroom. This trophy is passed from homeroom to homeroom each year.

They also received individual trophies which went to each player on the team.

After the game, the umpire commented on how well both teams played. Congratulations are certainly due to the homeroom champs of 79. (56, R, 9–12)

One step in creating continuing constructive groups in schools that are departmentalized (that is, high and junior high schools) is to group students into persisting homerooms, in other words, to put twenty-five freshmen in one group for administrative purposes, and leave them in that group for four years, as they progress on to seniorhood. Some schools do this, but many others regroup their homerooms (each year?) to facilitate various administrative purposes. Homeroom stability obviously assists students in getting to know a continuing group of people who share some common concerns (for example, they're taking the same kinds of courses).

These common concerns in homerooms can be constructively intensified if the school takes certain measures. These measures include structuring academic programs so most of the students in the same homeroom take many of their courses together; giving the group the same homeroom teacher over their entire four years in school; setting aside significant units of time during the school day for homerooms to operate as units (as compared to only being a unit for reading notices and taking attendance); and asking homerooms both to undertake school responsibilities and to present themselves to other students as a viable entities.

The School involved in the preceding item takes all of these steps. The clipping demonstrates one element of its program. Homerooms compete against each other in a volleyball contest. The contest is publicized, and the winning team receives a schoolwide trophy which it retains until next year. Such measures give each homeroom a significant sense of identity. For instance, the winning freshman class for its next four years will be under "pressure" to live up to its surprising early success. Whether it maintains its record or not, all of its members will be putting pressure on each other to keep trying.

But, we should note, this stimulation of vital homerooms is not inconsistent with overall school spirit. The School, even though it is small, recently placed second in the statewide girls' volleyball championship. Obviously the students don't see anything wrong with caring about both their homeroom and the whole school. It may be they can care more about the whole because such caring is not inconsistent with their caring for their homeroom units: the whole supports its parts, and is not their enemy.

I do not have access to precise analyses of the amount of vitality possessed by various high-school homeroom systems. Actually a wide variety of homeroom procedures are used, and different schools apply different ones, for example, they keep students stable and rotate teachers, or they rotate students and teachers but still leave significant time for homeroom activities. The constructive management of homeroom arrangements presents an important, but unrecognized, opportunity for the improvement of departmentalized schools.

330.   The students in the School never assemble in homerooms; all the administrative arrangements usually handled by homerooms are carried out by other means. The School does occasionally bring students together in their annual classes (for example, there are meetings of all freshmen or all juniors). However, there are only about four such meetings a year, and they are relatively large and formalistic. Despite the lack of traditional subentities, such as homerooms, the School retains a relatively high level of school spirit as a result of its extraordinary extracurricular program. Due to this program, a great majority of the students belong to—and participate in—a club, or are involved in sports (69, P, 9–12).

The item demonstrates the principle that there is not "an answer" to the problem of creating vital subgroups, but simply a concept. The School has created such groups without homeroom or age groups, but that creation has taken planning and effort. The clubs and teams are school-sponsored activities and are under pressures to relate their activities to the whole, which is the School. And, given that pressure, they meet the need for subgroups comparatively well.

There is another subgroup system that some American schools are exploring. It is based on a practice common in England. In that country most boarding schools, and many community schools, subdivide their students into "houses." Each house is comprised of a group of students from all age groups formed into a component of the whole school. The next item describes a Chicago public school which attempts to apply these English principles. (Incidentally, a number of other American schools have attempted to apply similar principles of subdivision.)

331.   The School is subdivided into four separate areas, each allocated to a separate student "house." Each house area contains a lunchroom, study area, and locker room for its students. Each house also has its floor and furnishings colored a common color, and the house is designated by that color, for example, Purple House. Students are assigned to houses as they enroll in School, and they generally stay in the same house for their four years. Thus, each house contains a cross-section of the School population.

One assistant principal, counselors, and some teachers are assigned to a particular house, and efforts are made to stimulate continuing contacts among the students and faculty of the house.

One of the major reasons for the houses was to help students to form close contacts with other students from different neighborhoods and ethnic groups (through having a process of student grouping which fostered intrahouse contacts, as compared to neighborhood or race based ones).

To enforce the patterns of intrahouse contact, students are given ID cards which show the colors of their appropriate houses. They are supposed to wear these cards at all times. The display of the cards should enable teachers easily to see if students are respecting house "lines" in using study and lunch space in the School.

In practice, students are not required to observe the card display rule. When we asked one student who his friends in the School were, he said, "Largely those I went to elementary school with." When we asked how he maintained those contacts, he said, "Although all of us are assigned to different houses, we eat lunch together, since the 'stay in your own house' rule is not particularly enforced."

The School has few significant responsibilities or activities allocated to students by their houses. There are no signs or symbols (apart from the color scheme) distinguishing the various houses. We were not told of any plan to give the houses more connotative designations (apart from their colors) or to imaginatively portray their identities.

In general, the students, and some of the faculty, see the house structure as an administrative arrangement that is unrelated to the quality of student life (14, P, 9–12).

Serious planning went into the development of the house system: the four separate areas, the color scheme, the color coding of the cards, and the assignment of students and faculty. However, the effort is floundering on the rock of day-to-day administration. The School lacks a vital discipline system to restrain and punish students who do not observe the "stay in your area" rule. It does not have a clearly written, widely distributed document that explains the rationale of the house system to students, teachers, and parents in a way that reveals its constructive potential. The students and faculty gathered in houses are not treated as potentially self-contained social units, with a network of intrahouse activities, for example, parties and group and intragroup responsibilities (such as seniors counseling freshmen). The houses do not engage in structured competition with other

houses to attain significant recognition. And there are no symbols to
identify the houses, apart from their color schemes and the names derived
from those schemes.

332. With the encouragement of the principal, a number of the
teachers stimulate competition among different rows of students in their
classrooms. The rows compete in matters such as improving attendance,
displaying good discipline, and completing certain class assignments.

This policy of intergroup competition is deliberately followed, to
mobilize peer support for desired conduct and learning. The more successful rows receive conspicuous collective rewards, while the students in the
less successful rows are encouraged to help and push each other to improve.

The principal said, "Students inevitably look towards each other to see
how they should apply themselves. And, in fact, sometimes students look
down on the responsible conduct of other students. Competition among
rows or other groups in the classes enables teachers to direct this process of
peer signaling towards desirable ends. In addition, the students generally
find it more fun the way they're talking to each other about their work,
instead of just listening to the teacher" (18, P, 8-9).

The concept of interrow competition is applied by many elementary-
school teachers on an ad hoc basis. In the Soviet Union, the concept is used
throughout the whole system of elementary and secondary education. The
conscious aim of the Soviet policy is to encourage students to (1) look
toward each other for academic help (and I mean "legal" help, not cheating), and (2) be prepared to frankly but tactfully criticize students whose
irresponsible or selfish conduct is jeopardizing the adult-determined goals
of the group.[4]

In contrast to these Soviet policies, American education patterns generally focus on individualized grading and responsibilities. The effects of
these policies are to encourage students to (1) assume that other students
will not help them, and that they should not try to help others, and (2)
ignore the irresponsible or wrong conduct of other students, unless such
misconduct is very immediately personally harmful to them.

The School is located in a community with a high level of disorder and
antisocial conduct. Presumably the principal has concluded that a partial
solution for this problem is for the School to develop student work teams
that are charged with adult-determined collective responsibilities. Perhaps
such groups can act as an antidote for the gang-oriented environment surrounding the students. Interestingly enough, the Soviet educator who is
principally credited with developing the process of collective responsibility
evolved his procedures from conducting training programs for juvenile
delinquents (though the Soviets would undoubtedly say that their procedures are equally appropriate for youths from all types of backgrounds).

Discussion

There are a variety of intellectual conflicts focusing on the nature of social life in the past, and of youth-adult relations in particular. These conflicts implicitly ask: were there really powerful communities around our young in the historic past? That question is of more than rhetorical interest. For, if such communities were rare, then the plea today for community in schools may be essentially utopian and unnecessary. This is not the place to definitively settle the issue. However, some overlooked general principles can be uttered.

As some historians have observed, the young in the American past were frequently geographically mobile, and not tied down to settled environments. Furthermore, the multi-generational extended family was quite uncommon, due to the relatively short life-span of typical adults; most adults matured and died before their own children bore grandchildren. Because of advances in modern medicine and public health, grandparents are actually more common in our own times than they were throughout most of the past (for example, during the nineteenth century).

Despite these drawbacks on neighborhood and intergenerational intimacy, we must recognize two overriding facts about the "past": most families (and their children) were poor and lived in rural—and farm-related—environments. As a result of these patterns (1) there were many important tasks that could be done by comparatively unskilled labor (and could thus be done by young persons), and (2) many of these tasks required younger and older people to work together. Thus the brute processes of survival created powerful bonding ties between the young and their coworkers, regardless of whether these people were relatives or long-term neighbors.

Today, of course, mechanization, urbanization, and comparative prosperity have extinguished many of these vital patterns. It has actually become difficult in our time for some educators to conceive of ways that their students can significantly work with others to contribute to school operations. And, indeed, the school spirit contest described in item 307, which provided a striking example of community in action, was in many ways an "artificial" activity. This is not to belittle the contest. Still, the example does illustrate the contrast between our current situation and that which prevailed (for most young persons) 100 years ago, when the students (in a rural area) might have helped the school by working with others to carry out numerous essential chores.

The conclusion that arises from the preceding discussion is that young persons at this time are more disintegrated from both their peers and older persons than they were in the past. This disintegration has probably played a significant role in stimulating the trends in alienated youth conduct described in the final chapter.

During the same period that the bonding forces among youths, and among youths and adults, have declined in vitality, changes in education policies have tended to diminish communal vigor in schools. Many of these changes have already been discussed in earlier chapters, such as increases in school size, the specialization of teachers, and the growth in bureaucracy and rationality. These changes conflict with the procommunity practices described in this chapter. Thus it seems evident that schools should move more actively toward fostering school spirit.

Unfortunately, this necessary move may be impeded by the complexity of the challenge, and the comparative ineptitude of many of the persons who must handle the necessary planning. And communities, in part, are deliberately planned—by people who write and publish school songs, establish schedules for assemblies, design school buildings that permit semiindependent, houses and who decide to publicize teachers' and students' birthdays.

The ineptitude of the planners is not essentially due to general incompetence. Instead, it is specifically caused by (1) the peculiar ignorance many modern educators have about the nature of community, and (2) the emotional and intellectual styles that have been favored by our processes of training and selecting educators.

The ignorance about community is revealed by the remarks, scattered throughout the chapter, about communities evolving "naturally," or about the "spirit of the times" being hostile to community—when, after all, the speakers are in control of school, and can help make their own "times." It is as if man has no ability—or responsibility—to reshape a man-made environment that is not working well. Of course, this attitude of "things are beyond our control" gratifies one important emotional need: it permits those who, in fact, do have some control to evade their responsibility.

Another cause for the general ignorance is that creating school spirit—or community—is like inspiring an orchestra, or getting 350 students to collect 106,000 signatures. In other words, some formal skills are helpful in such tasks. However, musical knowledge alone does not make a great conductor, nor does a college course in planning teach one how to galvanize 350 adolescents. It is not solely a matter of being "born" with such abilities. Some learning is involved. But the way such talents are learned is not by taking courses, but by apprenticeship, wide reading, varied occasions for practice and observation, and actually living in communities and helping them work.

And this proposition leads to my second handicap to improving in school community-building. The current processes of training and selection for teachers and administrators do not help them become community builders. Indeed, young persons with a strong interest in (and flair for?) community-building in education would probably find themselves repulsed by the barriers they might have to face before their interests could be refined and applied. For instance, their first few career years might have to be spent in a self-contained classroom, neither helped by others nor given a chance to help. Their reaching-out instincts might be frustrated in work environments where people don't have parties, where students are passed off to counselors, and where symbols and traditions are treated by many administrators as trivial and phoney. At the end of such an indoctrination, it is hard for aspiring community-builders to have a good perception about how to go about attaining their end. And so, by the time they become adults with significant power, they end up reciting solecisms about the "spirit of the times," and being afraid of making fools of themselves or of showing feelings about things that deserve feelings.

7 Conclusion

A friend who is a minister is fond of the following story:

> *I was walking down the street one morning not long ago. A fine-looking man came alongside and kept pace with me.*
>
> *"I am the devil," he announced.*
>
> *"Well," I said, "I have always been very curious about you and I'm glad to see you at last. And what are you doing this morning?"*
>
> *"Oh, my usual business. I am going about corrupting the works of man."*
>
> *We chatted pleasantly, for I have never been a devil-hater, and kept company for some distance. I was surprised to find the devil such a pleasant and well-spoken gentleman. After a time, we noticed a man in front of us who gave all outward indications of having been struck by a good idea. He stopped suddenly still, his face lighted up, he struck his hand to his head in joy, and rapidly walked away to execute his idea. Thinking that this gave me at least a temporary advantage, I said, "Now there's a man who has an idea, and I venture to say that it is a good idea. That's a point against you. What are you going to do about that?" "Nothing easier," said the devil, "I'll organize it."* [1]

I will first generally discuss the implications of the items and analyses presented, and then indicate some of the writings and authorities that have shaped the perspective of this book.

The array of items and comments portrays a variegated scene. At first, one can be understandably reluctant to generalize about the schools described—except to say that the practices presented are very diversified. It seems that many educators are dedicated and imaginative, that some are well intentioned but confused, and that there are many time-servers.

But one can generalize further. Many persons have commented on the close interrelationship between schools and society. But the items translate this abstraction into specific details. From the items, we can see that what happens in the outside world has important effects on what is done by people in schools.

Thus our courts—and many of our intellectuals—have gradually changed their views relating to guilt, punishment, and the relationships between youths and adults. And, lo and behold, principals, teachers, and students discover that the power of schools to restrain or punish certain forms of behavior is constrained.

Again, the intensity of egalitarian attitudes in our society has increased in the recent past, and, as a result of that general shift, the rigor of academic demands, grades, and student groupings (by ability) have all declined. .

Furthermore, American society has had a continuing and intensifying attraction for economies of scale, solving problems by spending more money, the efficiencies generated by specialization, and the benefits of bureaucratizing and formalizing public institutions. The effects of these trends on the schools studied are obvious.

Finally, the long-term increase in prosperity and economic security in society has apparently caused us to assume that we can support high proportions of adults who are either incompetent or engaging in prolonged career exploration. This assumption has made it more difficult for educators to make competence and diligence important educational goals.

None of the preceding is meant to say that schools are powerless to quarrel with social trends. No trend is ever all-embracing. And we have seen, through the items, that not all schools have acted in ways congruent with the trends just described. But if we are distressed at some of the schools presented by in items, the "blame," unfortunately, can be shared by many institutions and persons beyond schools and educators.

Our efforts to generalize about the items can be assisted if we recall an important principle affecting interpretation: one set of facts can acquire richer meanings if it is related to other (perhaps formerly ignored) information. For example, we could understand the reports much better if we could discover an equivalent body of information about what was happening in Chicago-area schools twenty or thirty years ago. If things were much "worse," we could then say that the situation was "looking up," or vice-versa. But it would obviously be very had to get such information. And the significance of even the historical information available is problematic. For instance, one of my students reported on his "old" high school. He concluded that the situation had significantly deteriorated during the years since his graduation. And he presented reasoned evidence for his conclusion. However, as in many such instances, the neighborhood surrounding the school (and the socioeconomic mix of the student body) had also changed. As a result, it is hard to segregate the impact of general social and educational change from local neighborhood shifts. In effect, when we see things microcosmically—and look at only one school—they can be confusing. While some schools have gotten worse, new schools have opened that never existed before, and others have become larger. What do we compare the new and the much larger schools to? That question is important; if we conclude that all the new and enlarged schools are good, then they "make up" for the older ones that have deteriorated.

But, despite these barriers to acquiring perspective, we do have some long-term information to help us sharpen our judgment. This information consists of the most recent available aggregated, long-term, national statistics about certain trends in youth conduct. I will present these statistics below. My presentation will be brief, since I have written extensively about these developments elsewhere. The statistics will be about whites, since they represent our generally "most favored" social class. While they are nationally aggregated, the disaggregated data for Illinois (and for Chicago, to the extent they are available) follow congruent patterns.

Between 1950 and 1976, the rate of death by suicide for white males, ages fifteen through nineteen, increased 260 percent. The suicide rate for older adults remained relatively stable during this period.

Between 1959 and 1976, the rate of death by homicide for white males, ages fifteen through nineteen, increased 177 percent. Most of the assailants were other white male adolescents. This was the highest rate of increase for any group of white males.

Between 1950 and 1976, the estimated number of illegitimate births for unmarried white females, ages fifteen through nineteen, increased 143 percent. The rate of increase among these young persons far exceeded any increases among older females.

The level of white adolescent illegitimacy is at the highest rate in this century; the levels of homicide and suicide are about 10 percent below the century's maximums, attained in 1975.

In an affluent suburban community, the number of seventh-grade boys who began drinking during the previous year increased from 52 percent in 1969 to 72 percent in 1973. A 1974 national survey disclosed that 24 percent of the respondents of both sexes between thirteen and nineteen reported being drunk four or more times during the previous year.

Between 1957 and 1974, the number of delinquency cases disposed of by U.S. juvenile courts increased 96 percent.

In two surveys of national samples of students in American research universities, the proportion of students who admitted engaging in some form of cheating rose from 5.4 percent in 1969 to 9.8 percent in 1976, an 87 percent increase.

Between 1960 and 1973, throughout the country, arrests of males under eighteen for narcotics violations increased 1,288 percent.

National surveys report no significant declines in levels of youth drug use, and surveys of high-school graduating classes of 1975 and 1977 found that the percentage of males who had used marijuana before tenth grade had increased from 18.2 percent to 30.6 percent.

A variety of surveys of youth attitudes and conduct between 1948 and 1973 have disclosed a steady increase in attitudes evincing withdrawal, cynicism, loneliness, and hostility to authority. Two national surveys of adult attitudes found that the level of tension and worry among young adults (ages twenty-one through thirty-nine) increased from about 30 percent (in 1957) to 50 percent (in 1976). These developing attitudes are clearly inconsistent with a serious acceptance of social responsibility and with a sense of wholesome self-respect.

Two careful surveys of school crime and violence both concluded that the level of school crime has increased gradually since (about) 1955, and that, if the increase has leveled off, there has been no sign of any decrease. Students are in more risk of being criminally victimized in school than in any other environment where they ordinarily spend their time.

The patterns of increases revealed in these statistics also generally apply to blacks. However, there are minor differences. These differences may be more related to the lower socioeconomic status of blacks (as generally compared to whites) than to the issue of race itself. Essentially, while all the black statistics go up like those of the whites, the homocide and illegitimacy rates for black adolescents are higher than for whites, and their suicide rate is lower.

These distressing statistics justify the conclusion that there have been substantial changes in the feelings and conduct of American youth over the past twenty to twenty-five years. And, obviously, these changes extend far beyond the conduct explicitly described by the data. For instance, the suicide rate is only a direct measure of "successful" suicides that have been detected; however, it also indirectly measures undetected suicides, attempted suicides, and severe depressions. When the measured suicide rates go up, we should assume that all the other indexes similarly shift.

The data do not mean that all or most American youths are distraught. We are a huge country, and there are many pockets of health, maintained by individual families or wholesome local institutions. Still, there has indisputably been a significant general deterioration.

The conduct and attitudes described by the statistics can be characterized in terms easily understood by laymen. The statistics demonstrate the steady spread of loneliness, boredom, purposelessness, selfishness, and anger among our young. These shifts were understandably accompanied by a decline in capability of the young to accept delayed gratification. I describe the attitude changes in these harsh terms because the understanding is that persons prone to grievously hurt themselves or others, or to irresponsibly explore drugs or sex, are likely to be leading emotionally empty lives. They have very little to do that is worthwhile, and what they have to do that is constructive is not important, and they do not know how to do it well.

None of these remarks is a serious criticism of our children and youths. It is true that the conduct and attitudes just sketched are undesirable. But young people, in general, do what they are "told" to do by adults and adult institutions. And, if adult institutions treat them in a trivial and disengaged fashion, they will respond appropriately. Of course, the young people responding will not say, "We don't want to be treated trivially!" Indeed, they may even explicitly say, "Adults aren't leaving us enough alone," or, "We aren't permitted to do what we want." But adults who try to teach or act as mentors to the young should interpret what they say, rather than simply respond literally. And the young, when "left alone," are increasingly prone to engage in activities harmful to themselves and others. One should interpret this conduct to "say" they really want engagement and consequential demands. If we try and satisfy this request from the young, many adults must engage in hard but gratifying work.

The conduct and attitudes that young persons display are learned from outside environments (and from the persons operating in those environments). Evidently, certain of the environments around our young have changed for the worse over the period described. From the items in the text, it seems likely that schools represent one of these changed environments. In other words, it seems clear that many schools are trying to take their students for granted, and children and adolescents spend a great deal of time in such schools. Twenty-five years ago, when they spent almost as much time in attendance, the conduct of the young was much "better." From this sequence, it is logical to conclude that schools have deteriorated.

Unfortunately, the adults in many schools portrayed do not think the conduct of their students is important enough to warrant serious criticism or praise, nor do they care enough about youth conduct to really try to shape it. There seems to be a fervent hope that if we leave the students alone, they'll do the same for us. But in some cases the adults involved do accept the responsibilities of professionalism, or the students involved force themselves into the lives of their educators. In such cases, these adults have to worry about being good role models; enforcing discipline; arguing with parents and worrying about court decisions; insisting on homework; flunking students; or trying to inspire them. In all of these demanding activities, the educators have to think about whether they'll be backed up by (1) the administrative norms of their school, (2) their entire school system, or (3) external agencies such as courts. Obviously many educators lack a firm base to stand on in resisting these multitudinous potential conflicts I have just sketched.

Such educators want to execute a peace pact with their students: let me go may way, and you can go yours. The problem is that neither the students nor the educators are sovereign nations. They cannot enter into such arguments. The students do not always know what is best for them—as demonstrated by the statistics just outlined. The educators are employees. They are paid to accept certain inescapable responsibilities. And they have chosen to accept the task of caring for other peoples' children. They were not drafted.

Such "pacts" between students and educators do not produce peace for either camp. The students become bored and angry, and some educators are frustrated from the beginning, and others (who thought the pact might pay off eventually) become disillusioned. Unfortunately, many of the disillusioned educators still hope there can be a renegotiation of the same pact. And there's the flaw. The true proper parties to any such pact with educators are not the students. They are (1) the parents of the students and (2) in some large sense, the society existing in the present, past, and future. This proposition does not foreclose the involvement of educators with students. But students should not and cannot decide what treaties about school policy the proper parties should negotiate. The students cannot decide because (1) they cannot vote because they are immature, (2) they are, in general, not contributing to the support of the schools, and (3) they are, not supporting themselves. Given such extraordinary dependency, it is not appropriate for students to decide how teachers (paid by others) should act toward them in school, while they are living at home (typically supported by their parents).

None of my remarks is intended to suggest that all student wishes or opinions should be disregarded. The more school-related responsibilities students accept, or have thrust on them, the more in-school authority they should have. But even in the schools portrayed where the students had significant responsibilities, they only met a fraction (perhaps 5 to 10 percent) of the operating costs. In fact, in the 5 to 10 percent schools, it seems the students actually exercised more than 5 to 10 percent authority. And, in most of the schools portrayed, the students' contributions to school operations as crossing guards, tutors, fundraisers, hall guards, helpers in planning, members of athletic teams, and newspaper staff were probably less than 5 percent of the total adult contribution in money and time.

In sum, if the students pitch in and help the school "work" in important and responsible fashions (comparable to the contributions of adults), then it is appropriate for them to really assume power. But the fact is that the more the students do contribute, the closer their attitudes come to those of the adults. In such circumstances, student power is an extension and refinement of adult power. It simply makes many elements of adult power more effective. And, where there are apparent differences between adult and student power in such cases, these differences are only the frictions that occasionally arise between all people with common aims and slightly different perspectives.

Unfortunately, the policies of many of the schools studied seem to have been deliberately devised to frustrate the desideratum just sketched. Too many schools rarely ask—or demand (for we are not just "invited" to pay taxes)—that most students make contributions to the whole. And many of these same schools which tolerate or encourage student parasitism also (1) invite students to make a variety of decisions, (2) give the students freedom to make choices paid for by the other people's money, or (3) permit students to act in an indifferent or slovenly fashion without criticizing ineptitude or selfishness, or praising efficacy or dedication. This is the worst of all possible worlds. It is understandable why it results in boredome or disengagement from adult-sponsored concerns, and why it ultimately leads to more serious consequences.

Other Authorities

Social scientists have continuously stressed the basic tendency of human beings to perceive and construct the world in terms of their subconscious assumptions.[3] A typical description of this pattern was articulated by Berelson and Steiner:

> [Man] tends to remember what fits his needs and expectations; . . .he sees and hears not simply what is there but what he prefers to see and hear; he will misinterpret when correct information is too painful; he seeks out congenial groups in order to be comfortable about his actions and his opinions; he is skilled in engaging in private fantasies and "defense mechanisms" in order to lighten the human load; he tends to believe that people around him agree with more fully than they in fact do. . . .[4]

These thoughtful cautions apply to social scientists as well as to all other human beings. There are various conventions that have evolved in the sciences to try to protect readers from the effects of this tendency of evaluators (such as myself) to warp and distort "reality." One protective convention is for a researcher to locate her or his work and perspective within some intellectual tradition. This does not assure readers that the tradition is correct, or that the author has properly applied its perspectives. Still, the process of locating stimulates the author to test her or his perceptions against those of others, and gives readers intellectual landmarks to use in evaluating the work. And, because these landmarks have already been subjected to evaluation elsewhere—which is why they are landmarks—the readers can use such criticism or approval as tools for considering the work before them. Now let us consider the intellectual roots or *Looking at Schools*.

There is a widespread and persisting intellectual tradition of looking back toward some past era which was more favored than our present environment. The anthropologist Mercea Eliade identified instances of this pattern in non-Western cultures.[5] One of his examples was the basic tale of the Garden of Eden. Again, in Western society, Jean Jacques Rousseau launched his prolific and influential career by writing the *Discourse on the Origin of Inequality,* and the major theme of that essay was founded on a sympathetic sketch of the hypothetical life of the first primitive peoples.[6] We may look at protrayals in this tradition as examples of poetic and simplistic myths. But if we routinely consider them as solely charming and naive, we may fail to perceive their potentially profound intellectual merits.

When societies are under stress, they will pursue, via discussion and reflection, solutions to their problems. One element of such pursuit is to consider alternative modes of social organization. The most significant modes of alternative organization are those that have persisted for long periods of time: they have withstood the "test of time." And so the study and respectful appreciation of the past are highly appropriate responses to serious social stress. This does not mean we are always right in our analysis of the nature of the past; after all, even the Bible gives us few details about what the Garden was like, and anthropologists have concluded that Rousseau's vision of the primitive past, which even he called "hypothetical," was factually incorrect. Furthermore, just because the reign of Pharaohs persisted for 3,000 years does not mean we can or should create equivalent dynastic structures.

This posture of sympathy toward, and interest in, the past can be contrasted with affinity for a dynamic present. Essentially, such presentism is characterized by a strong belief in "progress"; the most pejorative term applied by persons who sympathize vigorously with progress is "old-fashioned," as if old were automatically bad, and new, good. And most readers will recognize that there is an elaborate literature founded on the assumption that new policies and programs are likely automatically to be better than their predecessors (for example, the New Deal, the New Frontier and the Great Society programs, and President Carter's efforts to popularize New Foundations).

Let me state the issue perhaps oversimplistically. One can conceive of two forms of utopianism. One form looks to the past and believes that it was as good as, or perhaps better than, the present. One can easily criticize such a perspective, which we might call conservative. The other form identifies with the concept of progress and implicitly believes that, after 100,000 years of human experience, we can probably do something which makes the 100,001st year generally better than its predecessors. The progressive perspective is widespread among Americans. However, it does seem to conflict with certain statistical probabilities. This implicit criticism of progress does not mean that there has never been a "desirable" change; what it does mean is that changes we call desirable often have bad secondary consequences. For example, the sciences which have rendered us so many benefits have also created nuclear weapons and ICBMs. What computation system should we use to cumulatively evaluate the medley of all scientific discoveries? Or, to bring the question closer to home, the schools which have raised literacy may also have provoked increased youth drug use and suicide. How do we add up such things?

Berelson and Steiner, whose work I quoted, would predict that "progressives" who look at schools would tend to focus on school innovations and formalistic improvements in evaluating the current education situation. They will see alienated youth conduct (such as that portrayed in the previous statistics) as a disturbing but essentially irrelevant issue. To the extent they do confront the question of youth alienation, they will attribute it to nonschool causes, or "acts of God." They will be reluctant to admit that the changes in the schools—to advance progress—may really be a major cause of these distressing, unintended outcomes. Furthermore, many correctives proposed to deal with youth alienation will be derided by progressives as traditional, old-fashioned, or in conflict with current (and thus correct) values.

This discussion about progressives and conservatives may appear somewhat abstract. However, it goes to the heart of the question of school evaluation. When we evaluate any activity, we first have to ask ourselves exactly how broad our perspective should be. For instance, we can look only at the long-term rates of increases in enrollment (and average length of enrollment) in schools and colleges, without even considering whether those rates have already surpassed some optimum point. And, based on such criteria, education is doing fine. Even if we turn to more qualitative data, such as the average level of student reading scores, education is performing adequately. Of course, during the past decade, those scores have regressed slightly.[7] However, that decline fades to inconsequence when compared to the distressing shifts in the measures of youth alienation I have presented. The limited perspectives applied in looking at enrollment rates and reading scores represent the implicit progressive view. Or we may choose to look at a much wider spectrum of student conduct. We may even make inferences about the connection between such conduct and the development of the character of students (and their future roles as adults). *Looking at Schools* has applied such an atypical perspective.

When viewed from this broader approach, things look very different. Which perspective, the narrow or the broad, should be stressed? One might say we should use both of them, but efforts of such scope are very costly. Indeed, they may even be technically impossible. Furthermore, the more restricted measures, for example, reading scores, or student attendance, are admittedly more precise and cheaper to collect.

Conservatives, when assessing education, will inherently be more sympathetic with the broader measures, and the progressives, to the narrower ones. Conservative have an inherent suspicion of (1) formalistic state involvement in issues of interpersonal relations, (2) assumptions that significant variations from traditional modes will usually turn out well, and (3) short-range assessment of complex phenomena. These suspicions are founded in the conservatives' leaning toward the past on the basis that, whatever, its deficiencies, it persisted, and that is no small virtue. The suspicions provoke conservatives to rest their opinions on general, wide-ranging analyses. The progressives, with their affinity toward experimentation and optimism, will more often rely on (1) more focused and immediate evidence and (2) generalized abstractions about the way people "should" be. And shouldness, since it is based on semimoral considerations, is viewed beyond evaluation. The progressive emphasis on immediate evidence tends to encourage reform (since the reforms can hopefully be managed to improve such concrete outcomes) and removes the barrier of having to satisfy abstract objections about the "tendencies" underlying certain proposed change. Thus the progressive can more often urge, as evidence, that the proposed change "works," at least in the short run.

This is not to characterize the progressive's tactics as dishonest. If one is optimistic, but responsible, then one is naturally prone to look for short-range evidence. Then, one may say, "Look, the reform works—reading scores are improving, or average days attendance have increased, or children say they find school more pleasant." Conversely, the more pessimistic conservative will try to broaden the scope of the argument and bring in apparently more remote, but tangible, considerations. Now in any particular educational controversy, what issues are short- or long-range are subject to shifting determinations. And almost no one is entirely progressive or conservative. Thus, apparent conservatives may make simplistic appeals to past traditions, while progressives may bolster their proposals with comparatively complex analyses. However, I would still contend that thoughtful conservatives have generally applied comparatively wide-range perspectives in their approaches to analyzing and evaluating change. As a result, in the end, one's evaluative approach is significantly affected by one's general perspective, whether progressive or conservative.

Of course, one might say that a person's conservatism or progressivism is based on genes, toilet training, or the like. Thus, why bother to weigh the pros and cons of these perspectives? But books, almost by definition, presume the worth of logical argument. As a result, let me persist in defense of the conservative perspective applied in *Looking at Schools*, so readers can ultimately make their own advised judgments. And my defense will incidentally be an identification of the intellectual roots of the book. By considering their own reaction to those roots, readers can finally decide what evidence should be weighed—and how it should be weighed—in looking at schools.

There is a long and rich tradition of Americans applying progressive perspectives to innovations and institutions. Leaders and intellectuals such as Franklin, Jefferson, Horace Mann, and Emerson have articulated and implemented such positions. In our own time, political figures such as President Franklin D. Roosevelt and Lyndon B. Johnson have espoused such views, as well as intellectuals like Arthur Schlesinger, Jr., and John Rawls.

It is not as simple to identify significant political conservative themes in the American intellectual and political mainstream. Important elements have been found among creative writers, such as Hawthorne or Melville, and one can follow this pattern into our own time. But unfortunately, in the political sphere, we usually fail to realize how essentially conservative the radicals in our past were. And it is this muddying of distinctions (when we look toward the past) which has obliterated much to the conservatism in our history. Really, many of our historic "radicals," when measured agains contemporary ideology and educational practices, would probably be counted as conservatives. For example, Jefferson, for all his egalitarianism, designed an education system for the state of Virginia which unabashedly assumed that only a small portion of grade-school students (who showed "genius") would be advanced to higher levels at public expense.[8] The idea of supporting marginal students in schools for long periods of time because they might be late bloomers would have been antithetical to his thought.

Again, Jefferson stated the goals of what he called "primary" education in the following duty-oriented language.

> To give every citizen the information he needs for the transactions of his own business;
>
> To enable him to calculate for himself, and to express and preserve his ideas, his contracts and accounts, in writing;
>
> To improve, by reading, his morals and faculties;
>
> To understand his duties to his neighbors and country, and to discharge with competence the functions confided to him by either;
>
> To know his rights; to exercise with order and justice those he retains; to choose with discretion the fiduciary of those he delegates; and to notice their conduct with diligence, with candor, and judgment;
>
> And, in general, to observe with intelligence and faithfulness all the social relations under which he shall be placed.[9]

And while Horace Mann was at least agnostic in his religious views, the following story demonstrates his intense concern with character in the schools he was helping to vitalize:

> He sought out the most distinguished authors of the day for his district school library series, including Washington Irving, George Bancroft, Nathanial Hawthorne, and Richard Henry Dana, Jr. However, he considered fiction dangerous unless it was carefully edited and its prose studded with moral teachings. Mann conceded to Elizabeth Peabody that

her young friend, Nathanial Hawthorne, had written *Twice-Told Tales* "beautifully," but for schools, he needed "something nearer home to duty and business." . . .Viewing most "popular literature" as "a popular curse," he would not conceive of giving his authors free rein. [10]

In other words, it is true that many of the progressives of our past were in favor of what some of their contemporaries saw as educationally radical ideas. But these same progressives simultaneously wanted to maintain policies that today we would call conservative. Undoubtedly, if our historic progressives had been asked to justify their conservative values, they would have said, "But this is the way societies have always worked," or, "The values I want to maintain are congruent with the inherent needs of human beings."

In our own era, it may appear that our education policies are simply carrying forward traditional American values; and we have a tradition of favoring change and experimentation. But, in our past, our proposed changes were tested against a relatively traditional, and conservative, view of human nature. In contrast, many of the schools surveyed were, in practice, indifferent to the cultivation of excellence, character development, or patriotism. Jefferson and Mann, from their writings, would have found such priorities distressing.

In sum, a careful reading of the American political tradition suggests that our early leaders would have been highly critical of any school evaluation largely focused on reading scores. Furthermore, they would have assumed that schools should first be dedicated to shaping responsible and patriotic citizens, with high capabilities for deferred gratification.

Unfortunately, one problem with using the American tradition as an intellectual resource is that many of our thinkers were dealing with society in the process of being born. As a result, they were under great pressure ot focus on the creation of essentially new institutions, to fill comparative voids. Thus their writing seems to stress novelty. And, perhaps, such a pattern of constraints has given a progressive cast to their words. In contrast to the American situation, European writers could easily draw contrast between a rich and engaging past that was sliding away, and the future that was steadily evolving. This elaborate resource may be part of the reason that the intellectual quality of nineteenth-century European conservatism was richer and more explicit than that which prevailed in America. And now that America, like nineteenth-century Europe, has a complex institutional past, it may be time for us to give greater weight to tradition and history to help interpret the present. After all, the American past was fairly "successful": the policies and institutions of our past helped produce a prosperous and relatively secure present. While we are changing education—and change we must—we should strive to identify and retain the patterns of the past which generated our current success. In this process of conservation, we may learn much from the perspectives of the nineteenth-century conservative European intellectuals.

A seminal figure in articulating conservative thought was Edmund Burke (1729-1797), who sympathized with the American Revolution and was able to perceive important distinctions between it and the later one in France.[11] Burke stressed the need for change to be rooted in realistic views of both human nature and the traditions of the societies involved. In one of his famous passages in *Reflections of the Revolution in France,* he forecast the rise of a dictatorial military figure over the then revolutionary government in France, nine years before Napoleon's appearance and seizure of power,[12] His "forecast" was based on his description and interpretation of historic and current trends affecting France. Burke, in particular, was profoundly critical of changes based on abstract views of the way people "should" be, or of efforts to make them virtuous in spite of themselves. In criticizing such dogmatic efforts toward reform, he said, "The bulk of mankind, on their part, are not excessively curious concerning any theories whilst they are really happy; and one sure symptom of an ill-conducted state is the propensity of the people to resort to them."[13] Any thoughtful reader of Burke can easily draw inferences as to his views on some of the educational practices portrayed in *Looking at Schools.*

Thomas Chalmers's (1780-1847) stature among his contemporaries did not approach Burke's. Still, his social theories, which were propounded in extensive writings,[14] were also supplemented with actual administrative efforts. As a result, they attained a special precision and vitality. Chalmers was a Scots clergyman and economist. He concluded, from his personal observations, that the Poor Law payments (or, as we would say, "welfare") distributed by government agencies were essentially disabling to their receivers. He was determined to develop an alternative "system" based on voluntary giving to poor parishioners through local religious organizations. He believed that only such structures could help the receivers overcome the handicaps engendered by economic dependency; furthermore, he concluded that in many situations the economic needs of the receivers were actually second to their emotional ones (for example, loneliness, insecurity) and that systems of personal, voluntary charity could alone satisfy such needs. Again, we see in Chalmers the repetition of traditional conservative themes: the issue is not simply getting government help to people, but dealing with them wholistically and without excessive formalism and bureaucracy. However, he did not assume that all recipients were deserving or honest.

In 1819 Chalmers volunteered to become pastor of a large Protestant parish (with 10,000 inhabitants) in the industrial city of Glasgow, Scotland. It also held the highest concentration of poor persons in the city. He persuaded his parishoners to adopt a policy of keeping Poor Law assistance out of the parish. He organized and motivated the parishioners so that they alone ministered to the economic and emotional needs of one another. His system persisted for eighteen years, and he concluded it was highly success-ful, so successful, in fact, that poor persons in other parishes who received Poor Law support tried to move from their parish to his, and in the process give up public support. Chalmers contended his demonstration showed that nonbureaucratic forms of assistance were both cheaper and more effective. For the rest of his life, he continued writing and working to advance com-munitarian forms of assistance. Of course, the exact evaluation of Chalmers's demonstration is difficult, though he approached his effort with considerable rationality and kept elaborate records. Furthermore, even if we conclude that it failed, how much of the failure should we attribute to unreasonable bureaucratic intrasigence? For example, while the members of Chalmers's large parish received no Poor Law benefits and effectively supported their own poor, they were simultaneously still taxed to pay benefits to other parishioners. This double tax policy was partially respon-sible for the decline of the demonstration after Chalmers left the parish.

In any event, it is not hard to deduce what perspectives Chalmers would apply in comparing state-supported schools to schools supported largely by parents' contributions. And Chalmers, in making his evaluation, would look at far more than reading scores, for, speaking with reference to the use of statistics in his own times, he said that "in former times the tendency was to proceed on principles without facts—as if to keep the greatest distance from this error, the incessant demand now is for facts without principles. Ands so our empirical statesmen would commit questions of the most momentous import into the hands of mere collectors and emperics like themselves."[15]

Chalmers's evaluation of institutions such as schools would consider the whole medley of values communicated by locally supported institutions, in contrast to institutions financed by remote systems of taxation. He would have no trouble in understanding the prevalence of vandalism in many schools (which seems so strange, when we consider how many benefits the state is giving to these students). And his solutions would focus not so much on greater giving, and not even on direct repression, though he believed in fostering morality. He would simply say, "Until the students, their families, their friends and neighboors make—and choose to make—contributions to support these schools, things will stay bad." Maybe he would have a point. Now, exactly how we create the sense of community on which such systems rest is very complicated. And it is no accident that Chalmers was a clergy-man and an economist (a interesting nineteenth-century combination). But a first step in any such process of creation would be for us to realize that we may have been going in a wrong direction.

There are other significant nineteenth-century English and European intellectuals whose names might be mentioned, though I will not analyze their works here. Some that come to mind are Henry Sumner Maine

(1829–1890), who articulated a careful—and even sympathetic—analysis of the contrasts between ancient and modern concepts of rights and obligations.[16] The Frenchman Fustel de Coluanges (1830–1889) subtly and imaginatively portrayed the nature of human life in ancient Greece and Tome, and suggested ways that such beliefs shifted as the societies moved toward urbanization (the shifts were not necessarily attractive).[17] James Fitzjames Stephen (1829–1894) presented an insightful critique of John Stuart Mill's work *On Liberty.*[18] And John Henry Newman (1801–1890) shifted from the Church of England to the Roman Catholic Church and justified his move in a variety of writings which contained a powerful dissection of many popular trends.[19] I should finally mention the vital Frenchman Emile Durkheim (1858–1917). Durkheim appreciated many of the dangers and tensions inherent in his changing times, although he was perhaps more sanguine than some that the changes might be made beneficient, through the intervention of social science.[20]

It would be absurd to characterize these intellectuals as enemies of change. They all would accept change as a basic law of life. But it would be fair to say that they all argued that whether any change is to be judged constructive must be determined in the light of some overall view of human nature. And this view of human nature would depend on a long-term perspective. They would ridicule arguments that a change was good just because it:

Was popular with adolescents;

Treated children as equal to adults;

Signified that more money was provided to deal with some concern;

Gave the state more power to deal with an issue;

Increased the amount of cognitive knowledge (become some reasonable level of literacy) acquired by students;

Made schools apparently more like the other institutions (for example, factories or bureaucracies) in the society; or

Satisfied some abstract view about how human beings *should* conduct themselves, without any reference to any image of how they have generally conducted themselves in the past.

These conservatives might well approve of changes that incidentally had some of the effects listed above; however, their justifications of the changes would rest on far more profound generalizations. In a way, the conservative intellectuals were "losers" in a struggle to determine the shape of modernity. To the extent that Americans think at all about the European debates on these issues, they are more likely to recall English intellectuals such as John Stuart Mill, George Bernard Shaw, or the Webbs, whose propositions were more egalitarian, optimistic, and interventionist.

I will conclude this Anglo-European educational tour by sketching a conflict in which the conservatives and progressives were arrayed against each other.[21] The themes of this conflict prefigure many of the problems identified in *Looking at Schools*.

During most of the nineteenth century, English children received their education in church-related schools, largely supported by direct parental payments plus occasional charitable contributions. They did not have the American system of tax-supported schools (although, during the same era, American tax-supported schools actually relied on far higher tax rates on parents, as compared to taxpayers in general). The English progressives proposed that the government should provide broad-scale tax support for state schools and, in effect, should simultaneously begin to phase out the existing structures for church and parental control of private schools. The change was allegedly urged to insure that all children, regardless of their parents' income level, received a decent education. The opponents of the change contended that (1) the current system was reaching an adequate proportion of children, (2) it was effective partly due to its close ties to families and the church, and (3) the proposed system would diminish family and church ties and become a stifling bureaucracy. Even many of the proponents of the change were embarrassed as state intervention into education, a peculiarly "family" matter. As justification for the intervention, they argued that it would be short-term. As soon as an adequate level of general learning was attained (in perhaps two or three generations), the state-supported system would be dismantled. Then, the responsibility for paying for education (and controlling it) would return to families.

Between 1879 and 1880, laws were passed establishing an elaborate system of state schools. The role of the government enlarged, and that of families and churches gradually declined. E.G. West, in his authoritative study on this controversy, plotted the growth of education in England both before and after the decision on public support. He demonstrated that, during the whole nineteenth century, the level of education, (for members of all social classes) throughout England steadily grew. It is impossible to tell, from looking at this growth data, when state support was phased in. In sum, there is no evidence that state support was needed to sustain the long-term pattern of a steady increase in education. There is now a great deal of objective evidence that state support has undermined the power of churches, families, and other local entities over education, and has enlarged that of elected officials and their intellectual allies. In addition, there is no sign now that literacy in England has reached levels far surpassing that of the nineteenth century, that those who now hold power over education want to return it to parents and churches. Furthermore, since these families and churches have been weaned from their responsibilities for about 100 years, it would also be difficult for them to take them back.

I am not familiar with any American work which portrays the issue of state support in quite the light applied by West.[22] But, from my understandings of American nineteenth-century developments, it appears that essentially the same contentions against state intervention in education were raised as in England. Furthermore, the evidence suggests that local and privately supported education institutions in America were doing fine on their own. In other words, the issue was not so much support and assistance, but control. Perhaps the English conflict was more clearly articulated due to the generally more coherent level of conservative thought in that country. Also, in England the "state" that was intervening was the whole nation. In America in the nineteenth century, the "state" was the "State" and not the federal government.

I described this conflict in detail becuase the "conservatives" deserve some credit for the effectiveness of their prediction. State-supported schools—as evidenced from *Looking at Schools*—are not a big success. It is true that they do manage to educate large numbers of students. However, from the historical evidence presented by persons such as West, it seems that parents might have ended up choosing to pay for their own childrens' education, if they had been left to their own devices.

At this time in history, it may not be feasible to encourage a gradual shift back to greater parental payment. (Still, such a possibility should not be precluded. While public school enrollment is declining; private enrollment has not only stabilized, but is increasing.) Regardless of whether such a shift occurs, we should look seriously at what has been happening within the private schools, where parents, through their purchases, make deliberate decisions about what they think is best for children.

Many of the private schools described in the items, in particular those related to the Roman Catholic Church, seemed to be doing quite well. The status of the secular private schools described in the items is more complex. Their academic performance is adequate, but this is partly explained by their high pupil selectivity. In the area of character development, these schools (see items 29, 33, and 179) appear to be doing poorly. I believe this deficiency is due to the perspective of the parents involved. Upper- and upper-middle-class American parents who send their children to nonresidential secular private schools have chosen these schools not for moral indoctrination or to socialize children into community living (as might occur in a boarding school) or to teach the children about heterogeneity, but essentially to have them attain high college entrance scores.[23] Thus, some of the private secular schools portrayed actually seemed to represent the most extreme aspects of our individualistic American traditions. Indeed, the vitality of the conservative tradition in many Catholic schools is probably due to their roots in an Old World religion and their frequent ties with ethnic groups. In contrast, the secular private schools (except items 69 and 70) were studiously unethnic and agnostic. In a way, vitality of the Catholic, parent-oriented schools represents more evidence in support of a conservative perspective in education. These schools are doing well not because of their borrowings from progressive perspectives, but in spite of the borrowings, and because of what they have retained from conservatism. To identify a Catholic school that borrowed too much, consider item 71. That school has gone out of operation since it was studied.

It is understandable that some contemporary American readers may feel that the conservatives I have cited—and the doctrines they articulate— are implicitly antidemocratic and hostile to the spirit of our society. Unfortunately, in the current context, the issue of "democracy" is a misleading concern. It is true that some of the nineteenth-century conservatives took positions in their day which today might be called antidemocratic. However, in evaluating those positions, it is more appropriate to judge their proponents by the standards of their time, instead of using hindsight. Similarly, if we apply the basic perspectives of the conservatives to many of the educational concerns of our era, the conservatives—and not the progressives—will appear the more committed democrats. And here, I'll say some blunt words. Many of our contemporary progressives have incidentally evolved into authoritarians in their desire to impress their vision of the future onto a recalcitrant majority (or on the majoritys' children)[24]

For instance, many of the public schools described in *Looking at Schools* are engaged in frustrating the will of the majority of the parents using those schools. Do many readers believe that the majority of parents under government pressure to send their children to school 38 think that school should compel their children to sit beside other student exercising their right to wear T-shirts advertising marijuana? Similarly, what proportion of the parents using school 15 think they should be pressured to send their children to a school where fourteen-year-old boys are allowed to dress like pimps? And how many parents want their children pressured to attend schools where teachers assume they can pass and graduate everyone without their meeting some minimal standards? (During much of the period studied, this "pass them on" practice prevailed in most Chicago public schools, for example, see item 142.) And, turning from parents to taxpayers in general, what proportion of taxpayers want to support such policies?

The awkward truth is that the private schools are essentially democratic: they reflect the wishes of their users—and the public ones are often authoritarian—many parents only using them due to state-generated economic pressures. Of course, some educators may say that children, and not parents, are the true constituency of public schools. But my conclusion is that many (most?) students are in favor of firm and consistently enforced rules to make their schools safer and more pleasant. And, anyway, any public institution that justifies its role by playing children and adolescents off against their parents is sapping the vitality of the commonwealth. The Pied Piper was an enemy of both parents and their children.

Now, it is true that when a school "gets tough" with a particular student, that student's parents may resist (especially if the school does not generally seem to know what it's doing). But such occasional resistance is no sign of the nature of implicit will of the majority. Unfortunately, one could write another book as to why schools at this time do not reflect the majority will. And the reasons would include matters such as the intervention of courts (a nonrepresentative and essentially nonaccountable entity); the appeal of egalitarian ideas among a small but influential intellectual group; the inertia which develops in large bureaucracies; the susceptibility of upper-level governmental entities to nonmajoritarian ideologies; the complexity of the problems that have developed; and the lack of adequate comprehension among the majority as to what can and should be done.

In any case, the fact is that, at this time, the position of nineteenth-century conservatives is approximately democratic, and those who support the schools as they are, and have been tending, may be the true antidemocrats. In effects, at this time the majority is not deemed capable of rearing its own children generally according to its own desires.

Incidentally, we should perhaps consider the effects of such usurpation of parental authority on potential parents. At this time, the demographic data show that growing proportions of better-educated persons are avoiding marriage, or getting married but choosing not to bear children. These trends are not socially desirable. Such persons represent the more enriched portion of our gene pools (if we want to discourage childbearing, we would be better advised to discourage less able persons from such responsibilities). In any case, I speculate that one of the many factors fostering this undesirable trend is the perception by many intelligent young persons that, if they choose to have children, the public schools will not offer them much support in their responsibilities as parents. From my contacts, many such persons view schools more as obstacles or challenges that parents must confront, compared to valuable assistants. I believe they partly ground such opinions on their own experiences in schools as students. It's not that they were suppressed while they were in school; they simply are reluctant to bear children because the schools might give their children the same offhanded license which they received. Essentially, these young adults are grown-up enough to see they received an inadequate education, and are not experienced or powerful enough to articulate or create the elements of a better one. But meanwhile they choose to defer—or reject—the responsibilities of parenthood.

Let me shift now from an historical review to a consideration of some contemporary Americans who have articulated themes congruent with the

European conservatives just covered. These Americans, like the Europeans, argue that proposed changes must be analyzed in the light of their inherent tendencies, and that such tendencies must be inferred from a general consideration of human nature. They warn us that there are many institutional and intellectual interests underlying the promotion of egalitarianism and government intervention. As a result, in making our judgments about institutional evaluations, we must often go beyond simplistic and questionable data, and rest our conclusions on more persisting and commonsensical bases.

Some of the more prominent of these writers, such as Wilson and van den Haag, have directed themselves at the problem of crime prevention.[25] Perhaps this has occurred because the flaws in the progressive approach to crime have become so conspicuous and aggravating. After all, it is remarkable that at the most prosperous time in our history, when so many "reforms" have occurred, the level of crime has not declined, but either stayed constant or risen. Thus the way is open for conservative perspectives to be considered. And it should be noted that the conservatives, true to their tradition, base their analyses and prescriptions on (1) the best data available and (2) a careful discussion of what seems typical and inherent in human beings.

Of course, other conservative theorists have risen in areas such as poverty reform. Edward Banfield represents a typical member of this group.[26] Incidentally, it is, I believe, significant that Banfield's first major work was a study of social patterns of helping and disengagement in a contemporary rural Italian village.[27] I suspect that this research provided him with a perspective which affected his consideration of American urban problems. Again, we see the basic conservative theme: what is pervasive and permanent among human beings?

I should also mention controversies arising in the field of psychology. There, some prominent researchers—including Donald T. Campbell, in his presidential address to the American Psychological Association—have begun to ask, "Have we gone too far in our glorification of self-fulfillment, to the detriment of maintaining satisfying communities?"[28] Campbell even suggested that many of the "traditional"—and note the connotations of that word—folk proverbs about social controls and self-restraint expressed a form of vital wisdom.

There is no doubt that many educators, social scientists, and intellectuals are dissatisfied with what have been happening in education over the past ten or twenty years.[29] Many policies and innovations have been criticized, or ever more general criticisms articulated. But these criticisms often fail to quarrel directly with some of the basic premises underlying the alleged errors.

The critics are often reluctant to say that children and adolescents cannot be "invited" to choose between honesty and dishonesty; that they must be indoctrinated to honesty and good citizenship. They are afraid to propose that the wishes of the majority of the students' parents should be critical test of a school's legitimacy.[30] Or, when they talk about parent power, they envisage additional elective and bureaucratic structures (such as "parents' councils"), as compared to simply letting parents choose through devices such as voucher systems.[31] And, when reformers allegedly offer parents' choices, these choices are often surrounded with endless hedgings, to insure that parent preferences do not impinge on the values with which the reformers want to indoctrinate their children.[32] Finally, too much of the serious research on education issues ignores the immediate values students are expressing in school, and by the term "immediate" I mean such simple matters as refusing to cheat, helping to make the school work by doing vexsome chores, and in general displaying good character through observable conduct.[33]

It is understandable why many critics have trouble discussing our educational problems in terms of the perspectives supporting the preceding propositions. The relative newness of our society has caused us to undervalue the importance of social continuity. Thus many American ignore the role of education as a deliberate socializing agent, and pay excessive attention to cognitive growth (as if IQ alone could be equated with either virtue or significant talent). Furthermore, our tradition of individualism makes us reluctant to accept the inherent need to indoctrinate children. But, of course, we simultaneously practice such indoctrination in our families and schools. Jefferson and Mann better articulated the true American tradition regarding such indoctrination by impliciting saying, "Of course, we must indoctrinate children—up to some point; the only valid and interesting issue is, who will decide the content of what indoctrination?" Criticism has also been immensely complicated because to the interaction between the processes of education and innumerable dynamic other social forces, for example, comparative affluence, the mass media, the bureaucratization and enlargement of schools. Because of this complexity, critics are compelled to qualify and elaborate their analyses and prescriptions. As for research on observable student conduct (which demonstrates values in action), I have already outlined some of the barriers, intellectual and technical so such research. But, obviously, they are not insurmountable.

The suggestions and implicit criticisms woven through *Looking at Schools* spring from a conservative perspective. They rest on a cross-cultural and historical view of the nature of man. I apply that perspective because I believe the track record of the nineteenth-century conservatives I have mentioned is good. The insights they offer greatly enrich our understanding of what schools are, and should be, doing. They do not tell us exactly what we should do now—indeed, they would view such prescriptions for the future as inappropriate. However, they can help us see what is wrong in the light of persisting human imperatives. And, from that light, we can begin to plan our own process of correction.

Theoretically, it may be possible for us to technically and precisely evaluate the effects of suggestions such as revitalizing dress codes, or the other approaches I propose. I'm all in favor of attempting such evaluations. But during the many intervening years before definite evidence come in (if it ever does) we should give greater weight to a conservative tradition in making our judgments about schools and children. From the evidence in *Looking at Schools,* it seems that educators now applying such conservative principles—in both our public and private schools—are performing a precious service for their students and our society.

Appendix: School
Descriptions

The schools described in the items represent a sample of forty derived from a total of 167 reports. The sample was not selected on a highly systematic basis; the principles applied in choosing were semiintuitive. In general, I favored longer and better-written reports on more "interesting" schools. "Interest" meant the school's practices illustrate some point as to what is either good, bad, or highly typical. To my mind, there seemed to be little merit in making the sample more precise, for instance, by trying to bring in more or less suburban or elementary schools. After all, there are differences in size among high schools; should we "compare" one large school to three smaller ones? Or, in the case of elementary schools, it is my conviction that the effectiveness of such schools—because they often have self-contained classrooms—is more affected by idiosyncratic factors, either good or bad, prevailing in individual classrooms, than is the case in departmentalized schools. As a result, my studies of schoolwide factors have given greater considerations to departmentalized schools. If these considerations are accepted, I believe the items presented (accepting the limitations of a book of this size) provide a good qualitative picture of what has been occurring in schools in the Chicago metropolitan area during the 1970s. If some publicized education issues do not appear much in the items (for example, busing for desegregation), it means that those issues were not immediately affecting many students or schools, though they may affect families' decisions about where to move, or whether to move.

The precision and currency of the statistical data available on the schools in the sample vary considerably. Furthermore, precise and current statistics are often not important for evaluating many of the items presented. Thus the information set forth below represents my estimate of what is adequate for the purposes of productive analysis. (Incidentally, as already mentioned, my reporters did not usually collect schoolwide reading score data; such information can be useful, but my helpers lacked the time and training to place such data in an appropriate context, and, without contextual data, the scores are very misleading.)

Each numbered item set out below presents its information on a school in a uniform sequence, as follows:

1. The grades enrolled in the school;
2. The academic year the school was last studied;
3. The number of students enrolled;
4. The racial or ethnic mix of students;

5. Whether all the students are all of the same sex (only noted if this is the case);
6. The proportion of students from low-income families (as defined by the standards of the U.S. Bureau of the Census) or the evaluator's or staffs' estimate;
7. The annual tuition charged in private schools (in church schools, there were some unnoted variations for several children in one family, or for nonparishoners);
8. If it is a high school that uses test scores as part of its admission criteria, that fact is noted;
9. The item numbers in the text which refer to the particular school.

To demonstrate this process, here are two examples: School 20, a Chicago city public high school, is described as follows: 9–12; 77–78; 350; 52 White/48 Black; 43%.

School 60, a church-related high school, is described as follows: 9–12; 78–79; 1,000 (all boys at time studied); 75 mixed ethnic/25 black; upper-middle to lower class; $1,000; test scores examined.

I must also mention that the data on Chicago public schools, for the purposes of consistency and precision, are derived from the 1977–1978 data in *Selected School Characteristics, 1973-1974—1977-1978,* a publication issued by the Chicago Public Schools, rather than from my students' reports. This means that (1) the data given are rather precise, and (2) some of the descriptions for schools, in fast-changing neighborhoods, may portray environments somewhat different from those described by the data. I do not believe the effects of this latter discrepancy are significant.

In general my students did not make racial breakdowns in describing school staff, and I have not placed such information in my descriptions. However, readers may be interested to know that (1) during the total period studied, there was a moderate level of staff racial integration in many Chicago public schools, and at the very end of the period (through a major staff shift) all school staffs were, for practical purposes, desegregated; (2) the proportion of black staff members in various suburban public school systems was probably proportionate to the number of black students enrolled in each system; and (3) private secular and church-related schools, except those with high proportions of black students, had few or no black staff members. I would not suggest that the staff patterns in private and suburban schools are the result of racial discrimination. Many private schools have lower salary schedules, and this undoubtedly affects the job preferences of some black applicants. Furthermore, some blacks who live in the city may not want to travel to suburbs for their work.

City Public Elementary

1. K–8; 73–74; 615; 65 White/35 Latino; 35%; and 6, 63, 185, 188, 199, 236.
2. K–8; 77–78; 655; 60 Black/40 White and Oriental; 60% and 106, 147, 258, 297, 324.
3. K–8; 74–75; 1250; 75 Latino/25 White; 12% and 105, 260, 289, 291.
4. K–7; 77–78; 1,000; Black; 60%; and 5, 46, 137, 145, 173, 215.
5. K–8; 77–78; 1,200; 58 White/30 Latino/12 Black; 10%; and 113, 214, 234, 238, 318.
6. K–8; 77–78; 570; 99 Black; 65%; and 20, 24, 28, 42, 49, 60, 64, 96, 146, 200, 246, 327.

City Public Secondary

12. 9–12; 72–73; 1,950; 48 Black/40 White/12 Latino; 40%; and 30, 114, 166.
13. 9–12; 77–78; 2,400; 100 White; 3%; and 139, 149.
14. 9–12; 77–78; 2,320; 53 Black/47 White; 26%; test scores examined; and 39, 44, 133, 134, 135, 189, 202, 212, 226, 239, 265, 273, 308, 321, 331.
15. 9–12; 76–77; 2,200; 99 Black; 60%; and 10, 53, 102, 165, 172, 176, 178, 190, 193, 197, 201, 227, 263.
16. 9–12; 77–78; 2,500; 99% Black; 80%; test scores examined; and 92, 156, 191, 192, 197, 205, 242, 266, 274, 304.
17. 9–12; 78–79; 3,300; 100% Black; 88%; and 112, 161, 164, 168, 170, 171, 203, 211, 235, 253.
18. 4–8; 78–79; 560; 100 Black; 80%; and 11, 18, 104, 111, 115, 121, 123, 154, 163, 169, 233, 261, 281, 282, 320, 332.
20. 9–12; 77–78; 350; 52 White/48 Black; 43%; and 55, 88, 95, 103, 141.
21. 9–12; 77–78; 4,600; 72 White/28 Black; 19%; test scores examined; and 75, 84, 93, 97, 110, 143, 144, 152, 187, 248.
22. 9–12; 77–78; 3,200; 55 Black/45 White; 30%; and 67, 81, 159, 216, 218, 219, 222, 237.

Suburban Public Elementary

27. K–8; 78–79; and 27, 48, 99, 195.

Suburban Public Secondary

30. 9–12; 77–78; 3,000; 100 White (90% Jewish); upper-middle class; and 14.
31. 7–8; 77–78; 600; 100 White; upper-middle and middle class; and 19, 23, 45, 86, 101, 107, 155, 209, 228, 243, 322.
32. 7–8; 77–78; 800; 100 White; upper-middle and middle class; and 73.
34. 9–12; 77–78; 1,300; 100 White; upper-middle class; and 1, 68, 79, 230, 301, 323.
35. 9–12; 75–78; 1,500; 100 White; upper-middle class; and 194, 286.
36. 9–12; 78–79; 4,200; 96 White/4 Black; upper-middle to lower-middle class; and 2, 22, 31, 41, 58, 77, 80, 117, 118, 153, 160, 213, 259, 269, 288, 299, 311, 315.
37. 7–8; 78–79; 825; 100 White, upper-middle class; and 17, 69, 78, 94, 129, 184, 225, 232, 244, 245, 316, 319, 325.
38. 9–12; 77–78; 1,800; 85 White/15 Black; upper-middle and middle class; and 74, 119, 120, 127, 181, 207, 210, 254.
39. 9–12; 77–78; 2,500; 100 White; upper-middle and middle class; and 43, 76, 109, 151, 167, 177, 179, 186, 221, 278, 284, 285, 290, 298.
40. 7–8; 76–77; 1,200; 100 White; upper-middle and middle class; and 62.

Church-Related Schools

All church-related schools are Roman Catholic. The proportion of faculty members in a Roman Catholic school who are members of a religious order is, I believe, significant in affecting the ultimate character of the school. It is significant because order members have undergone a lengthy socialization process different from the training of lay teachers; made a lifetime commitment to their "profession"; agreed to accept a relatively high level of external discipline; and have living arrangements which often place all order members in a school in a common residence. These factors greatly increase faculty cohesion in many church schools. Still, I would not say that the proportion of order members is the sole determining factor in ascertaining the character of a Catholic school.

My students did not collect consistent information about the proportion of order members in the church-related schools they studied. And sometimes there are substantial variations in these proportions, ranging from a low of zero to 10 percent, to a high of perhaps 80 percent. From my general understanding, I would estimate that all the Catholic schools listed below had 40 percent or more order members in their faculties, except schools 55 and 58. As readers may observe, 55 is a carefully managed school (and the proportion of its religious faculty is still significant); the school described in 58 had very few order members when it was visited and, since the visit, for all practical purposes it has gone out of business.

I should also note that the term "ethnic" was sometimes used by my students in describing the social class of students in Catholic schools. Perhaps its significance needs amplification. It connotes children from nonblack familites whose parents range from foreign-born to third-generation Americans. In some "ethnic" schools, one nationality (for example, Italian) was strongly dominant, but in others the mix was highly diversified and included students of Polish, Irish, Italian, and Mexican descent.

Church-Related Elementary

47. K–8; 77–78; 340; 95% White, ethnic; upper-middle to lower class; $375; and 131, 132, 148, 208.
49. K–8; 78–79; 245; 50 Italian/40 Latino/10 Other; middle class; $250; and 4, 13, 21, 32, 47, 59, 61, 100, 124, 128, 175, 217, 229, 262, 270, 292, 326.

Church-Related Secondary

56. 9–12; 78–79; 355 (all girls); 100 White ethnic mixed; middle-class; $500; test scores examined; and 8, 16, 16, 38, 52, 37, 65, 89, 183, 204, 224, 267, 277, 279, 294, 295, 305, 310, 329.
57. 9–12; 74–75; 450; 50 White/30 Black/20 Latino; middle and lower-middle class; $450; and 71, 125, 287.
58. 9–12; 78–79; 3,300 (all boys); 85 White/15 Black; middle class; $750; test scores examined; and 3, 7, 12, 26, 35, 37, 50, 57, 98, 116, 122, 126, 138, 174, 206, 231, 247, 193, 302, 314.
59. 9–12; 77–78; 700 (all girls); 100 White; upper–middle and middle class; $600; test scores examined; and 9, 70, 72, 108, 150, 280.
60. 9–12; 78–79; 1,000 (all boys at time studied); 75 mixed ethnic/25 Black; upper-middle to lower class; $1,000; test scores examined; and 25, 40, 521, 84, 90, 140, 158, 196, 198, 223, 250, 268, 276, 283, 300, 303, 312.

Private Secular

66. 9–12; 78–79; 70 White/30 Black; upper-middle class; $2,800; test scores examined; and 91, 130, 180, 220, 240, 306, 313, 317, 328.
67. 9–12; 72–73; 250; 99 White; upper class; $1,800; test scores examined; and 33.

68. 9–12; 73–74; 870; 99 White; upper class; $3,000; test scores examined; and 29, 34, 182.
69. K; 75–76; 50; 100 Black; lower class; no charge (government and private agency grants). and 275, 296, 330.
70. 7–10 (new and expanding); 75–76; 100 White; upper-middle and upper class; $1,000; test scores examined; and 66.

Notes

Introduction

1. Michael Rutter et al., *Fifteen Thousand Hours* (Cambridge, Mass.: Harvard University Press, 1979), p. 21.
2. Frank C. Macchiarola, *Mid-Year Report of the Chancellor of Schools to the New York City Board of Education* (New York: New York City Board of Education, 1979), p. 11.
3. Ellis Page, "Interview with New AERA President," *Report on Education Research,* April 18, 1979, p. 4.
4. Rutter, *Fifteen Thousand Hours.*

Chapter 1

1. John Henry Newman, *On the Scope and Nature of University Education* (New York: E.P. Dutton, 1956), p. 124.

Chapter 2

1. National Panel on High School and Adolescent Education, *The Education of Adolescents* (Washington, D.C.: Government Printing Office, 1976), p. 25.

Chapter 3

1. G.W.M. Hart, "Contrasts between Prepubertal and Postpubertal Education," in *Education and the Cultural Process,* George G. Spindler, ed. (New York: Holt, 1974), p. 358.
2. Stanley K. Clam, ed., *A Decade of Gallup Polls on Attitudes Towards Education, 1969–1978* (Bloomington, Ind.: Phi Delta Kappa, 1979).

Chapter 4

1. Brewster M. Smith, "Competence and Socialization," in *Socialization and Society,* John A. Clausen, ed. (Boston: Little, Brown, 1968), p. 310.

2. For an instance of a different type of grading arrangement, see, for example, Edward A. Wynne, "Learning About Cooperation and Competition," *Educational Forum* 40 (March 1976): 279–288.

Chapter 5

1. Ernest van den Haag, *Punishing Criminals* (New York: Basic Books, 1975), p. 134.
2. U.S. Department of Health, Education and Welfare, National Institute of Education, *The Safe School Report to Congress, V.I.* (Washington, D.C.: Government Printing Office, 1978); U.S. Department of Justice, *Crime Victimization in the United States, 1976 [et seq.]* (Washington, D.C.: Government Printing Office, 1976), p. 13; and Robert J. Rubel, *The Unruly School* (Lexington, Mass.: Lexington Books, D.C. Heath and Co., 1977).
3. "Analysis of CTU Survey," *Chicago Teacher,* March 1978, p. 2.
4. National Institute of Education, *The Safe School,* p. 37.
5. For another perspective on the theme of "how bad are things?" see Daniel Linden Duke and Cheryl Ferry, "What Happened to the High School Discipline Crisis?" *Urban Education* 14 (July 1979): 182–204.

Chapter 6

1. Lucius Annaeus Seneca, "On Benefits," in *Moral Essays, V.III.* (Cambridge, Mass.: Harvard University Press, 1935), p. 241.
2. The point about incentives for cooperation is raised by James S. Coleman, "New Incentives for Schools," in *New Models for Public Education,* ed. James W. Guthrie and Edward A. Wynne (Englewood Cliffs, N.J.: Prentice-Hall, 1971). See also Wynne, "Learning About Cooperation."
3. "Seventh Annual Gallup Poll on Education," *Phi Delta Kappan* 57 (December 1975): 237.
4. For a full discussion of the Soviet patterns, see Urie Bronfenbrenner, *Two Worlds of Childhood* (New York: Russell Sage Foundation, 1970).

Chapter 7

1. Willard Waller, *The Sociology of Teaching* (New York: Russell & Russell, 1961), p. 441.

2. For references on the data presented, see, for example, Edward A. Wynne, "Behind the Discipline Problem: Youth Suicide as a Measure of Alienation," *Phi Delta Kappan* 59 (January 1978): 307–315; and Wynne, "Facts About the Character of Young Americans," *Character* 1 (November 1979): 1–8.

3. For presentations of this position, see, for example, Peter L. Berger and Thomas Luckman, *The Social Construction of Reality* (Garden City, N.Y.: Doubleday Anchor, 1967); and Orrin E. Klapp, *The Collective Search for Identity* (New York: Hold, 1969).

4. Bernard Berelson and Gary A. Steiner, *Human Behavior: Shorter Edition* (New York: Harcourt, 1967), p. 199.

5. Mircea Eliade, "The Yearning for Paradise in the Primitive Tradition," *Daedalus* 88 (Spring 1959): 255–268.

6. Jean Jacques Rousseau, "Discourage on the Origin of Inequality," in *Great Books of the Western World,* v. 38 (Chicago: Encyclopedia Britannica, 1955): 98–140.

7. Advisory Panel on the Scholastic Aptitude Test Score Decline, *On Further Examination* (New York: College Entrance Examination Board, 1977).

8. Thomas Jefferson, "A Bill for the More General Diffusion of Knowledge," in Ray J. Honeywell, *The Educational Work of Thomas Jefferson* (New York: Russell & Russell, 1964), p. 204, sec. XVI.

9. Jefferson, "Report of the Commissioners Appointed to Fix the Site of the University of Virginia," in Honeywell, *The Educational Work,* pp. 249–250 (Jefferson was the author of the report.).

10. Jonathan Messerli, *Horace Mann, A Biography* (New York: Knopf, 1972), p. 345.

11. For one of many edited collections of Burke's works, see Edmund Burke, *Selected Works* (New York: Modern Library, 1960) W.J. Bate, ed.

12. Ibid., p. 420.

13. Ibid., p. 212.

14. For a basic presentation of Chalmers's work, see Norma Masterman, ed., *Chalmers on Charity* (Westminster, England: Archibald, Constable and Cox, 1900).

15. Ibid., p. 12.

16. Henry Sumner Maine, *Ancient Law* (New York: Holt, 1906).

17. Fustel de Coulanges, *The Ancient City* (Boston: Lathrop, Lee and Shepard, 1873).

18. James Fitzjames Stephen, *Liberty, Equality, Fraternity* (New York: Holt, 1873).

19. For one of Newman's many relevant works, see, for example, Newman, *University Education.*

20. For some of Durkheim's relevant works see, for example, Emile

Durkheim, *Moral Education* (New York: The Free Press, 1973); *The Division of Labor In Society* (New York: The Free Press, 1949); and *Suicide* (New York: The Free Press, 1966).

21. Edward G. West, *Education and the State* (London: Institute for Economic Affairs, 1955).

22. For some discussion of the American situation before state-supported schools—especially in New York State in the 1840s—see Edward G. West, "The Political Economy of American Public School Legislation," *Journal of Law and Economics* 10 (1967): 101–128.

23. The following anecdote demonstrates the importance of cognitive scores in these schools. I recently was informed that one of these schools hired a reading specialist to work with teachers and students in its middle grades. The specialist was hired because the school and the parents were worried about their children's measured reading performance; *they were only reading two years ahead of the published national norms.* I'm not suggesting it is undesirable for parents to stimulate their children to excell; still, many observers might conclude, from the picture presented from the items, that there are other areas of conduct where the students might need more help than in reading.

24. For a critical general discussion of recent patterns of legal interventionism, see Franklin Hunt, "The Lawyers' War against Democracy," *Commentary* 64 (October 1979): 45–51; and also see Donald Horowitz, *The Courts and Social Policy* (Washington, D.C.: Brookings Institution, 1977).

25. Ernest van den Haag, *Punishing Criminals* (New York: Basic Books, 1975); and James Q. Wilson, *Thinking About Crime* (New York: Basic Books, 1975).

26. Edward C. Banfield, *The Unheavenly City Revisited* (Boston: Little, Brown, 1974).

27. Edward C. Banfield, *The Moral Basis of a Backward Society* (New York: The Free Press, 1958).

28. See, for example, Donald T. Campbell, "On the Conflicts between Biological and Social Evolution and between Psychology and Moral Tradition," *American Psychologist* 30 (1975): 1103–1126; and Lauren G. Wispe and James N. Thompson, Jr., eds., "The War between the Words: Biological Versus Social Evolution and Some Related Issues," *American Psychologist* 31 (1976): 341–384.

29. For representative works on current proposed criticisms and reforms, see, for example, Bronfenbrenner, "The Origins of Alienation," *Scientific American* 23 (1974): 51–53; James S. Coleman et al., *Youth: Transition to Adulthood* (Chicago: University of Chicago Press, 1974); Lawrence Cremin, *Public Education* (New York: Basic Books, 1976); and A. Harry Passow, *Education Reform: Retrospect and Prospect* (New York: Teachers College Press, 1976).

30. For some discussion of the potentially conflicting roles of parents, taxpayers, and citizens in determining education policy, see Edward A. Wynne, "Accountable to Whom?" *Society/Transaction* 13 (January–February 1976): 10–27.

31. For an example of efforts to increase parent authority over education through involving them in formal decision-making, see some writings on the New York City school decentralization controversy; for example, Melvin Zimet, *Decentralization and School Effectiveness* (New York: Teachers College Press, 1973).

32. For some discussion of voucher proposals, see, for example, Institute for Contemporary Studies, ed., *Parents, Teachers and Children* (San Francisco: Institute for Contemporary Studies, 1977); and John E. Coons and Stephen D. Sugarman, *Education by Choice* (Berkeley: University of California Press, 1979).

33. For some examples of research concerned with the nature of students' conduct in schools, see, for example, Roger G. Barker and Paul V. Gump, *Big School: Small School* (Stanford: Stanford University Press, 1964); Jacquetta Hill Burnett et al., eds., *Anthropology and Education: An Annotated Bibliographic Guide* (New Haven: Human Relations Area Files Press, 1974); James S. Coleman, *The Adolescent Society* (New York: The Free Press, 1971); Philip A. Cusick, *Inside High School* (New York: Holt, 1973); Philip Jackson, *Life in Classrooms;* Rutter, *Fifteen Thousand Hours;* and Waller, *The Sociology.* Jackson's book is perhaps the most "optimistic" of the studies, but it must be remembered that his data are largely based on self-contained classrooms, and come from schools as they were twenty to thirty years ago. There is a periodical, the *Journal of Anthropology and Education,* that is largely devoted to studies of this general nature. One cannot simply evaluate the entire ouvre presented there. However, I believe many of its articles suffer from their authors' tendencies to overidentify with statistically deviant students and social groups—and, conversely, with the authors' failures to accept the legitimacy of many demands for social control in schools. My suspicions of these articles are supported by the conclusions of others. Thus, an on-the-scene evaluator of a group of anthropological researchers doing studies of school desegregation emphasized the limitations of the studies due to the "politically liberal and radical" perspectives of the researchers, and "their snobbish and basically unsympathetic attitudes towards educators." Joan Cassell, *Studying Desegregated Schools* (Washington, D.C.: National Institute of Education, 1978), p. 20.

Index

Index

Student Assistants

As already noted, my research assistants were my graduate and undergraduate students in a variety of classes in the College of Education of the University of Illinois at Chicago Circle. About one-third of the reports in *Looking at Schools* were done by graduate students, usually operating individually; the remainder were done by undergraduate students, usually operating in teams of two to five students.

To provide my many students with some recognition for their essential contributions, I have set out here the names of the students whose reports are quoted in the text. The nature of their contributions varies widely; some have contributed a great deal of material, and others much less. But I cannot make such distinctions in recognition, since my calculations would be highly problematic at this point. I should also mention that the credits may contain one or two omissions, since there may have been some errors in correlating students' names to reports.

Eyda Alegret, Gary Anderson, Sandy Arrigo, Debbie Asher, Robert Baker, Geraldine Banks, Linda Baro, Mary B. Bazel, Vivian Bell, Connie Bendewald, Kornelia Benhalmi, Steve Berngard, Maria Blanco, Marge Bohus, Mary Bonnett, Gregory Bowden, Christine Boyadjian, Vera Bozinovich, Eileen Camacho, Gwen Carter, Sara Caswell, Jean Coconate, Yanna Cotsiopoulos, Vince Cybourn, Sue Daidone, Jane Dean, Diane Dedo, Deanna DeFlorio, Jeff Dillon, Martha Dominguez, Kathy Duddy, Carol Dusek, Juanita C. Dyson, Bill Eggert, Larry Field, Terri Finkelstein, Maureen Fitzpatrick, William Fowler, Olema Galceran, Evert Guerrero, Sheila Hall, Sandra Hansen, Helen Harris, Joanna Helenowska, Dave Hudik, Ellen Huska, Brenda James, Lois A. Janotta, Cheri Jones, Debbie Kalupski, Annie Karleski, Bruce Kelly, Barbara Kerber, James Klise, Julie Kneip, Gloria Komaras, Roger Konow, Helen Kordela, Tom Lalagos, Vicky Leonardi, Marcela Licea, Martha Lizcano, Sylvia Lizcano, Linda Lucchetti, Sharon Mahoney, Susanne Marder, Becky Mark, Mary Martens, Melva Mason, Barb McCague, Peter Meach, Mary Lou Medina, Mary Meza, Contessa Miller, Ruth Mingelano, Maryann Moats, John Mochel, Virginia Mondragon, Dawn Moriarty, Nancy Nowak, Arthur Nehemow, Debbie Newton, James Otave, Edna Padilla, Janice Pajonk, Betty Papapostolou, Rhonda Patten, Toni Pedroza, Nilsa Perez, Kathy Piechowski, Linda Porch, Wayne Porod, Carmen Quinn, Julie Rice, Ray Richard, Sharon Roberson, Cheryl Roe, Linda Roshinski, Ken Sahnas, Brad Savage, Cathe Scalise, Anita Scotese, Gail Shaeffer, Melinda Shambo, Thomas M Starcevich, Richard J. Starman, Fay Stewart, Kay Stewart, Steve Surak, Thomas Tiernan, Randa Touquan, Mary Ann Urka, Efrain Vargas, Mark Vieceli, Lina Vlcek, Cindy Vujtech, Lydia Warman, Brenda Watson, Harold Weatherford, Gloria Williams, Debra Wilson, Bruce Witschorik, Raymond Woliel, and Gail Yokubimas.

About the Author

Edward A. Wynne received the Ed.D. from the University of California, Berkeley. Dr. Wynne is a sociologist and associate professor at the College of Education, University of Chicago at Chicago Circle. He is also the editor of *Character,* a monthly periodical focusing on the public and private policies affecting youth character development, and the chairman of Socialization to Adulthood, a special-interest group in the American Education Research Association.

Dr. Wynne is the author of several books including *Social Security: A Reciprocity System Under Stress* (1980) and *Growing Up Suburban* (1977). He has worked as a practicing labor lawyer and as a planner for government antipoverty programs.